Dragged Up Proppa

Dragged Up Proppa

Growing up in Britain's forgotten North

PIP FALLOW

MACMILLAN

First published 2023 by Macmillan
an imprint of Pan Macmillan
The Smithson, 6 Briset Street, London EC1M 5NR
EU representative: Macmillan Publishers Ireland Ltd, 1st Floor,
The Liffey Trust Centre, 117–126 Sheriff Street Upper,
Dublin 1, D01 YC43
Associated companies throughout the world
www.panmacmillan.com

ISBN 978-1-5290-5085-1

1 3 5 7 9 8 6 4 2

A CIP catalogue record for this book is available from the British Library.

Typeset in Sabon LT Std by Jouve (UK), Milton Keynes
Printed and bound by CPI Group (UK) Ltd, Croydon, CR0 4YY

Visit **www.panmacmillan.com** to read more about all our books
and to buy them. You will also find features, author interviews and
news of any author events, and you can sign up for e-newsletters
so that you're always first to hear about our new releases.

Learning to read and then write has given me a voice. I'd like to dedicate this book to a whole generation who suffered the same lack of opportunity but have not been as fortunate as me. A mute generation. An under-represented and marginalised generation. A socio-economically disadvantaged generation with no voice. My generation.

To the many that didn't make it, RIP.

To those who can still stand, 'Take care and keep ya timbers in!'

Contents

1. My privileged background   1
2. Pennies in my eyes   15
3. The man who voted to strike   33
4. Starting school   44
5. My mother   57
6. Comprehensive school   65
7. Leaving school   82
8. The 1984–5 strike   96
9. Lucky breaks or theft?   116
10. Black money   124
11. London: One year on   131
12. Running away   140
13. The great cock and dole swindle   148
14. West Ruislip tube station, north London 157
15. Back to Blighty   173
16. London   187
17. USA   197
18. The stable twenty   209
19. Why lay bricks?   220
20. The organised chaos we all call life   228
21. My education   238
22. The north/south divide   247
23. So where are my politics today?   262
24. My village and me   270
25. The collapse of the red wall   283
26. Why write this book?   301

Acknowledgements   306
Where did it all go?   309

1

My privileged background

I don't remember being born. They say it's a messy business. Growing up was certainly a messy business. Probably should have guessed at the beginning what I was in for later. Half a dozen boys, all born in the same small bedroom in a pitman's cottage on the east coast of Durham. Almost exactly two years between each of us and me the last of the six lads. No lasses. My mother so wanted a girl and I was to be her last chance. Sorry, Mam.

No men allowed in the bedroom at a birth then. This was 1966, when babies were women's business. The women in the family, my aunties and grandmother, would be there but no men. The men and boys would be called in when everything had been cleaned up and when mother and baby were ready to be seen. That's if the men weren't down the pit, of course. Like I said, I can't remember being born but I can almost see it now. A circle of doting females staring down at me. 'Ah, what a shame, another boy. Another pitman!' It's as if I *can* remember. I can imagine the women then filing out: job done! Then my father, with my five brothers, filing in, a circle of different-sized heads blocking out the light and smiling down at me, pleased they didn't have a sister or daughter. Pleased they had another pitman.

My definite earliest memories were of when I was merely twenty months old. I can be accurate about this because we moved from that house when I was that age and those almost black and white images etched on my new brain, I believe, were of the inside of that first cottage. I can remember which cupboard the cheesy biscuits were kept in, I remember finding out soap powder didn't taste very nice and I remember pushing my four-year-old brother, Nigel, down a steep set of wooden stairs and watching him break his skull on the tiled floor below. I clearly remember him being sat on the top stair and me walking up behind him, putting both hands on his shoulders and pushing him with all of my tiny might. I can see him now trying to spin and grab at the multicoloured curtain strips that hung from the top of the landing and missing them with his frantic grasps. Funny really because, years later, Nigel would be the only one in my family to attend university after his schooling. He went on to do a masters in Civil Engineering. Perhaps I should have dived down after him, thus sustaining myself the apparent good knock on the heed required. However, I didn't. Not sure why; probably not having spent a full two years on planet earth, I was still unaware of the benefits a good education could bring. After all, I'd just graduated from soap powder to cheesy biscuits and to me then, even at such a young age, smashing your skull didn't quite present itself as a way of moving forward. I was still quite naive.

I do remember the house move. I didn't know then why we were leaving all I knew behind but I do now. We had outgrown it. Six kids, a Labrador called Brit and a mother and father in a one-bedroom cottage I suppose was a bit of a squeeze. My father had decked out the loft and my three eldest brothers slept up there. As I got older, I found myself questioning if I had actually pushed my brother to his near death. I looked to my mother for confirmation but I don't think she could bring herself to believe I could do such a thing. As I reached my mid-twenties, I was for some reason driven by a burning desire to prove my murderous guilt and actually knocked on that door. I had heard that the house had remained relatively untouched since we had moved on. The man who lived there was a friend of my father and knew who I was. When I explained why I was there he had no hesitation in letting me in. As I walked in, I closed my eyes and peered deep into my mind's library at what I could actually see. When I opened them, I was astonished! It was a perfect match to the worn-out picture I had stashed there. Even the multicoloured curtain strips were still in place. I was tickled pink. I had been right all along and I was left in no doubt I was, in fact, a real-life attempted murderer!

I was not to know at this particular time of my life, but the village where we lived existed because of coal. About seventy years before my being, coal had been found over one thousand feet underground and because of that, my village had been immediately built. My grandfather, my father's father, who had died because of hard work and whisky just before I existed, had belonged to the team of sinkers who had first dug that experimental shaft and struck black. It had probably once been an idyllic meadow with trees and hillocks covered with lush, green grass before they discovered what lay underneath. However, there was little evidence of anything that nice for us to admire now; instead, a purely functional grid-like system of *Coronation Street*-style red-brick terraced houses, named First Street, Second Street and so on, all the way to Eleventh Street, now smothered its once green hills. At the top of the village, running its full length, was West Street, at the bottom of the village, running its full length, was East Street and right up the middle, hosting its shops, churches, pubs and school, was, of course, Middle Street. No architectural flair required, just small, tightly packed houses for pitmen and their big families.

If you wanted a garden, there were allotments situated across the top of the beach and sprawling up to and around the sky-scraping pithead. Most did without and made do with small backyards.

I don't suppose there was, or ever will be, a way of getting billions of tons of black filthy rock from underground without turning the earth's crust upside down. It was the only way, and anyway, I knew little else. However, what I did know from very early on was the pit and coal trumped all and my father spent more time down it than he did at home.

If I was to look out of my bedroom window and down onto the streets at certain times of the night or day, I would see a flow of weary men streaming one way, against a flow of fresh men gushing the other in a hasty bid to get back down that dark hole and do what they knew best. Cutting coal. I knew them all. There would be a scattering of unleashed dogs, like in a Lowry painting if you take the time to stare into it deeply, free to search out their returning masters. I knew all of the dogs too. The men looked strong, like ants. Busy black soldier ants working perilously around the clock, each one capable of carrying a load of hardship and suffering, equal to one hundred times their own body weight. I would observe their distinctive walks and stare deep into their faces before recognising my father as one of them.

The council house we were allocated and moved into was only one mile down the road and a field full of retired pit-ponies away from the grid-like system we had escaped. It had four bedrooms and a back garden. I think the architect who'd designed the house and the surrounding estate had perhaps taken his inspiration from rabbit warrens. This was perfect. Two boys in each bedroom, a lot better than we had been used to. The fixed bath and a toilet were actually *inside* the house. I was paired up with Nigel in the smallest bedroom. By this time, he had made a full recovery from my attempt on his life. Fortunately for me and due to the very nature of the crime, he had no memory of the incident; and as I, the only true witness to the crime, had not quite got around to constructing full sentences, it seemed I had escaped justice.

This was to be my home for the next seven years or so. The estate was surrounded on three sides by industrial yards and farmland chopped up by busy railway lines that seemed to have a constant stream of coal trucks rumbling around on them in all directions. The fourth side was a black polluted beach. For a child growing up, it was bliss, a nice oily beach and plenty of railway tracks to play on.

Although I'm certain my senses were keener back then, I can't seem to remember an autumn or a spring. Just winters and summers with nothing in between. The winters seemed bitter, dominated by long, dark nights with deep snow and massive snowmen. The summers seemed hot and dominated by bright sun that woke before everybody. It would burn high all day and then blaze orange through my bedroom curtains well into the night. Perhaps it wasn't that my senses were keener, though I'm sure they were. Perhaps it was because this was before central heating. When it was summer outside, it was summer inside and when it was winter outside, we lived like Eskimos. We didn't have to buy spray-on snow for our windows at Christmas then. We had the real stuff. On the inside.

I owned nothing of value, but felt rich. I had everything in life I needed, yet apparently I was poor. I wasn't aware I was poor; I felt like the richest kid alive. Some of my friends were a lot worse off than me. I never went to bed hungry, and had a solid family and loving parents. One of my friends told me whilst we played in the street that his dad had run off and his parents were going to be divorced. Divorce was statistically much rarer back then and to a young boy trying to work life out, I recall it holding the same intrigue as death, or even sudden death. A shocking event. I probably related the two traumas so closely based on the evidence I was presented with: a deep haunted stare and a look of worry that I don't think ever left him.

I realise now looking back into that council estate in the seventies that though divorce was still rare nationally, I probably witnessed more than the national average. After all, if a marriage was to explode then, the chances of a woman buying her own home was zero. And as for the colliery houses . . . well, they were only for people who worked down the pit (men), leaving the fragmented shrapnel of shattered families only one place to land: on my estate. And the thousands like it.

I had trouble understanding broken families. I lived in such a tight-knit clutch, I had difficulty working out how they were supposed to function. Probably because some I encountered didn't. I lived in a house where everybody did their best to help one another and could not comprehend any other way. I had another friend, in the surrounding streets, who was fatherless and I was amazed how he would treat his mother with disrespect. None of it made sense. He would steal money from her purse. This confused me, but I suppose it would have. I had no need for money. I was rich.

My father had three jobs. He worked down the village pit six days a week, sometimes seven. And any spare time on the surface would be spent flying about in his van either fitting a new device that had just been invented called an 'automatic washing machine' into somebody's washhouse or climbing on a roof to fit another high-tech, state-of-the-art piece of technology that had been named the 'TV aerial'. Or – sorry, he had four jobs – he also had a window cleaning round. He never stopped. If someone asked him why he had so many jobs, he would always say, 'Oh! I can't afford to be poor!' Another piece of double Dutch or working man's philosophy I've still to this day not quite worked out.

When somebody bought a washing machine in the local town, they would be given our phone number. They would ring and my mother would write down the address on the reverse side of cardboard strips salvaged from cut-up cereal boxes and kept on the telephone table just inside the front door. My father would then go and pick up the machine from the store, deliver it and fit it for a fee. We were the only house in the street that had a phone. The same would happen if somebody was affluent enough to actually buy a TV. The phone would ring, an address would be taken and off he would go, in his van with his ladders on the roof (and sometimes me sitting next to him) and erect the aerial for a fee. We were the only family in that street with a motor vehicle too.

My father would never open his miner's wage packet. It would be given to my mother every Friday, unopened, for her to keep the family. He would survive on his other work. His fiddle. He would also buy gifts with this and bring them home. In May 1973 he came home with a massive wooden box that we soon realised was a colour TV. He climbed on the roof and fitted an aerial and came down and plugged it in. The following day we watched the Leeds v Sunderland FA cup final in colour on one of its three channels. The Sunderland goalkeeper, Jim Montgomery, pulled off a stunning double save and Ian Porterfield went on to score a screamer. Sunderland were second division giant killers and beat the almighty first division Leeds United 1–0. That particular day there must have been fifty people dancing in our living room and a further fifty in the front garden staring through our front window. We were the only house in the street that had a colour TV.

That TV arriving into our lives was big. The only people allowed to turn it on or off were my mother or my father. We knew when it was on because it would buzz loudly and when it was not in use it would have to be unplugged from the wall. There was no walking in the room and flicking the telly on to see if there was anything worth watching then, oh no. The telly would be put on when everybody was sat down quietly, ready to watch something that we knew we wanted to see. It was a true window into the outside world and beyond. I recall going into space and being scared of the Ogrons that were trying to kill the time traveller Dr Who. I believed he was real! As real as the colours and the sounds of the Bay City Rollers. Sitting in front of that screen could be a trip to the zoo. I would stare at animals on the Johnny Morris show I hadn't realised existed. Then there was Concorde, full of human beings, taking to the skies before going two thousand miles per hour and I have an image of George Harrison's fingers making up the chords as he sang 'Here Comes the Sun'. I'd heard the song before in my brother's bedroom, on his record player that looked like a fat square briefcase, but to actually see where that sound came from was something else. There was a close-up of his fingers moving around the frets. His hands surprised me. They looked just like everybody else's and gave me a feeling that anything was possible. I can't listen to that track today without being transported back in time and finding myself sat with my face just inches away from that big wooden box housing its small screen. That's real time travelling, done properly. Not like that phony Dr Who.

When I was seven and a half, I got my first job delivering newspapers, the only criteria for getting the job being that you had to be ten. But lying came easy, if for the right reasons. I remember delivering newspapers on a warm summer day and my father driving past in his van. He stopped and asked me why I was on foot.

'Because my bike is knackered,' I told him.

'Finish your round and I'll see you back at the house,' he said.

We met back at the house and he had a look at my bike. I'd found it at the local tip and had brought it home some months before. My brothers had fixed the punctures and got it on the road but it had seen better days. The tyres were bald, it had no brakes and was brown with rust.

'Right,' he said, 'jump in the van.' I did. We drove into the local town of Hartlepool and he walked me into a bike shop.

'Which one do you want?' he asked. It was like all my Christmases had come at once. I walked out of that shop with a brand-new Raleigh Chicco. It cost £23. That bike was my world. After getting home and showing everyone my pride and joy, my father asked me to run an errand.

'Could you go to the pit and pick up my wages?' he asked. I pedalled the one mile and with my head in the clouds I entered the local village. I pedalled up through Middle Street and into the numbered streets and freewheeled down Third Street to the colliery offices. Leaving my bike outside, I entered the wage office and I spoke to the wages clerk.

'I'm here for me dad's wages,' I said.

'What's his name?' he asked.

'Tommy Fallow.'

'Full name?'

'THOMAS Fallow.'

'Middle names?'

'None,' I replied. And the cash was handed over in a little half see-through and half brown-paper envelope. That was the level of security then. No bank transfers needed, just a near eight-year-old boy on a shiny bike. I tucked the money down my sock and pedalled home and gave it to my mother. His weekly wage for working six days underground was £22. One pound less than the cost of my bike. Collecting my father's wages became a regular event.

If I was to send a near eight-year-old kid to that street today, he would find no pit and no wage office next to it. There is no trace of *any* of it. If it *was* there and he left his shiny bike outside, it would be gone when he came back out. If he had money on him, he would be stopped and robbed. In the days back then when I rode proud on my new bike, people took drugs to make themselves better. Today it seems they take drugs to make themselves worse.

I walked down Third Street last week and it was all police-taped off. Apparently somebody forty years old who has never owned a house and whose rent, drugs and wages have been paid for by me and you got beat to death with a hammer for a £10 bag of crack cocaine. This is common. The experts say the social problems in the area cannot be directly linked to the recent deindustrialisation of the area or the particularly high level of unemployment it left. All I can conclude from that is that there is no such thing as an expert.

The bike made my paper round more efficient, so I took on a second and an evening round too. This earned me £1.80 per week. I would collect this on a Saturday morning in a sealed brown envelope and give it to my mother, unopened, of course – just doing my bit! Like I said, I had no need for money. I had a brand-new shiny bike and was the richest kid alive.

Though I was living rich, I still have small triggers in my memory that remind me we must have been financially very poor. One of those memories still stands clear today. A few friends and I had one day wandered about four miles and were just outside a railway yard, swimming in an industrial slurry pond. I lost my shoe. It got sucked from my foot and disappeared into the mustard yellow mud. Despite my valiant efforts I couldn't find it and returned home just before dark with only one shoe. My mother went mad! Now, to put things into perspective it wasn't even a shoe but a plastic sandal. We all had them. Thinking back, they must have been the cheapest way of keeping six kids shod. They were the light brown equivalent to a modern-day pair of crocks and probably cost less than a pound a pair, in today's money. And I only had one. My mother made me wait up for my father coming in from the pit. It must have been near midnight when he arrived through the door. She was still very upset as she explained to my father that I had no shoes to wear for school the next day.

'Come on then,' said my father, 'jump in the van.' We travelled as near to the pond as we could get by road and then travelled the last half mile across fields on foot. He had his miner's cap lamp in the back of the van, which he used to fit TV aerials to chimneys in the dark, and he put it on his forehead. We reached the pond and I showed him where it had been lost. The image of my father plodgin' in thick muddy water in the early hours of the morning, with only a cap lamp for light, and finding that shoe which was probably worth less than 50p is still an image that haunts me today. He wasn't angry; he never was. He was just getting on with doing what he needed to do. In the morning I cycled to school. Tired but shod.

Another story I have trouble forgetting happened when I was probably only about five or six. I was ill and absent from school. In fact, if I was allowed off school, I must have been near death. I think I had mumps. I had been in bed for several days, had not eaten and came downstairs feeling a little better. I was hungry and my mother, pleased I was recovering, asked what I wanted to eat.

'Mushrooms, fried in butter,' was my answer. We didn't have any mushrooms in the house and my mother, happy I had an appetite, had an idea.

'Come on then, let's go out and get some. Quick, there's

11

Charley's van outside.' Those days a large box van would come around the streets and sell groceries from the back door. Charley looked exactly like Benny Hill. We stepped onto the long slatted back step and looked into the mobile shop.

'Afternoon, Charley, could we have half a pound of mushrooms, please?' my mother asked.

'Only if you pay off what you owe me from last week,' Charley replied, lifting his eyebrows.

'He's been ill and it's the first time he's wanted something to eat for days,' my mother said, picking me up, sitting me on her hip and stroking my hair. She emptied her purse onto the counter. He counted it out. One pound and sixty-six new pence. I can still remember the exact amounts today for some reason.

'Thank you very much,' said Benny Hill as he scooped up all my mother had. 'But you still owe one pound and fifteen pence,' he said as he marked the debt off in his little black book.

'Can we have some mushrooms?' my mother asked again.

'Not until you have paid off what you owe from last week,' he repeated as he looked around my mother and me for a customer that might have money. A queue of neighbours had formed behind us and as we stepped down off the step and walked past them empty-handed, I could sense my mother's shame. We got home and I pretended I had gone off the idea and said I fancied toast. I watched her making toast. It was the first time I'd seen my mother cry. Before the bread had charred there was a knock at the door and it opened. It was Old Mrs Butterfield from across the street. She stepped inside and handed my mother a brown paper bag full of mushrooms.

'Pay me when you can,' she said. My mother thanked her, she turned and was gone. I knelt on a stool at the table and chopped the mushrooms whilst my mother melted butter in a pan. It was the second time I had seen my mother cry.

My privileged background

Today this would be described as a 'disadvantaged background', but was it? If I had been born in Chelsea to rich parents and had one thousand pairs of shoes, how could I have learned the true meaning of the word 'value'? If I could have afforded a field of mushrooms and I had never seen Old Mrs Butterfield come through my door, how could I ever have known the true meaning of the word 'community'? I suppose rich kids would rely on the dictionary definition for such words. Well, they should be careful; the dictionary is only black and white, and can read like lies. In my book, I think perhaps the words 'disadvantaged' and 'privileged' might be more honest if they were to steal one another's meanings.

For my eighth birthday I wanted a zoom-lens camera. I must have thought for a moment that I *had* been born in Chelsea. There wasn't a hope in hell, they cost hundreds of pounds. I had seen them in the thick photography magazines that once a month I delivered to a big posh doctor's house that sat on its own hill just outside the village. I would hide in the bus shelter at the bottom of the hill and stare at the glossy pictures of brand-new cameras and the close-up images they could achieve and dream that one day I might own one. They could steal a snap of an oblivious wild bird from hundreds of yards away, yet when I stared hard at the image, I could imagine I was right there with the wild creature, sharing its freedom. I would admire every image and wonder what the words might be saying before folding up the far-too-expensive-for-me magazine and slipping it through the door. What I actually got for my birthday was a small cardboard box of Quality Street. It was the type with a cellophane front, so you could see the sweets inside. My brother Glen asked my mother if *he* could wrap the present ready for me coming in from school. My mother, busy with teatime, agreed and he wrapped it. What my mother didn't know was that before he wrapped it and left it on top of the giant TV he had stuck an empty toilet roll tube on the back, so when I picked it up, I might think it was something else. I did. I picked it up, looked at the shape of it and, much to the amusement of all five brothers, shouted, 'Yes, a zoom-lens camera!' My mother came in from the kitchen, saw what they had done and was not amused. We still laugh about this today because it *was* funny. Who the hell did I think I was? A zoom-lens camera, for God's sake! Had I taken leave of my senses? I definitely needed bringing back down to earth. Bet that's never happened in Chelsea. If you look in the dictionary under 'disappointment', it says, *Fail to meet expectations. To not achieve fulfilment. To feel let down.* Not a mention of the word 'learning', or 'valuable lesson'. See, I told you the dictionary was only black and white and tells lies.

'Disappointment' was not something I really understood. I suppose if I was to define its meaning in my dictionary, it might read, *An emotion experienced by only spoiled people when they cry because they didn't get something that was never theirs.* No, we didn't do disappointment. How could we? We had just had to cancel my seventh Christmas because my father had been on strike. Ah! Yes, the miners' strike of 1972, I must tell you about that. But before I do, let me tell you a little more about the man in our house who chose to strike.

2

Pennies in my eyes

My father was a hero. Not just to me but to his country. He lived to the age of eighty-seven. He had been one of eleven children, but only five survived to be adults. The consumption killed six. So called, because that's what it did. It consumed all it touched and took them away. He could remember being a child and seeing his brothers and sisters laid out in open coffins in the living room of their colliery house. They would lay old pennies in the sockets of the dead child's eyes. He never did tell me why; tradition, I suppose. My father contracted 'the consumption' at the age of seven and unexpectedly survived.

'Even my mother had written me off,' he told me. 'I remember waking up on the floor at the foot of my mother's bed and flicking the pennies off my eyes. I could sense a commotion in the room. I'd been tightly wrapped in a stiff cotton bed sheet and it took me a while to wriggle out. I eventually got to my feet and looked through the cast-iron bars of the bed-end, just in time to see my mother give birth to our Ray, my youngest brother. The doctor who had only one day before pronounced me dead and laid me out, ready for my coffin, had just delivered my new brother. My mother was overjoyed. She would always say to me, "That day, I had twins!"'

Can we imagine that today? How does someone deal with watching most of their offspring slowly die? I'm a father of three now and I have thought long and hard about how they could have dealt with such losses yet managed to get on with their lives. At one stage of my quest to fully understand their strength, I even dared to have the audacity to question if they could have actually loved their children as much as we do today. But I think we know the answer to that, don't we?

My father once said to me whilst we worked in the garden, 'If I ever wrote a book about my life, I would call it *Pennies in My Eyes.*'

Hence this chapter's title. It was the least I could do.

He had started working down the mine as a boy of thirteen and on his third day he had seen a man killed by a fall of stone. He'd helped dig him out and stretcher him to the surface. Headed by the colliery manager in his top hat, they delivered the dead man to his miner's cottage by hand cart before laying his body out in the backyard. The manager then paid the shocked and distraught widow what he had been owed to date, before issuing her with eviction papers that said she and her children had seven days to get out of their pit-owned house. He then ordered my father and the team of men and boys back down the shaft to get on with their work.

He was seventeen when Hitler invaded Poland and he gave up working the pit. He walked from Durham to Coventry to work in a munitions factory with a friend of his from our village. Coventry was heavily bombed and my father was blown up and buried alive in rubble. His friend dug him out. Both legs were broken just below the knee and one of his arms was shattered too. He told me about this.

'The air-raid sirens were going off but we thought we'd

chance it and try to make it back to our digs. We were running down the street laughing and carrying on. All of a sudden, we could hear the whistle of bombs coming down. They say they travel faster than sound and you can't hear them coming but believe me, we could hear them all right. The whistling got louder and louder. Joe went one way and I went another. I ran down three small steps and dived into an air-raid shelter and then there was a thump. I can remember not being able to move at all and being completely covered in pieces of concrete. Every time I tried to breathe in, my mouth filled up with dust,' he explained. 'I could hear Joe, my mate, shouting my name and I could feel the rubble piled on top of me getting lighter and lighter. Eventually Joe lifted a concrete block off my face and I spat out the pellet of dust that had formed in my mouth and started to breathe. He then laid me out on a batten door and dragged it up the street and onto a playing field.'

My father said he could remember lying on that door and looking down the high street which was completely ablaze. He said there were about thirty firemen directing hosepipes into the tall burning buildings and he watched as the front of a building toppled slowly into the street, killing them all. He then lost consciousness and woke in a hospital which was to be his home for the next four months. He told me that from all the things that had happened to him in his life, the thing he remembered most vividly and could not forget were the screams of those firemen that day.

While he was lying in his hospital bed, he signed up to join the RAF.

'Why?' I asked him.

'Anything but the navy, always been terrified of drowning,' came the answer. He then spent nearly a year on twenty-six airfields on the south coast of England shooting down the Luftwaffe. The RAF were building an elite parachute regiment and told him the training would take six months. He signed up, his thinking being, by the time he had completed his training the war might be over.

Two months later he was being dropped by parachute behind enemy lines and fighting the Japanese in Singapore, India and Burma. He was in the Special Elite Parachute Regiment 2810. Google it and you will realise that it was against all odds that my brothers and I were born. There were forty in his squadron and they would jump out of a Dakota plane in the dead of night and sabotage strategic points, destroying everybody and everything in their way. After one year he was the only original member of his squadron left. They formed and retrained a new squadron and after only a few months he was one of only three original members left. They formed and retrained another squadron and by the end of the war, he was one of seven original members left.

The evidence of my father's past decorated our house. I grew up thinking it was normal to have an SLR 303 rifle hanging around on the landing, bayonet and all. He had removed the firing pin, of course, so we were unable to murder one another whilst we played. We had a couple of hand grenades as ornaments on the mantelpiece (decommissioned, of course) above a couple of empty tank shells on the hearth and below a criss-cross of samurai swords mounted on the chimney breast that he'd kept possession of after killing a couple of highly decorated Japanese generals. Then there were his two sets of straw-filled army issue boxing gloves we would put on if there were any disputes that needed to be settled. This was a fair system that would be strictly refereed and if one brother was much bigger than his opponent, handicaps such as having to kneel down or keep one hand behind his back would be handed out. Being the smallest, this worked well for me and was often a good opportunity to reap revenge. And then there was his

tent. His big green army tent had been his home and had travelled around the world with him. It would also be our
accommodation every time we went on holiday. He would put
all of us in the back of his tiny Ford Anglia van, drive up to
Scotland, we would pitch it in a farmer's field and when a
farmer came and asked what did we think we were doing, he
would tell them to fuck off! And that would be our home for
a week. My mother only tried it once. I don't think it was her
thing.

One of my older brothers, Raymond, had got in on the act
and had built lots of model Airfix war planes, painted them up
in the finest of detail and hung them from his bedroom ceiling.
We would lie on his bed for hours and imagine what it must
have been like to stare up into the skies of Dresden in 1945. By
the age of six I knew every British aeroplane involved in the
conflict and still do today. My friends loved coming to my
house; I think they thought it was a museum. I grew up feeling
I had just missed the war. I had, I suppose, by a mere twenty
years.

As the years moved on my mother was quite successful in
demilitarising our home. The ornamental hand grenades were
demoted to the shed, the guns and swords were put in the loft
and the tent and boxing gloves disappeared. Some thirty years
later my father took everything from our home that reminded
him of his time at war, including his medals, and donated it all
to a museum in York. He never explained why. I was
devastated.

It's probably fair to say that being the youngest in any large
family has its benefits, if for no other reason than the passage
of time; things get better every day. Looking at how we lived
then and how we live now amazes me. In fact, if you look at
my grandparents, then my mother and father, then my wife and
me and then our children, it could be argued, the longer you

can stay in the womb, the better; I should know, my generation were the first to not be landed with the option of remaining hungry or eating tripe. I suppose there's a time when you just have to pop out and face whatever comes your way. There were a lot of changes in the brief snippet of time from when my eldest brother left home to the point when I did. Despite The Beatles, he had to leave home if he wanted long hair, whereas I got to sit and watch *Top of the Pops* with a mullet. I think our parents probably mellowed a little and moved with the times. My mother was always very trendy and my father certainly changed. My eldest brother, Tony, tells a story that typifies this change.

There were two reasons for having to keep quiet in our house. One was, 'Shhhh! Your father has been on night shift and is in bed!' And two, 'Shhhh! Your father is watching the news!' Well, picture this, me at about eight, walking into the living room full of silent brothers whilst my father is halfway through the sacred BBC *Six O'Clock News*, walking up to the telly, pushing one of its four channel buttons and jumping on my daddy's knee. My brothers look on amazed.

'What's this?' he asked, smiling.

'It's called *The Muppet Show*, Dad. It's much better than the news!' I informed him. To my brothers' astonishment, he watched and enjoyed the whole show. He particularly liked the old men on the balcony. My older brothers always mention this. That and the fact that I never had to go to Sunday school. Actually, there were six of us and only the first three had to go through the ritual of getting dressed in their Sunday best once a week and attending Sunday school. Even though they hated it. I think it had been my father's decision to spare his youngest three of this agony and I can remember a very fresh-faced, young-looking minister knocking at our front door one Sunday afternoon to find out why my brothers had not attended that morning. We had seen him pull up at the front of our house in his white Morris Minor and because it had been my father's decision, my mother had asked him to deal with it. I hid behind a door to one of the spare rooms near the front of the house to hear what was said. I was probably no more than six.

'The boys were not at chapel this morning, Mr Fallow,' said the man in black-and-white dress.

'That's right!' said my father. 'And they won't be there next week.'

'Do you mind me asking why?' asked the minister very politely, to which my father replied:

'Listen, young lad, if you had been to war and seen what I've seen, you wouldn't be stood there dressed like that and believing what you believe.' I couldn't see the reaction on the minister's face, I was hiding behind the door, but he said little more than goodbye and left. I remember thinking, *WOW! My dad tells vicars what to do!*

At Sunday dinner that afternoon my mother asked, 'So, what did the minister have to say?' to which my father replied:

'He'll not be back!'

The only other reference regarding religion I can recall from my father was as he drove his van on the way to one of our camping trips. We'd packed the tent and supplies into the van before jumping in the back. He had a week off work and the weather forecast was brilliant. It was common for the whole street to come out, stand at their gates and wave us off and this particular time I'm sure all six of us plus our dog were there. As we headed north through Northumberland it started to rain heavily. My father switched on the wipers and growled.

'The only reason God is making it rain is because the bastard knows I don't believe in him!' Quite confusing for a kid.

Shortly after we returned from the camping trip our dog disappeared. He escaped one morning and was found later that

21

day, running about in a field full of sheep doing his very best to land himself a lamb dinner. He had been successful and killed two sheep. A few days after, I came in from school only to be informed by my mother that Brit the Labrador had gone to live on a farm in a faraway place called London because there was more space there for him to run around and that's what dogs like best: space. I did at the time find the idea of a dog that liked nothing better than to kill sheep going to live on a farm a little hard to work out. In fact, it was so hard to work out, it took me about another ten years.

I was living in the epicentre of a number of relationship circles surrounding me like the many skins of an onion or the layers that make up planet earth. At the centre, inside the hot inner core, was the nucleus of me, my brothers and our parents. In the next and slightly bigger outer core was my extended family of which there were many. Uncles, aunties, the grand-parents who had not yet managed to die and lots and lots of cousins. In the next ring of warm inner mantle were my friends. People I chose to be with. After that, the ring of slightly cooled mantle was full of neighbours and friends of friends. After that was an even larger ring. The crust. This cold, rocky outer layer contained teachers, shopkeepers, everybody at school. The people I knew well enough to know that I didn't want to know them any better, if you know what I mean: the postwoman (Christine), the insurance man (Stan), the milkman (Frank; he did magic tricks), the rent man (Clem) and many more. Clem the rent man was funny. This was only two decades after the war and if you were unfortunate to look exactly like Adolf Hitler (not a good look today, and definitely not a good look back then), you'd think the least Clem would have done was not grow a tash. But he did. He would walk into our house (nobody knocked and doors were never locked) once a week and my mother would have his rent waiting for him in the middle of the kitchen table. He would count the cash, put it into his leather satchel and then proceed uninvited to check out a few rooms around the house, sometimes even going upstairs. He would go outside and have a look around the garden and then fill in a form to say the house was being looked after but before he left, he would always have a comment.

'That grass needs cutting,' or 'Take that washing line down – it's on next door's fence post,' or the like. I think he fancied my mother. Everybody did. To us, he was just a public servant, doing his job and looking after the council's house. Making sure it was kept right for the next tenant when we had gone. We didn't mind. After all, he was helping to keep the whole estate looking tidy. It was not our house, and we were grateful for what we had.

To me, our back garden was huge and was an extension to our larder. I don't know how my father found the time to plant it but plant it he did. There were long rows of cabbages, sprouts, cauliflowers and all. There were what looked to me through such small eyes like acres of onions, peas, beans and leeks and next to the brick shed there was a greenhouse. All built by my father. The garden came with rules. No footballs and no activities that might result in the veg being damaged and no eating the tomatoes from the greenhouse. All produce had to be brought indoors, cleaned, handed to my mother and evenly distributed to the family.

I wish I could be pleasantly nostalgic about my mother's cooking but I can't. Sunday dinner would be almost like a ceremony and I think my mother would start boiling the veg and incinerating the meat on the Wednesday. All the veg would be boiled into such a mush, it seemed to run into one. Every Sunday the whole family would sit around the table only to be presented with a dinner that looked like it might have *once* appeared appetising before it had spent a night locked outside on the back step in heavy rain.

We would have cereal every morning. School dinners were fine, I liked them, and we got a bottle of milk as soon as we got there. I'm sure we must have qualified for free school dinners; however, we were never made to go through the ordeal of having to stand in the queue in the dining hall to claim free dinner tickets. My mother would set our dinner money out on the mantelpiece every Sunday night. Six piles, mine on the left and the rest to the right in order of age.

'Make sure you get seconds,' my mother would say when we picked up our money. 'There'll only be a sandwich for you when you get in.' That's what life was about. If you paid for something (even though we probably didn't have to), you got your money's worth. I'm still like that today. I can't walk past a skip in the street without having a mooch and seeing what people are throwing out and I never leave anything on my plate. And anyway, it worked fine and, like I said, unlike some of my friends, I never went to bed hungry.

The house itself wasn't complicated. In fact, it was a giant box. There were four bedrooms surrounding a small bathroom upstairs. Downstairs there was a small kitchen and three large rooms, of which we only ever used one, circling a central staircase, plus a small downstairs toilet. The kitchen had a small shelved larder, full of tins, off to the side. The larder was essential. It was our fridge. I'm not sure what the science was behind it, but it was supposed to be cooler in there than the rest of the house. There was an air brick at floor level and an air brick up high and if you looked through them, you could see into the coal house which was only accessible from outside. If there was any milk left after breakfast (which was rare), the tall glass bottle would be stood half submerged in a bowl of tap water in the larder in order to keep it fresh. As high tech as it was, it didn't always work and that system still has me having a good smell of anything before I drink it, all these years on.

I'm not sure to this day why we didn't use all the rooms. Perhaps my parents couldn't afford to furnish them or perhaps they saw living there as temporary and it wasn't worth moving in fully. Or more likely, my parents and us had been born and lived in such cramped conditions we simply didn't know how to grow into the space provided.

There was one neighbour who for some reason stood out in my life. He lived just around the corner and was called Tommy Robins. He looked and sounded like a northern Sid James, was always ridiculously happy and would always be doing or going somewhere interesting. He was, I suppose, just a neighbour but to me he was part of that hot inner core and I do not have a memory from the day we moved into that house of this person not being my best friend. Strange we got on so well really. We had been born thirty-nine years apart and he had actually attended school and the pit with my father's younger brother Ray.

We would go everywhere together and he would always introduce me as 'Pip with the honest face'. I'm still not sure today why. I'm not sure if I had a sly face and he was taking the piss, he was just doing it for his own amusement or he actually thought I had an honest face.

'Look how honest that face looks!' he would say to strangers as I would stand there looking as honest as I could. Another strange thing about Tommy was he no longer worked down the pit. He had worked there from school but after returning from his two years' national service in the navy and going back down the shaft only to be buried under a fall of stone, he had quit. He had been buried for a while and where the black stone had cut through his flesh it had left greyish-blue tattoos on various parts of his body and face. He had also lost his pointing finger from his right hand, leaving only a stump at the first knuckle that he would use as a prop to get laughs by poking up his big nose and asking anybody who had just met him for the first time, 'Could you help me pull this out, please?'

He had a fish shop but sold it. He delivered bread for a bakery but got sacked for lining his own pockets. He had worked as a bus conductor for a few years but got sacked because he didn't feel right taking money from people when the bus was already going there anyway. He had his own ice cream van but not for long. He then worked for British Rail, transporting crews of maintenance men around in a giant yellow Bedford bus. He called it his Yellow Submarine. It had a little cooker, sink and bench seating around a table where men could eat and play cards. We went everywhere in it.

'He's had more jobs than Tommy Robins!' is still a saying in and around the colliery villages of Durham today to describe somebody who can't hold a job down. It makes me smile when I hear people using the saying when they don't know who he was.

I think up to this particular point in my life I was probably the most content and happiest I could be. I probably had a sense of *it doesn't get any better than this*, making me sceptical of change. At eight years old, your thinking is probably, *if it ain't broke, don't fix it*. It wasn't that I lacked ambition, I did have ambitions. I wanted to know how coffee tasted and after watching American TV adverts I had also been asking my mother if I could keep a little of my paper-round money and buy a packet of Wrigley's Spearmint gum. There was a white, metal vending machine that looked like a giant upright packet of Wrigley's Spearmint gum on the wall outside the newsagent's, behind the bus stop, that the miners would use on their way to the pit. The miners used gum because once down the pit they were not permitted to smoke because of explosive gases. I would pick up the shiny, silver wrappers discarded on the pavement and hold them to my nose. If I'm truly honest, I probably had a little lick. I had tasted Beech-Nut before – that was a cheap British equivalent and only a penny a packet – but the smell (taste) that came from the Wrigley's foil was something else. I was convinced I had discovered the taste of America. The idea of slotting a new five-penny piece into the front of that machine, turning its clunky wheel and hearing a small packet of gum drop out of the bottom excited me more than anything else I can remember. One Saturday, I gave my full wage packet to my mother to open and hoped she would remember I had asked for a little back. She did and gave me 5p. I must have pedalled through the streets and back to the newsagent's at over one thousand miles per hour. I clearly remember the packet of gum falling from the machine with a thump and me grabbing it before putting it to my nose. 'This I must show to my brothers,' I whispered to myself as I pedalled off again at the speed of light with the United States of America in my pocket.

All of my brothers were in the house and I remember walking around the living room offering them a piece of gum. I was cool! My mother refused but they all took one and then I asked my father, 'Would you like a piece of American gum, Dad?'

'Oh yes, I'll take that to the pit with me tonight,' he said, lifting his eyes from his newspaper as he took a piece from the packet and dropped it into his shirt pocket. It was the last one. I can recall the deep level of grief I felt when realising my time had not yet come for me to sample the delights of the USA. I snuck away up to my bedroom and cried in my bed, my only comfort being that I had been generous and done the right thing. I think there's probably a lesson in life there somewhere. Anyway, I got to try some Wrigley's Spearmint gum sometime later and it was not that cool. I think this was the dawn of me realising the difference between advertising and lies. None! As for coffee, one of my brothers started studying at a polytechnic and used to pinch sachets of Mellow Bird's from the canteen for us to try at home. I still prefer tea today. With no milk.

It all makes me wonder about happiness. Have you ever asked yourself, *At what point in my life was I the happiest?* Try it!

If your answer is the day I met my husband/wife, the day I got married or the day when my children were born, well, I'm sorry but those answers for me were not truly honest. Concentrate hard and be completely truthful to yourself. Don't be polite and give a manufactured answer designed to please others. When you first met your partner, did you really know what would come of it, and if it was so long ago, can you really remember your exact emotions? And as for your wedding day, was that 'happiness' or was that relief it was all over, all the planning had paid off, things had gone well and you were satisfied everybody seemed to have a nice day? We all feel joy when new life comes into the world, especially when you have helped create it, but let's be honest, that joy *is* loaded. It is joy with grown-up weights piled on top, anticipation, responsibility, worry and probably relief again, that's if everything went well. That is not true 100 per cent happiness. The type of true 100 per cent happiness I have been looking to find definitely does not have things piled on top holding it down.

Being completely 100 per cent honest with oneself was harder than I imagined but I did get there in the end. To find true happiness I had no option but to go to a place where I did not know anticipation, responsibility or worry. After searching for a time, I found that place. There it was, buried deep in my childhood, when I was just six or seven years into my life and lived in that large four-bedroomed council house with my mother, father and five older brothers. On Saturday mornings the whole family would be there. Apart from my father, of course. He was normally down the pit six or seven days per week and if he did get a day off, it would be the odd Sunday. But for the rest of us, there was no school, no college, no factories, nothing. I would always be first to rise. Sometimes I would be up so early I would actually see my father before he slipped out of the door into darkness to get down the pit before the sun came up. Occasionally, if I was very lucky, I would get to spend a few minutes with him. I would help him to light the fire and as the dry sticks snapped and cracked, he would whisper softly so as not to wake the others. He would ask me all about what I had been doing during the week whilst we shared a pot of black tea. The milkman hadn't been yet. He would then kiss me on the top of the head before leaving. The paper boy would soon come as morning broke and my brother Calum's *Look-in* pop magazine would drop on the doormat. I would sit in front of the fire and look at the brightly coloured images of new, glam rock stars like Mud dressed in their Tiger Feet, or Alvin Stardust with his black leather gloves, his Coo Ca Choo and his big silver rings, before placing the magazine carefully back on the mat. He liked to think *he* had seen it first.

My second from the top brother, Raymond, would always be next to rise and this is when that high level of joy would ignite.

'Can we play Sharks in the Carpet?' I would ask. To which he would hide his neck, slide out his bottom jaw and teeth, and wiggle all his fingers as he pulled a face that he and I thought was shark-like. The idea behind Sharks in the Carpet was simple. If you touched the carpet, the sharks that lived in it would gobble you up. He would get on all fours and follow me around the room as I leapt from one piece of furniture to the next in a desperate attempt to stay above sea level. Like a monkey, I would fly through the air from the armchair to the coffee table, only for the shark to then tilt the table slowly from one end. The fear of sliding off into a shark-infested carpet would soon have me leaping through the air again to the next piece of furniture, making sure that not so much as a tip of a toe got wet or bitten off. I would throw cushions into the middle of the sea. These were islands I could fly to but these were dangerous. The noisy shark, who roared like a lion, would pull at them, dragging them around the floor as I clung on, like a limpet to a rock.

This was bliss. Ecstasy. The level of euphoria from having survived those shark attacks I guess can't be measured, but for myself it could go no higher. At the time it felt like Sharks in the Carpet lasted for most of the day, but I'm sure the shark must have run out of steam in no more than an hour. Thinking back now, it seemed so real. Survival was an achievement and I'm sure I can actually remember seeing shark fins sticking above the pile of the carpet. The noise and the chaos downstairs would, I think, wake everybody upstairs because it wouldn't be long before the room would be full of siblings demanding we curb our behaviour. That would be it, the shark's neck would reappear, its teeth and jaw would slide back in, his fingers would become limp and the roar would cease as the beast that lived in the carpet would metamorphose into nothing more than an older brother for another week.

I've tried to relive that ultimate high. I suppose we all do it, chasing something you're not sure can be reached. What I did was to think hard and compare me now to me then, and concentrate on the differences in me today at fifty-five to the differences in me then. *That's easy*, I thought, *everything is different*. If I was to stand on an armchair now and leap through the air landing on all fours on the top of a wooden coffee table, it, together with my legs and wrists, would, I'm sure, shatter into a thousand pieces. But there are more than just the physical differences. Back then I knew no consequences. I didn't know I could crack my head and I definitely didn't know our council house rent was £19.60 per calendar month and my father only earned £32 for a seven-day week.

Another massive difference I found within myself was that I have lost the ability to pretend or play. My brain has been packed with truth, with fact and with grown-up 'think'. I've been ruined. Soiled with logic. How sad. Have I gone so far into being real and sensible there is now no going back? I could give it a go. I could jump around on my furniture and try my utmost to stretch my imagination but I know in my inner self, it does not matter how hard I throw myself about or how intense I stare, I will never be able to see those Sharks in the Carpet.

I have tried beer. That helps me play, but it has consequences in the form of a hangover and giving me empty pockets. I've sampled my fair share of fast women and slow horses. They're as disappointing as one another. I've jumped out of an aeroplane. I had sixteen seconds before my chute opened and then a further thirty-four seconds before I landed softly in a field. It was all right, I suppose. I've considered religion. *That might help me play!* I thought, but I fear I was ahead of the game on that one, having already filed that 'big man in the sky' stuff into my junk box years before emails were even born. However, I must admit, I am a little jealous of those gospel singers when I see them on TV. They look like they can see sharks. I thought about trying drugs but they sound expensive and all that grown-up logic I've picked up on the way just wouldn't allow it. I've tried the cinema. I went the other day. It killed an hour or so, but I'm not entirely sure that even a miserable hour deserves to die that way.

I suppose I'd almost given up. Succumbed to the fact the highs in life have come and gone. I have a five-year-old grandson now and last week he stayed with us for the first time. At six a.m. I heard him creeping down the stairs and I quietly got up and followed him down. I walked into the lounge and our eyes met. Immediately I transformed into a shark. There was no need for an explanation of how the game worked. Perhaps it's instinct or perhaps the rules of the game are passed on genetically, but he certainly knew how to survive. It's a serious game, life or death, and we dived around the room for what seemed like for ever. It only stopped when my wife eventually came down to see what the racket was. She pointed out that his head looked like a tinned tomato and he was near to hyperventilating. And me!

Perhaps there's a message there somewhere. *Don't give up! The highs come back!* Don't get me wrong, I didn't actually get to see fins sticking out of the floor but it was certainly the closest this old man has been for years to seeing Sharks in the Carpet!

3

The man who voted to strike

When I was about ten or eleven my father surprised me by discussing a mission he had taken part in when he was in Singapore.

'We had to take Kallang airport back because we were having trouble getting in supplies,' he explained. 'The briefing and planning took four days. We studied maps and aerial photographs for hours on end. We made detailed plans of what gear would be needed and exactly how, what and when my squadron would attack the airfield. We were to be dropped at midnight the following Sunday and secure the airport tower and surrounding buildings. The rest of the men would then secure the airport while ten of us would take charge of the two fire engines we knew were there from surveillance. Five men in each and I was to drive the first. We would drive out of the airport and head north, all bells and lights blazing until we reached the heavily manned Japanese checkpoint, one point six miles from the airport's gates. We would stop side by side, blocking the road, and flash our lights and ring the engines' bells as if attending an emergency. When the Japs walked down the road to see what all the noise was about and got within twenty yards the second squadron who had set off the day before us and were to be hiding in the jungle either side of the road on the British side of the checkpoint would give it to them.'

'Did it work, Dad?' I asked.

'Not quite,' he explained. 'Taking the airport was simple, we only lost two lads and one of *them* was a roman candle.'

'What's a roman candle?' I asked, intrigued.

'That's what we called it when a chute got tangled and failed to open, just flapped about,' he explained. 'The second man took a bullet when we stormed the building but it was easy and all the Japs ran for their lives. We picked the tell-tales off and took the fire engines and everything looked to be going well.'

'What's a tell-tale?' I quizzed.

'Somebody who could spread news and blow our cover. We couldn't have the checkpoint finding out we had landed so we shot them all as they ran away across the airfield,' he said in a manner like he was talking about shooting at paper targets and not real people.

'What happened at the checkpoint, Dad?' I was desperate to know.

'Well, we stopped short, parked the fire engines side by side and started to make a noise. Within a minute there were forty or more Japanese solders walking steadily towards us. They got past halfway. Nothing happened. The headlights dazzled them and they couldn't see our British faces inside, yet they were getting closer and closer with each step and still nothing from the hidden squadron. "Let's go!" I whispered and we all jumped out and started firing. Some dropped, some turned and ran and some stood and fired back. Within half a minute the only men left on the road were the dead and dying but quite a few had made it back to the checkpoint. We jumped into the fire engines and I shouted to the boys to get their grenades ready. We raced forward as fast as the heavy engines would let us and as we passed the checkpoint building, we showered it with bullets and grenades. We could hear the hand grenades thumping and men screaming as we stopped about fifty yards up the road. We jumped out and finished the last ones off. We had taken out over sixty men and secured the checkpoint but they had taken four of us.'

'Where was the hidden squadron?' I asked.

'The commanders had not sent them. They had calculated my squadron would all be killed at the airport and had dropped the second squadron in behind us thinking *they* might make some headway if we had caused some damage. There was even a third lot ready if they were lost.'

'How did that make you feel?' I wanted to know.

'Ah, everybody had their job to do,' he commented.

He didn't talk of conflict much. It was rare. You would have to mention something relevant first, he would then play it down and you would have to nudge gently if you wanted a little more. I would get a little snippet of his life out of him from time to time and over the years I slotted the pieces together. I think there is an element of truth when it is said the people who experienced first-hand what it was like don't like to talk about it. I have a theory about this. It is based solely on my father's behaviour and his reactions to others. There were several occasions in my life when I have been in the company of someone who has boasted about what they did in and after the war. My father would always just sit and say nothing. I would think to myself, *If I had done half of what he had done, I would be telling everybody.* But there lies the difference. I was not there. The people who went and done it don't brag. They can't. My theory is, the reason they don't brag is because they feel that, unlike their fallen comrades, they didn't give every-thing. They came home. I believe it's guilt that keeps them quiet, a guilt that only they will ever know. I might be wrong

35

but it stacks up in my father's case. He hated American films that glorified war. He would laugh at the telly and then tell us to switch it off. I remember watching a war film. John Wayne was complaining he'd been hit in the shoulder by a bullet and my father laughed out loud.

'Why are you laughing, Dad?' I asked.

'Because it's not really like that,' he explained, still laughing. 'I've shot men in the top of the chest and in the shoulders and watched them spin on the floor like a dying fly and rip their own cheeks off because of the pain before I've put them out of their misery,' he said, switching it off.

He told me of a time when he had been fighting in the streets of Singapore.

'I stuck my head around the street corner and there were about two hundred Japanese troops running towards us down the street.'

'What did you do?' I asked him.

'Shouted to everybody to run like hell,' he explained as though stating the obvious. 'But I knew we wouldn't get to the end of the street before they came around the corner. The first few got around the corner and started to fire at us and the men I was running with started to hit the deck. You could hear the bullets cutting through their flesh before they went down. Unmistakable sound, that,' he said, in a very reflective manner. 'A bullet cutting its way through flesh.'

'What happened next?' I asked, intrigued.

'I jumped into a shop doorway and there was a door set back about three feet from the street. I smashed through it with the butt of my gun and went inside. It was a public toilet and there was a row of brick cubicles down one side with a single sky light above them. I shot the sky light out. The Americans had just joined the war effort and we'd been issued with new semi-automatic rifles. If you held the trigger in, it kept on firing. I jumped up, like a cat, sitting on top of the cubicles and I could hear the shuffle of the Japs' boots as they started to make their way in. I aimed my gun at the doorway and gave it to the first one that came in. I think I caught the second one as well. The rest backed off, giving me time to jump out of the skylight. It was a flat roof and I ran and jumped straight off the back of the building and luckily the wind had blown a pile of soft sand up against the wall below me and I landed in it. I hid in among some trees and within a few minutes a British army wagon came by and I jumped in the back and got back to base. Don't know why they didn't just slip a grenade in with me. I would have been knackered. Can't have been very well trained,' he said.

'How old were you then, Dad?' I remember asking.

'Nineteen,' he replied. I had a friend with me when he told that story and to this very day, whenever I bump into him, he will recite the story word for word from the very beginning to the very end. He has never forgotten any of it. Nor I.

He had killed hundreds of men, liberated British prisoners of war and seen things probably no man should see. He was a very well-built, handsome man and all my friends would joke he looked like Tarzan from the old black and white Johnny Weissmuller films. He did, I suppose, but to talk to he was more like Tommy Cooper.

He was also very upbeat and a witty man who rarely said a sensible word. He stayed in the forces for four years after the war setting up governments and councils and sorting things out. He referred to this period as 'mopping up'.

He got kicked out of the RAF. A dishonourable discharge. He killed a man for stealing blankets from the British army stores in Singapore. He had wanted to set an example of what happens to people who steal by throwing the thief head first down a well. He died of drowning. My father was then made an example of by the very government he had just set up. He was given a life sentence for murder but after receiving a personal letter from Lord Mountbatten, the Singapore judge agreed to let him serve his sentence in Britain so he could be visited by his family. He was locked up in a Singapore jail for two days and two nights before being escorted by military police and his CO and put on a ship to HM port of Southampton. His commanding officer followed him onto the ship and issued him with his prison papers.

'Now, Tommy,' he said, 'there are two things that you can do with these papers. One: you can take care of them and when you reach Blighty you can hand them over to the local authorities so they can deal with you. Or two: you can wait until this ship leaves the harbour, roll the papers up into balls and throw them into the sea. Do you understand?'

'Understood, sir!' he replied. He talked of the eleven-week journey home seeming like eleven years. The ship was a rusty old boiler that had definitely seen better days. It had been condemned and was supposed to have been scrapped some two years previously, but the navy had patched and bodged it as part of their effort to repatriate almost a million men after the war had ended. The job was nearly done. It was her last voyage and if it did reach Southampton, it was to be scrapped there. He said it would bang and crack and sometimes its steel frame would let out a scream as he laid trying to sleep in his makeshift hammock.

'I would lie there thinking, *I can see it now, I managed to avoid the navy, I've survived everything I've had thrown at me and this ship is going to snap in two and my mother will receive a telegram saying,* LOST AT SEA.'

Despite the dubious seaworthiness of the ship, and after almost three months of tormented sleepless nights swinging around in his hammock, his feet eventually touched the dry land of Southampton where he was demobbed. One week later, he was living in London and had joined the police force.

That didn't last long either. The sergeant who was training them had somehow managed to avoid going to war and had taken a dislike to a chirpy scouser my father had got to know on the ship. My father hated bullies and had stood up to the sergeant.

'Why don't you pick on me instead?' he had asked. The sergeant tried and died of his injuries a month later in hospital. My father had knocked him through the wall of a mess hut that was made from corrugated cement sheets and as he laid unconscious in the hole he had just made, a large piece of the sheeting had slipped out and fell onto his head. Another dishonourable discharge.

One hot summer my father took me and a friend of mine camping in Eyemouth in Scotland. We were teenagers and my brothers, I think, had probably seen enough of the inside of the big green tent. He was a good singer and the pubs would pay him to perform. He would leave us in the tent while he went out singing. We didn't mind this because he would always return in the dark with a bottle of Newcastle Brown Ale and fish and chips each. It was heaven. He returned with the goods one night and I remember him staring into the embers of the campfire. We were right near the beach high on the grassy clifftops.

'What are you looking at, Dad?' I asked him.

'That's just what it looks like before you jump down onto a town that has been heavily bombed,' he explained, his face glowing orange as he continued to stare at the hot embers. Now, if your father fought in the war, you have for sure, as a kid, asked this question.

'How many people have you killed, Dad?'

'Enough to get tired of it,' was his delayed reply. He went on to explain that after the Yanks had dropped two atomic bombs on Japan the Japanese had lost heart and given up. He explained that the war in Europe had been won but until then the Japanese had been fighting on.

'I remember finding a Japanese conscript hidden in a pile of rubbish in a back street in a small town in Burma and pulling him out so I could get a clear shot at him. He knelt before me, put his hands together and said prayers as I rested my gun on the top of his skull.' He poked at the ashes with a stick. 'I didn't pull the trigger. I put my foot on his chest and kicked him back into the rubbish.'

'Why?' I asked.

'Because I'd had enough of killing,' he said softly, still staring into the campfire. My friend never forgot that story either. Nor, again, did I.

'What was the worst thing you had to do, Tommy?' asked my friend.

'Killing our own,' he said. 'When we went into the Japanese prison camps, they had kept our lads in such squalid conditions, they were knackered. They could never have made the journey home.' He went on to explain how the Japanese had made the captured British servicemen dig what they thought were their own graves, made them lie in them and then put thick bamboo cages over the top. This was where they had remained for the whole time of their incarceration. Some of them had been living in shallow graves under the hot sun and had not been let out for almost two years.

'The majority of them were skin and bone and most were blind and had lost their minds,' he went on to explain. 'Our job was to get them out of their pits, clean them up and present them to the army doctor. If they could tell the doctor their name, rank and number, they were sent to the hospital but most of them couldn't stand, see or talk and we had to take them around the back of the building, put a bullet through their heads and bury them. Awful,' he said, his big face still holding the orange glow of the campfire.

Ah, yes! Sorry, the 1972 pit strike. The miners had a ballot and voted overwhelmingly to strike. British Coal was making massive profits yet the miners didn't feel like the profits were getting passed their way. The strike was over pay and only lasted a couple of months. The public had sympathy with the miners' plight back then. The country was brought to its knees, the power stations ran dry of coal, the electric died and the country was in darkness. Edward Heath's Conservative government fell and after a couple of months of striking the miners went back to work victorious. For me at six, it was exciting. I had never seen so much of my father. My main present for Christmas that year was a plastic football, which I later learned my eldest brother had managed to steal from his school. Because of the lack of coal and the subsequent lack of energy, Britain had been reduced to a three-day working week. We had no electricity most days and at night we lived by candlelight and we ate mainly soup made from veg my father had planted in our back garden, yet the memories I have of those few months still fill me with a fondness today.

The whole family slept downstairs in one room because it was the beginning of January and it was extremely cold outside. The room had an open coal fire and though I thought it great fun at the time, thinking back to those times now, it must have been very difficult for my parents. I have a memory of my mother being short-tempered and me not understanding why.

'Mam, the grill won't work.'

'I know, there's no electricity,' she explained.

'Mam, the light is broken in the kitchen.'

'I know, there's no electricity,' she explained again.

'Mam, the kettle won't boil.'

'I know! There's no bloody electricity, now bed down and keep quiet,' she shouted.

Everybody bedded down. About one hour later I needed the toilet and whispered, 'Mam, can I go to the toilet?'

'Yes, but hurry up and take a candle with you,' she whispered, sharply. I took a candle from the mantel and, careful not to step on a brother, left the room.

'Mam,' I whispered, sticking my head back through the door.

'What now?' she shouted in a whisper.

'Will I be able to flush the chain?'

I can still remember today being confused by the huge roar of laughter coming from that room whilst I did my wee by candlelight.

The news of the miners taking down the government was huge. Thousands of working men toppling the Tories, despite all their power and might. On the day Edward Heath accepted defeat and instructed his government to step down, every miner in every village marched behind their brass band to their pit-head and celebrated at its chained gates. The sight from the top of the village of nearly two thousand jubilant men shouting and jeering whilst the brass followed the thump of the big bass drums was something a six-year-old could never forget. I took a photo. Not with a camera, of course – we couldn't afford nowt like that – just a personal one etched on my brain. I prefer that type of photo to the ones we see on glossy paper. I find they can't be lost, or stolen, and they never fade.

My father had voted YES to strike action. I'm not sure why.

It must have been a huge decision to forfeit being paid for nobody knew how long with six kids to feed. I guess after the life he had lived he might have thought he deserved more than to be working three jobs seven days a week, only to see his kids walking to school in plastic sandals.

4

Starting school

My father had a tattoo. It was on his forearm and read
NEVVER AGAIN. It said NEVVER at the top and then there
was a crude drawing of a miner's safety lamp and then under
that, the word AGAIN. He'd acquired it during the war whilst
serving in Burma. Apparently, back then tattoos on a man were
a sign they had travelled. Unlike today, where you can get a tat
with your morning paper from most street corners. He was
never entirely sure if the NEVVER having two VVs in it had
been a spelling mistake or a deliberate act. He had written what
he wanted on a piece of paper, given it to the tattooist and let
him get on with it. When the artist finished, he looked at his
arm and was outraged by the two VVs. He had become even
more outraged when the tattooist demanded payment.

'Had he done it on purpose?' I remember asking.

'Aye, I think so. They didn't like us occupying their country,'
he smiled.

'Did you pay him?' I asked.

'No!' he said, laughing at the tattoo. 'There was a two-pint
jug of cooking oil on the table and I put my rifle to his head,
put my finger on the trigger and made him drink it.'

'Why did you do that?' I asked.

'Well, I thought if I have to live with a mess on my arm for

44

the rest of my life, at least he should have the shits for a couple of weeks,' he laughed. A stark reminder of how very different times must have been back then.

For my father to have been sitting on the other side of the planet in his mid-twenties and proclaiming he NEVVER wanted to go down the pit AGAIN says a lot to me about his then mood. He had been fighting for his country and for his very life for years yet felt he had escaped a worse hell.

My parents had made a ten-year plan. The idea was to use the rented big four-bedroomed council house to bring up the children whilst working hard and saving until they could buy their own home when a few chicks had become fully fledged and flown the nest. My father had been a fireman since his return from war, but after twenty years of fighting fire and just after my birth he had thrown in the towel. He needed a bigger wage and after biting the bullet, ignoring his tattoo, he had done the unthinkable and gone back down the pit at the age of fifty.

They achieved their ten-year plan in seven. They bought a run-down bungalow at the top end of our village a stone's throw away from the house where we had all been born. My father had six pigs in his allotment. He would travel in his van around four local schools after his shifts at the pit and collect their food waste for the pigs. Once they had eaten so much tapioca, semolina and custard that they were enormous, we put them in a trailer, put the trailer on the van and travelled two hours south to the Melton Mowbray pork pie factory. The money we got for six fat pigs that day paid for a kitchen and bathroom extension to be put on the back of our new bungalow. Another stark reminder of how different times were back then. It seemed silly paying rent with the bungalow standing empty. My mother got impatient and wanted to be in before we could afford it. They decided to take on a small mortgage. We were in. My father agreed to stay on at the pit until the mortgage had gone, my mother took a full-time job at a school as a nursery nurse and cleaned a local pub on a morning before she went there. This was how it would be until they were comfortable enough to retire. Despite what the tattoo said, my father did fourteen years at the bottom of that shaft. Until recently, I'd given this level of commitment little thought. I suppose I just thought he was doing what any man might do for his family. I suppose at the time I even thought I would do the same for my kids if needed.

I recently visited a coal mine. The National Coal Mining Museum for England have kept one open for the public to see in Wakefield. It is called Caphouse Colliery. Go, if you get the chance! I went with a friend who had worked alongside my father and he showed me what my father had been doing for the last fourteen years of his working life. What happened next was a massive shock. I was overcome with emotion to the point of sobbing and I think this happened for three reasons. The first being how dreadful the place was and how awful his time working underground had been. It was cold. It was dark. It was wet. It was filthy. It was hell! And the second, I had not realised how much he had given. His level of commitment to his family. To me. And third, I suppose the unexpected overspill of emotion stemmed from me not being able to discuss this with him and thank him whilst he was here. As for thinking I would probably do the same for my own family . . . Well, I'm not sure what it makes me, but I definitely could not.

Moving from that council estate and back into a privately owned house broke my heart. We only moved one mile, but to me at the age of eight or nine, it seemed so far away from all that had become my world. I think I worried the relationships I had made might quake and fracture or slip from under my plastic sandals. After school I would travel with my friends to my old home despite not living there any more and stare at the house from outside. After my friends had disappeared into their homes I would fly about on my bike, complete my two paper rounds, have a cup of tea with Tommy before pedalling or getting a lift in his stinking Land Rover that he now sold wet fish from the back of, back to my new address. Like a loyal homing pigeon confused and not wanting to be a stray.

The miners had won their battle for better pay. This was the seventies. The era today's mainstream media and modern-day politicians look back on as the dark days of high inflation, 'out of control wages', 'Something we must never go back to!'. Really! What stuck in my mind was, it was the first time we'd had owt! Anyway, that's not a rabbit-hole I want to venture down this early in the book but we'll come back to that one later.

Three chicks had become fully fledged and had flown. Tony, my eldest brother, had followed in his father's footsteps. No, he'd not started murdering people but had joined the fire brigade, bought his own house and married. Raymond, the second eldest, *had* followed in his father's footsteps and joined the RAF. Lucky for him it was peacetime and he was now living in Germany. And the third eldest, Glen, was in jail for stealing cars.

The crime he committed was hardly related to the modern-day crime of stealing cars and selling them for a profit. This was the birth of 'joy riding'. Glen and a couple of friends would take a car (the older types that could be started with a screwdriver as a key), drive around in it for an hour in the dead of night and then quietly replace it without the owner's knowledge. They had been doing it for months. They would even mark the tarmac with chalk so they could carefully return the tyres to their exact positions. However, theft is theft and they were caught when some poor soul got up in the middle of the night and tried to travel to the village pit to do his night shift, only to discover he had no car.

The gang of three attended court and were found guilty. They pleaded with the magistrates, saying they had only done it the once and they had fully intended to replace the car and said they were so sorry for any harm done. They even offered to pay for the petrol. My father attended the court and asked if he could get up and say a few words before they passed sentence. The magistrates agreed and my father, suited and booted, stood in the witness box. He explained about his service in the parachute regiment, in and after the war, his twenty years as a fireman and how he had served his community as a parish councillor for twenty years before more recently becoming a county councillor. He then let rip.

'This what you see in front of you today, your honours, is the new long-haired generation. They have no respect for their elders and no respect for people's property. I have watched them today as they have lied in court and tried their best to pull the wool over your eyes. I have tried everything with my son and it has all failed. He has been sacked from his job as an apprentice welder at the colliery twice for poor attendance and I have had to attend two tribunals and beg for them to give him another chance. Yet his apathetic attitude and his disrespect for his mentors still precede him. Let me tell this court today that if this young man does not receive a sharp short shock in the form of a prison sentence, he will only go on to cause good honest people more disruption and more distress and I can assure you that it will not be long before he will be standing in front of you again. Please lock him up for the good of all.' He stood down.

'Thanks, Dad!' Glen shouted across the courtroom before he was sent down for six months in a youth detention centre.

I think that's what they call 'tough love', or at least, what was once called tough love. It's not something we see a lot of today. Whatever it's called, it worked. He entered jail as a boy and came out a man. Even at the age of eight I could sense he was the black sheep. I remember how my four remaining brothers and I stared from our living room window at my very well-dressed parents as they returned from court. I can see them now getting out of the van, without Glen, surrounded by a dozen twitching curtains before heading, arms linked, down the garden path to the front door of our council house. It was the third time I'd seen my mother cry.

Some months later I recall moving house with my mother in the van whilst my father was down the pit and asking, 'Are you going to tell Glen where our new house is?' I remember her laughing at my lack of understanding of the situation. Under normal circumstances if you got six months in a youth detention centre, you could be released in four on grounds of good behaviour. This didn't apply to Glen; he did the whole six months because he had hit somebody over the head with a metal mop bucket in the showers. I still have an image of him now on his first day of release. Him standing to attention to watch *Top of the Pops* in our new house (my mother must have let him know where it was). He had a shaven head revealing a lot of acne on the back of his neck and looked startled or far too aware of his surroundings. However, he can't have been that aware; Queen's 'Bohemian Rhapsody' had been number one for twelve weeks and he'd never heard it.

His demeanour had changed; my father's remedy had worked and in just over a year he had bought his own house, not missed a shift at the pit and had married the girl of his dreams. She must have had an eye for the bad boy because she was the daughter of the man whose car he had stolen. It didn't last.

*

My first three years at infant school were easy. Looking back on those days now, all I can feel is an overall sense of mothering. Lots of what seemed like very old women fussing and being kind. I felt popular and liked, the food was hot and good and I remember being let outside a lot to play. Being let outside was very important to me then. It still is today.

The infant and junior schools were joined together. The building itself was a red-brick affair with separate yards for boys and girls surrounded by black spiked wrought iron and right in the centre of the village, under the massive daunting shadow of the iron pithead. It was under its shadow in every sense. It seemed the pithead, like the school building itself, was part of life's big plan. You started at the south end aged four and every year you were moved up a class and a step closer to the north end of the building. Eventually at the age of eleven you fell out of the north end of the building onto the cobbled streets, picked yourself up and started at the comprehensive school which was just that bit further north and just that bit closer to the dark hole that was to be your place of work for the next fifty-something years.

From my classroom window, I would look up at the massive cast-iron pit wheels spinning and listen to their hum, their whizz and then their clang. My father was the on-setter, which meant he sat at the bottom of the shaft, and was partly responsible for the sound. His job was making sure the men were safely in the cage before sending them, or coal, up when all was well. I would know when he was down there and felt connected somehow to that sound. It seemed its dominance and sheer might, together with its constant chiming, were the drive for a very slow-moving conveyor belt sucking me and all I knew towards that shaft. I felt glued to that belt and powerless to get off.

Following my five brothers through school carried

expectations and I don't think, for me, this was a good thing. I couldn't help thinking the teachers were disappointed and expected a little more. Number one son had been a high achiever and had passed his eleven plus, gone on to grammar school (too good for the pit!) and had later become a fire chief. Number two had been a very high achiever and had gone off to be a fighter pilot in the RAF (definitely too good for the pit!). He didn't make the grade actually and after two years of flying they had made him an aircraft engineer. Number three son was the welder at Easington pit but had been a very strong character and had definitely left his mark. Number four, Calum, had been excluded from the mainstream education system for violent behaviour. He had been getting bullied, had waited outside the school for the bully and had taken things a little too far. He was not allowed to mix with other pupils and had been removed from the comprehensive school and put back into the junior school where I was and spent his last year in the education system having one-to-one tuition because he was deemed a threat to others. I would often see Calum sitting face-to-face with his teacher in his own classroom, but I was not allowed to speak to him inside the school building. We would cross one another in the corridors and have to ignore each other, but then he would wait outside the gates for me and we would chat and walk home together.

It didn't do him any harm. Today he is the chief executive of some local government department somewhere or other, getting very well paid for doing a job I don't really understand. Number five son, Nigel, hadn't helped my cause at all. Perhaps I should have pushed him harder down those wooden stairs. I think he was a mathematical genius because he had been taken out of the system and sent to a college where they possessed the right resources for concentrating on his talents. He studied pure maths for a while before doing a masters in Civil

Engineering. Then there was me and for some reason I was having difficulty reading and writing and I think this was the time of my life that this started to become a problem. Today they would have a label for it. Dyslexia or dyspraxia or something or other. What the teachers called it then was 'backward'. I could recognise letters and know their sounds. I could build up the letters, put the sounds in order and read a word. I could slowly but surely build up the sounds in a series of words and read a sentence, but the effort involved would leave me with no recollection of what the sentence had said. This made most subjects difficult and all written exams impossible.

As I was moved a few classrooms further north, I started my four years in junior school and this was when things started to get sticky. I think I must have been a Marmite child. Some teachers liked me and would go out of their way to help me and others would only shout at me, wouldn't have me in their classrooms and would call me a dunce and a retard.

Things haven't changed so much. I have three sons and my youngest had exactly the same problems as me. I found myself at his school on three different occasions telling three different teachers, 'It doesn't matter if you don't like my child, your job is to pretend you do and to teach him.' They all took it on the chin actually and one young lady teacher actually broke down and cried and apologised for failing in her duties. I don't blame the teachers. I don't think I would have ever recognised these failures in the system if I had not once been that boy. It was the same with his reading and I was quick to pick up on that too before it became an issue. I think it is easy to solve a problem if that problem was once yours and you know it inside out. He is a very funny boy who puts humour above all else. He is good at sports, has never looked at a television in his life and hates walls around him. It was easy for me to teach him to read; all I did was make sure it was fun, and on a subject he would be interested in and then familiarise him with what he was about to read so he didn't have to concentrate so hard on the plot as he was concentrating on the words. I don't think he will ever read for pleasure but he is getting on very well in life. Back to the plot.

Apart from the dinners, things got quite unpleasant for me at school. I have very sad memories of being stuck inside the school building whilst everybody else was running about outside in the sun and air. One teacher, Mr Sanderton, would shout out ten words like completion, commotion, companion, and so on, and we would have to write them down on a piece of paper. We would then have to line up, present him with our papers and if they were spelled correctly, you would be allowed outside to breathe. This would result in me rarely getting out and the few times I did were because I had cheated. He was on my case and if all ten were correct, he would shake his head and say, 'I don't think so, boy!' The bastard would know and would make me write them out again in front of him.

Some kids could not spell at all and would be let out without question. I think they were seen as lost causes. The write-offs. Completely backward. They had it good, they didn't have to do anything to be allowed outside. I think the teacher wanted them out of his way so he could teach the worthy. I remember wishing I was fully backward like them and not only half backward like I was. I even had a few teachers hoodwinked. I would slow my words, slow my speech and limit my sentences so they would think I was a lost cause. A write-off. It worked and often I would be ignored and left alone. Anything for an easy life. It seemed it was survival of the thickest.

There were a few lessons that if you pretended you were interested in, you could get out of the classroom. Gardening was one. Being in the hottest, most boring greenhouse in the world was a thousand times better than being in any class, but it was seasonal and didn't save me for long. I joined the choir but that came to an end when they realised where the noise was coming from.

I hated Mr Sanderton and once stole his chalk and wrote SANDBAG IS A BASTERD in huge letters on the brickwork outside his classroom. I got caught for the crime and found guilty straight away because I was the only one in his class arrogant, yet backward enough to have a go at spelling bastard and fail. He beat me badly, which was frightening, but the bit I remember most about that beating was the reaction from the rest of the class. As he struck me repeatedly, all the boys stared down at the floor, whilst all the girls pulled their school jumpers over their faces and sobbed uncontrollably. He blamed me for making the girls cry and I clearly remember him shouting, 'Now, look what you have done!' as he beat me more. His weapon of abuse was called the slipper but was, in fact, a shoe. He kept it hung high on a nail to the right-hand side of his blackboard. It was blood red, ridiculously long and pointed and must have surely one day belonged to a giant clown. That day he grabbed the shoe, by the toe, with his right hand and my hair with his left. He swung at me repeatedly, hitting me with the heel until my hair came out in his hand. He threw my hair on the floor, grabbed my collar and continued.

Next time you are fortunate enough to be in the company of a ten-year-old child, look how cute they are, take the time to look at the size of their bodies. Their height, their small legs, look how thin their arms are, imagine how much they weigh. FFS.

A few days later, whilst in the bath, my mother realised clumps of my hair were missing and then spotted my arms were covered in bruises. I had sacrificed my arms to protect my backward brain from his blows. Sensing her high level of concern, I told her the truth about what had happened. The next day,

54

she told me I had to help her with her cleaning job at the pub and she would drive me to school. I thought I was in trouble. Those days if you got in bother at school and your parents found out, it usually meant you got a second round of bother at home. We arrived at the school and she told me to wait in the van while she had a meeting with Mr Sanderton. I could see her but not hear her through the window as she leaned across with knuckles pressed into his desk and shouted at the teacher with all her fight! She returned to the van composed and very calmly explained that if I kept my nose clean, Mr Sanderton would not be hurting me again, before explaining to me how very important it was that I didn't tell my father about 'any of this'. She then smiled and told me to get into school and do exactly as told. Not sure to this day why father was to be kept in the dark. Perhaps she knew he had at some point in his life become tired of murdering people and was scared he might relapse.

Mr Sanderton never hurt me again. Better than that, he seldom spoke to me thereafter. The only time he would speak to me was when he told me to get outside with the rest of the halfwits and write-offs so he could get on and teach the worthy. It felt like a huge weight had been lifted from my shoulders and I enjoyed the sun, the space and freshness of the air. I hated being in that room. I would stare out at the pit pulleys as they hummed loudly and spun so fast that their spokes would blur and vanish, before magically appearing again as they slowed and then stopped with their whizz and that clang. I would then look across the corridor at Calum, head to head with his one-to-one teacher before staring back at the slipper and realising there was no escape. It continued like that right up to the day I fell out of the north end onto the cobbles, picked myself up and started my five-year stint at comprehensive school. It seemed I was caught in a trap. It didn't matter what I did, I was being slowly drawn closer and closer to that 'provider of all' black hole at the bottom of the village and every time I tried to grab on to something solid, it would simply snap off and turn to dust in my fist.

5

My mother

Where do I start? At the beginning, I suppose. There was a twelve-year age gap between my mother and father which meant she had a much better deal in her childhood and lost only one sibling. Billy died before his second birthday. Poor Billy. Didn't even live to see the bottom of a pit shaft. Eight survived. My mother has very early memories of creeping down the stairs with two of her sisters in the dead of night and seeing Billy's tiny white coffin with its shiny brass furniture laid out in the middle of the front room. They were very young and had no concept or understanding of the finality of death. She remembers being excited and thinking the coffin containing her brother was a cake.

If my father looked like Tarzan, my mother looked like Jane. She was a beauty queen and beat thousands to win the Miss County Durham beauty competition three years running. She won it on the fourth year too but some bastard grassed her up for being a Mrs and not a Miss. And because she was married with two kids she was duly disqualified and asked not to enter again. She was, and still is, highly intelligent, but intelligence then was not something a woman should display or be recognised for. She was sent to grammar school at the age of eleven and excelled, but after a few years her father judged she was getting a little above her station and at the age of fourteen she was instructed to stop attending school, forget her studies, help her mother with the upbringing of her seven siblings and assist with domestic chores. Her wings clipped.

She was brought up with nine other members of her family in a two-bedroomed colliery house. The house, 67 Tenth Street, was straight opposite my father's house, at the top of the village, and as you can imagine was tightly wedged between Ninth Street and Eleventh Street. I remember the house well and would visit my grandparents at the weekends. To see a house like that today you would have to visit a museum. There was a coal fire burning in every room. All cooking was done on the fire and there was no bathroom. There was an outside toilet at the bottom of the backyard next to the coal house, a single external cold tap, a tin bath hung on the wall just outside the back door and a huge photo of Queen Elizabeth II on her coronation day hung above the fire on the chimney breast in the living room. I'm only fifty-five now and can hardly believe this is how people lived in my lifetime. When I tell my kids about how my grandparents lived, they look at me like I must be a phantom who has just celebrated his four hundredth year alive. Perhaps I've turned into one of those dads.

The house was always full of wonderful smells and if you weren't hungry before you went through the back door, you were starved by the time you got sat on the wooden framed two-seater sofa with its hard, brown nylon cushions. I don't think I was ever as hungry as Brocken, the skinny black 'n' tan Jack Russell who lived in the backyard but was secretly allowed on the hearth rug when my grandfather was not in the house. Brocken survived on humans being clumsy and was only ever fed if food was accidentally dropped or slipped to him by us sly kids.

I don't think I ever saw my grandmother sat down and I

can't remember ever seeing my grandfather stood upright. She was a large woman who didn't ever stop, was constantly on the go, tending to the two fires upstairs and the two fires downstairs or my grandfather's needs. My grandmother loved the Lord. My grandmother loved her Guinness, and my grandmother loved Brocken. I think she loved them in that order. Her twelve half bottles of Guinness would be delivered in a wooden crate by a wooden-backed brewery wagon every Friday. It must have been before off-licences or before women were allowed in pubs and every week the wagon would drive around the colliery streets dropping off beer in backyards for cash. Two bottles per night but nothing on a Sunday, Sundays being the day of the Lord!

I remember Stan the postman delivering a letter one Tuesday morning while I was there. It was from the brewery. It read that Brocken the dog had bit the brewery man on the back of his calf on his way out of the gate and if nothing was done, there would be no delivery the following Friday. I called around the following week and asked where the dog was.

'We had it destroyed on Wednesday, son. He was nee good!' she explained.

My grandfather was everything you would expect from a Durham miner. He looked like Clark Gable and shared the same perfectly trimmed moustache. He worked down the pit from the age of thirteen until the day he was sixty-five, always wore a three-piece suit with a trilby hat, had racing pigeons and was chairman of the committee at the working men's club for over thirty years. If I ever needed to prove my working-class roots, I would fall on this man. If I am a quarter of him, that should be enough to give me a bloody good pedigree. However, he was a man I never liked. Despite not ever doing anything for anybody he would constantly be ranting about somebody he had once asked to do something for him and because they hadn't, how useless they were and how they had done him wrong. He had no humour and thought the world revolved around him. It did.

They had two bedrooms upstairs, a cupboard-sized kitchen off the back of the house and two living rooms downstairs but only one would be used. The front room was 'kept for best'. It was full of all the best furniture that was not allowed to be sat on and had a china cabinet in the corner which contained the best plates that were far too good to eat from, teacups that were too good to drink from and in the middle of the floor, a mat too good to walk on. Not sure what 'kept for best' actually meant. Not sure if everything was kept for better people or for better days. My grandmother didn't get any better days. She dropped dead on the living room floor, looked down on by the cheap glossy print of the Queen in her gold, diamond-encrusted crown. She died between stoking the coal fire and making her man a mug of tea. A hard life lived. I remember one of my aunties commenting that at least she hadn't suffered, and my mother correcting her and saying she had done nothing but. My mother has always felt cheated in this respect. If her mother had only lived a little longer, they could have showered her with the niceties that today we refer to as the basics. Perhaps we can all learn from this.

After her death my grandfather fully expected his daughters (not his sons) to step up and tend to his every need; and they did. Much of his time spent down the mine had been on his knees shovelling coal and within a few years of retiring both legs had been amputated above the knee. He would shout out his one-word orders from his armchair.

'Sandwich! Tea! Biscuit!' And they would be placed on his knee. Or rather his lap.

I got the job of keeping his fire alight. I did this for about four years. I would call around early on a morning before

60

doing my paper rounds and liberating my chickens. My job was to put the kettle on the gas hob on entry, empty the teapot, put two pushes of loose tea into it, which came from a white bottle-shaped plastic PG Tips dispenser that was fixed to the wall with a big black button on it, pour the boiled kettle onto the loose tea, rake the fire, take out the ashes and put them in the metal bin outside, put coal on the fire, fill his two metal buckets from the coal house, pour his tea through a strainer into an enamel mug, which looked to me about the same size as the metal coal buckets I had just filled, and leave it next to his armchair for when he got up – a job he never once thanked me for. If I learned nothing else from this man, it was how not to be.

Every morning, as I went to leave, he would shout from his bedroom, 'Have you filled the second bucket?'

To which I would answer, 'Aye!'

To which he would say, '. . .' Nothing. One morning I filled the second bucket but he didn't ask if I had done so. My Auntie Rachel found him dead one hour later when she called to check on him. To this day, I still regret not going back and checking on my grandfather that morning. After all, I'd wasted two pushes of loose tea.

My mother was six when war broke out and almost twelve when it ended. She remembers those days very well. The village only suffered one air raid. The German bomber dropped three bombs before being shot down. One of the bombs hit a house only one hundred yards from where my mother lived and killed a family of four. She was in a concrete shelter with her brothers and sisters when the bomb thumped outside. The blast moved the shelter they were in a couple of feet across the street. There had not been enough room in the shelter for her mother and father and the children had sat in silence, wearing their gas masks and staring at one another thinking their parents had been blown to pieces outside. No wonder they remember those days so well.

When my father left for war, my mother was a kid in the street. Thirteen years later, he walked her home from a village dance and the rest, as they say, is history. My grandfather didn't quite like the idea of his daughter being involved with a man who had been away for so long and done and seen so much. Someone who had what we might call today 'baggage'. However, love is love and after a two-year courtship my twenty-year-old mother was married to my thirty-two-year-old father at the village chapel. I think they were very well matched in the sense that they both seemed to put humour above all else. If there is an ethos running thick through the veins of small colliery villages, it's 'if you don't laugh, you'll cry', and I think them as a couple personified this ethos. Another thing they seemed to have in common was they seemed to look down at the world from up above. They had a global view on almost everything. Whereas most people I knew would put their heads down, get on with life and question little, my mother and father would question everything. I think in my father's case it was because he was so well travelled and had seen so much. I think in my mother's case this was merely an indication and proof, if needed, of her intellect.

For six years I watched my mother study. I would get up to use the toilet in the early hours of the morning and she would be there in her chair, halfway through some assignment or other. A few hours later she would be getting us up for school, seeing us off and shooting off to school herself to teach. I really don't know to this day where she found the energy to achieve what she did. There were a few periods when she had to go away to university for a week. I think this only happened twice and I don't remember this for any other reason than my father was left in charge and we lived like savages. As soon as she walked out of the door it was like we were in an SAS training camp. There would be a huge pan of beef stew that he called 'scouse' and nothing else. Everything in that pan, apart from the meat, came from the garden and if you didn't eat it, you starved. Funny how things stay with you. I made a pan of that same scouse only two days ago. My kids took one look at it and went out for food. Don't know what's good for them!

After four years my mother had her degree and was employed full-time as a school teacher. After another few years my father had been made redundant, my mother was headmistress and my father would make tea for her coming in on an evening. She must have looked down at her plate each night and thought she had joined the Foreign Legion. My mother worked until she was sixty-three. They travelled and enjoyed a happy retirement together.

She is eighty-seven now and had a stroke shortly after the passing of my father. She fights her disability with such ferocity that sometimes I forget just how hard she has to fight.

It's quite common and a bit of a cliché to compliment someone by saying they taught you everything you know. But in the case of my mother and me, it really is true. In fact, she is still teaching me more and more each day and probably will do for the rest of my life. If I ever have to judge a person or a situation, my brain subconsciously checks it out with 'what Mother might think' before my decision is made. If I was to borrow my father's thoughts, I fear the very same method would land me in jail. So, I don't! However, the system of my mother guiding me through life without me hardly being aware seems to be reasonably successfully and the only time I appear to get it wrong is when I have misjudged what my mother might have thought. Perhaps I should listen to her more.

I suppose you are wondering, *If she is such a wonderful mother, then why didn't she teach you to read?* Well, I think the answer is this. At a young age, I would have to sit on my mother's knee and read a book. I hated this and knew the books were for someone half my age. I would slowly work through the book and then the next time we sat down it would be like I had never seen the book before. I would fill up and cry uncontrollably and my tears would splash onto the pages. My brothers would sense my discomfort and plead for her to leave me alone. I don't think I cried because I couldn't read, though I suppose if I could have read there would have been no crying. But it was more complicated than that. I think I cried because I disappointed. Have you ever tried to teach your own child how to drive? I have, three times and it doesn't seem to work. Each time I have tried, I have given up and handed the job over to a professional instructor. It works. Not only does it work but they think the instructor is cool and you're not. I have thought long and hard about my failures in this field and spent time wondering what they have got that I haven't. But that's a simple one: it is, I think, much easier to teach without the powerful and confusing presence of love.

Those days are over now and I'll let you be the judge but I think I might be getting the hang of this reading and writing thing. However, I do get everything I write proofread. By my mother, of course. Hope when you proofread this, Mother, *your* tears don't splash on these pages. That was not my intention. Love, Pip x.

6

Comprehensive school

There was a huge drop in the birth rate, here up North. I'm not sure why, probably because of the pill. But it had been too late for me – I'd missed that one and had already been born. Instead of everybody having families of sixes and sevens like mine, the rate had dropped to two point two. Some schools had closed due to the lack of numbers and some had fought to stay open. The comprehensive school in my village had been one of the survivors. How this affected me was that when I started the comp, I hardly recognised a soul. Double-decker buses packed with kids were being drafted in from the next pit village which had lost its school and I didn't know any of them. The new kids were a strange bunch and it didn't take long to realise their junior school had not been of a good standard. In fact, there was nothing they did or said that gave any indication they had actually attended a school.

This was perfect for me. My backwardness became so well diluted, I almost looked clever. Or at least average. There were seven classes of thirty-eight and within the first month we had been streamed according to our ability. There were no kids from the next village in the top two classes and I was placed in the fourth. It read like I was mid-table, which kept my mother happy, but what she didn't know was my class was like a box of monkeys.

It wasn't that the communication line between my school and my parents had been severed, it was more a case that it had never been put there in the first place. I can't remember a parents' evening and if there was one, I think the majority of parents would have probably felt too intimidated to return to the school. My parents weren't in that category but most were and a culture of 'parents should not interfere in their kids' education' had become a village norm. There had been several generations of poorly educated children churned out by the brutal system before us. Yesterday's under-achievers were now the mothers and fathers of today's under-achievers. Thinking about the state of that system now, I believe this was probably part of the problem. The chasm in the disparity of intellect between school staff and the people who had not long left, and were now parents, was so wide, a two-way understanding between both parties could never have been established.

The teachers drove in daily from afar and the headmaster's attitude was one of 'all the teachers are better human beings than you lot!' He would remind us of this at the beginning of every day. We would gather in the school hall and he would tell us how disappointed he was in us and how we should show more gratitude to his staff as they could be doing something better in life but had instead decided to give up their valuable time to help us. He would tell us how they were trying their best to make something out of us, but it seemed we were not interested and how it appeared to him we were happy to remain the 'nothings' that we would always be.

I can't remember anybody having a good relationship with a teacher. Apart from a girl in the fifth year that fell pregnant to a geography teacher. I think the headmaster was probably half right about the teachers being better humans than us because the geography teacher made an honest woman out of the girl and married her as soon as she was sixteen. I say only half right because by the time I was in my fifth year he had divorced her and had another pupil pregnant. The arts teacher was probably a better man. He had a sexual relationship with a boy but had the decency to hang himself before it became public and his wife found out. What inspiring mentors they were.

As I went from the first year to the second year, I was actually moved up a class. Don't ask why, but I was. I was average at maths and a few other lessons that didn't involve reading and I can only think this tipped the balance. My mother was pleased. On paper it looked like an improvement and a step up. But what she was oblivious to was that the teachers had given up on half the school and I was still surrounded by monkeys. Don't get me wrong, these were good monkeys, funny monkeys and definitely cheeky monkeys, some of who are still good friends of mine today. Who knows, perhaps I was the biggest monkey in that room? Whenever I meet someone from that time of my life, I am always reminded that I most certainly was. To put things into perspective, class six did nothing but the gardening around the school grounds and class seven picked up the litter, emptied the bins, kept the school's boiler stoked with coal and kept the teachers' cars clean. Inside and out.

It stayed like this for a while. It was fun. Half the school was learning very little and the other half was learning nothing. Half the school was treading water because as a man you weren't allowed down the pit until you were sixteen and the other half were treading water because as a female you couldn't be a housewife until you were eighteen. In our third year we got to choose what lessons we would like to take. The school must have been following some national curriculum that might have been understandable or relevant in Surrey or Kent but to us pit fodder it seemed like mush. The girls seemed to go one way (domestic sciences) and the boys another (technical skills).

Maths and English were compulsory and apart from them, I chose subjects that didn't involve reading. Before I knew it, I was in my last year.

The best way to catch a mouse alive is in a milk bottle. They had to be trapped; if left alone they would eat tomatoes, and tomatoes were money. What those hungry little bastards didn't understand was that when you are fifteen years old, money rules. A battle of wits, man against mouse and there could only be one winner. Me! After attending to my grandfather and finishing my two early morning paper rounds, I would release the padlock and heavy chain from the rusted old tin-sheet gate of my allotment, get myself, my panting dog and bike inside, before clanking it shut. Bliss. This was my world. The first job would be to lift the hatch on the end of the chicken shed. Now morning had broken and Mr Fox was safely back in his den, the hens could be liberated. They would squawk and flap as each and every one would compete to get their share from the enamel mug of corn scattered on the soil whilst I would enter the shed and steal their eggs, placing them carefully in the bottom of my straw-lined tin bucket. Just like tomatoes, these were also money.

With about four dozen hens and a long wooden greenhouse my father had built but then lost interest in, it was really quite an industry. It was all a daily routine to me: two paper rounds, collect the eggs, pick and bag up all ripe tomatoes, lock up, deliver three dozen eggs and four one-pound bags of toms to my customers before dropping off my dog, throwing on my uniform and pedalling off to school. However, casting my mind back now, there is one particular day in my last year at that school which seems to jump out and poke me in the eye.

How can I get out of today's English lesson? I wondered as I folded up and pushed the *Sun* newspaper through a letter box whilst lifting a pint of milk from the step and skilfully slipping it into my bag. Thatcher had stopped school milk so I pinched one every day. I always took them from *Sun* readers. The *Sun* had not been kind to us during the last strike so I'd decided if anyone was to be robbed, it should be the *Sun* reader. Probably Tories anyway. I never lifted milk from the same step twice, obviously; that would be suicide and a sure way to get caught. If a family lost one pint every day, my thinking was they would be out to get me, but if they only lost one every six/seven weeks, they were hardly about to build a hideout in some corner of the garden and camp out in an effort to bust me. Anyway, back to my thoughts that day. *How can I escape that one hour in a hot classroom doing English with Mrs Black?* I asked myself as I cycled, no-handed, whilst slurping at the warm stolen milk. God, I hated her, with her pink, thick-framed, pointed glasses and her wicked lust for embarrassing people. Especially me. Actually, thinking back to those times, I didn't hate all of school. It was only the dreaded English lessons I despised. Twice a week they came, Wednesday mornings and Thursday afternoons. English Language one day and then English Litera-ture the next. Who knew the difference, I'm not sure, only the teacher I reckoned! *I've got an idea*, I thought as I slipped the empty milk bottle into my paper bag and grabbed the Curly Wurly I had nicked from the newsagent's counter whilst pick-ing up my paper bag earlier.

I reached the garden, sorted out the chickens and entered the greenhouse. If you haven't caught a mouse in a milk bottle and you want to know how it is done, it is now time to pay attention. What you do first, and this is essential before setting the trap, is snap a truss from a tomato plant and rub its thick, pungent, green leaves into the skin of your fingers to rid yourself of all human odour. When your fingers are green and stinking then you can get started. The secret is to bury the empty milk bottle halfway in the soft soil at the foot of a plant you know has been recently ransacked by the thieving little bastards. The bottle has to be at an angle of about 45 degrees, then under the open neck of the bottle put a small block of wood, as a step, no bigger than a matchbox. Rub the bait (in this case the last inch of my melted Curly Wurly) all over the wooden block and then around the inside rim of the bottle neck before popping what is left of the chocolate down into the very bottom of the bottle. Time to retreat.

It doesn't take long before the mice appear. On this particular day it didn't take long at all. I remember it like yesterday. I collected the eggs and sat a safe distance away, hidden amongst the cabbages and brussels. I focused hard on the block of wood through the clear glass of the greenhouse. Inside a minute, a mouse appeared. He sniffed around the wooden block and another came from nowhere and jumped straight up onto the block. The first joined him as they sniffed around the open neck. I worried for a moment that they might feel the intensity of my stare but quickly dismissed the concept and, not daring to move my eyes, I focused harder still.

'Go, get in that bottle you little bastards!' I whispered under my breath. After what seemed like a minute but might have only been a half, one of them put his front legs and head into the open neck.

'Go, go, you little bastard,' and he did. His whole body disappearing out of sight as he slid down the glassy slide, not yet realising he'd been outwitted and when it came to getting out, his feet would slip on the smooth glass, sealing his fate. 'Wait!' The other little critter was looking into the bottle, watching his mate feasting on chocolate and toffee.

'Go on, go on, two for the price of one!' I whispered to myself, as the second slid in. 'Yes!' *Two in one bottle, double trouble*, I told myself as I jumped out triumphant from the brassicas.

After tipping the two new inmates into an empty biscuit tin on the workbench of the tool shed and watching them run about protesting at their incarceration for a while, I came up with a plan. My father had stacks of old green tobacco tins, each one containing a different category of rusty nail, screw, drill bit or whatever on a shelf above the bench. I cracked the lid from one and emptied what looked like some oily Stanley knife blades wrapped in brown wax paper onto the bench. *That will fit into my blazer pocket*, I thought. I stabbed a few air holes in the lid with my pen knife – they would be no good to anybody dead – and picking up the prisoners by their tails, I dropped them into the tin before firmly clicking down the lid.

'Git down, Sherry!' I shouted at my Jack Russell as I got on my bike. She was up at my pocket. She could smell the mice and wanted one for her breakfast.

It was Wednesday and that meant one dozen eggs and a pound of toms for Mrs Gorton in East Street, a quid! One dozen eggs and a pound of yellow toms for the Peacocks in Sixth Street, another quid! Two dozen eggs and two pounds of mixed toms for the Crossmans in the old police house outside the park gates. Only a quid! My father had told me Mrs Crossman's goods must be half the price. Her husband had been killed down the pit under a fall of stone and Mrs Crossman had been left on her own with four children and was struggling to make ends meet. My last delivery was to Old Mrs Bateman.

71

Now excuse me for going back in time at this stage of the tale, but I think it's important I explain how I came to know Mrs Bateman.

It hadn't started well. She lived at the end of her street and at the bottom of her front garden was a communal alleyway and a tall brick boundary wall separating her postage stamp garden from the park. A few years previously, probably when I had been no more than five or six, two of my brothers and I had developed a nasty habit of walking on top of the park wall and pulling faces at Mrs Bateman as she looked from the window. She probably found it funny at first, but as the novelty of three young kids sticking their tongues out and pulling at their ears had eventually worn off, she had reported our behaviour to my mother. We came in from school one afternoon only to be summoned to the kitchen and given a stiff lecture on how we had let the family down and how we should have more respect for our elders. The three of us were instructed to take an orange each from the fruit bowl, take them to her door and apologise. My mother only bought six oranges per week, one each, and I always kept mine for Saturday night. We were to give her the oranges as a peace offering and promise it would never happen again. We did as we were told and to our surprise, Mrs Bateman invited us in and thanked us for the fruit. It was brilliant. She made us tea in posh china cups and it was the first time I had seen or tasted a sugar-coated NICE biscuit. I dared to eat two and a beautifully sweet friendship was born.

Mrs Bateman lived on her own and would always be looking out of the window with the egg money ready. Sometimes, if I had a spare ten minutes, she would insist I went in and drink a cup of tea and if I was lucky, I would get a biscuit, a NICE of course, that she would refer to as a NEECE. She only got half a dozen eggs a week but would insist on giving me a whole one-pound note. I admired her generosity and would give her a free gift. A half-pound bag of toms or the odd cabbage or turnip or whatever I had too much of at the time. It worked well. I liked Mrs Bateman. She would tell me about her life as a child or what her husband had done during the war. He had inhaled mustard gas in France and though he had made it home he had not recovered enough to work again. At this particular point of my life the old lady was probably the nearest thing I had to a good book. The cover may have first appeared stale but once into the pages and their text there was always something sharp and interesting hidden there. She reached the age of ninety-nine and outlived her husband by over sixty years. Imagine that!

After bringing Mrs Bateman her eggs on that Wednesday, I put the dog in the shed, a pile of veg in the kitchen sink for my mother, the paper-round bag under my bed, blazer on, tie on, a tin of mice in my pocket, back on my bike and off to school.

Lynda Phillips was the love of my life. Pity I wasn't the love of hers. She had a blonde bob and an angelic face and would do my homework for a fifty-pence piece. It was a good arrangement. Any homework I received would be dropped into her bag and the very next day it would come back completed and exchanged for a ten-bob bit. I would sometimes give her a pound – perhaps I thought she could be bought. I would even pretend I liked Adam Ant just so we might have reason to talk a little longer. She loved Adam Ant and I hated him – perhaps I was just jealous. In fact, I think it was worse than that; so strong were my feelings for her I actually wanted to be Adam Ant. What did he have that I didn't? I had her believing I was too busy to do the homework myself and she didn't have a clue

I couldn't read. This was good and I was determined the situation stayed exactly like that. I needed every tool in the box if I was to win her over, but if she was to find out I had the reading age of a five-year-old, I was certain I would have been ruled out of the equation. She was in my English class and was clever. I had managed to escape attending English lessons very successfully. In fact, I had probably only been forced into turning up for no more than half a dozen all year. My favourite trick was to sweet-talk the metalwork or woodwork teacher and say I was a little behind on my work and if I could possibly get out of my other lessons, I could come in and get myself back on track. This worked for a while but it was not something you could pull off twice a week, every week.

I told nobody about the mice. Best if no one knew, it was safer that way. The clock moved fast and eventually the dreaded English lesson with the dreaded Mrs Black could be avoided no longer. Thirty-eight filed into her class. She was strict and as she stared down at her desk we would be expected to stand quietly behind our chairs until the noise of everybody's shuffling feet reached a level she found satisfactory. She would then look up sharply, wait for complete silence and when it descended, and only then, she would give us the instruction to be seated. The way it worked was simple: there would be a stale book on each desk and we would open it at the first page. She would start reading loudly from her copy of the same boring book and then stop. She would then call out a name and that person would have to read one page. It would start at her front right and work its way to the back of the room. The seats were arranged like what you would see in an aeroplane with a row of two tight up the right-hand side, then there was an aisle, three seats in the middle, another aisle and then another row of two up the left-hand side, all about six or seven deep, from front to back. She would work her way up the window seats first and then jump forward to the middle row and then work her way back through them. I would always position myself on her left and at the very back in hope that the one-hour lesson might finish before she reached me. This method of avoidance had worked a few times before but could not always be relied upon. If the book was short or the writing big and easy for people to read, I could soon find myself in deep water. Hence the mice. There were a few in the class who were known as 'non-readers'. Robert Chance was one. Mrs Black would miss them out, usually whilst uttering some derogatory remark about how she didn't need some degenerate retard ruining her day. Robert wouldn't even open his book. Neither did Jimmy Malcolm or Kev Laws. They were even allowed to look out of the window, across the rooftops to the tower of the pit wheels. I believe the thinking at that time was they were already destined to work down the pit, so they might as well enjoy the blue sky while they still could, and it was common knowledge that you didn't need to read to work down there.

It didn't take long for the reading to creep its way up through the window seats and leap across to the front of the middle row. It seemed the book was a quick read and combined with all non-readers being skipped past, it meant the reading quickly spreading like an aggressive cancer towards my corner of the classroom. In no time at all it had consumed all in the middle before leaping again and contaminating the front of my row. I stared in dread as it started advancing steadily towards me. There was still twenty minutes of the lesson to go and I was not going to be saved by the bell. Panic started to take over. Time for plan B. Out came the tin. I placed it on my closed knees, released the lid, and emptied the two mice onto the floor before clicking the lid back on and hiding the tin in my blazer pocket. Time to concentrate on the book. I held on to the book with both hands and looked as interested as I could as the reading reached the table in front of me and Lynda Phillips took the floor. Bingo! Suddenly the whole class exploded into a state of complete chaos. All the girls were standing on their chairs, Robert Chance was running around, scattering tables and chairs whilst trying to stamp the mice to death with his size thirteens, whilst Mrs Black stood on her desk and screamed at the top of her voice that they were God's creatures and must not die. Jackpot, job done!

The whole class was ordered outside and we watched through the windows whilst Mr Skirvin from the French class next door rummaged around on his hands and knees for ten minutes. He soon appeared outside triumphantly with two mice in a plastic sandwich box and like a hero released them in the grass behind the bike shed just as the bell went off marking the end of the lesson. Perfect timing. We all started to walk away.

'Where do you think *you* lot are going?' screamed Mrs Black. 'Nobody is going anywhere until I find out who is responsible for this debacle!' She was not amused. We were instructed to stand in a long line and look straight ahead. No talking.

'You will all stand there for as long as it takes for the culprit to step forward,' she explained, pacing up and down with her arms folded behind her back. After an hour or so in the heat, she started to soften a little and informed us gently of what a brilliant judge of character she was before starting to announce who she was certain it was not. She stood stiff in front of us whilst scanning every face for traces of guilt. Lucky I had an honest one.

'Susan Green, on your way. Collene Corfield, Lynda Phillips, on your way. Deborah Plant, on your way.' She continued this for a while until all the girls had gone. She stared at Alan Ladalor. Alan was quite camp and was the head of the school's drama group. He had been more terrified of the mice than anyone else, resulting in him standing on a windowsill and screaming louder than all of the girls put together, and he *definitely* wasn't that good of an actor. 'Alan Ladalor, on your way.' She smiled. He trotted off. I always felt sorry for Alan, for no other reason than I felt the place and time he had been born in didn't quite fit.

'Peter Clarke, off you go.'

Peter Clarke was known as 'Perfect Pete'. He was a large, overweight prefect who tried his very best in all subjects. The headmaster had once got him on stage in a morning assembly and given him an award for something or other and told us all to have a good long hard look at him because he was the model student and we should all be exactly like him. I remember Robert Chance whispering into my ear, 'I can't afford to eat *that* much!'

After a while there were seven of us left. The write-offs, of which I was one. I had no objection to working at the pit at this stage of my life. In fact, that's where I knew I was heading but I wouldn't be *down* the pit, I would be on the surface. If you were a welder, you didn't have to go down the mine. Welding couldn't be done underground because of explosive methane gases so it was done in workshops on the surface. I knew this because of my older brother Glen being a welder at Easington Colliery. All I had to do was pass my O level metalwork practical and there would be a place for me there. Perfect!

'I *will* find out who disrupted my lesson, and when I do, I promise you now, the person responsible will never walk into my classroom again,' she exclaimed. Robert and I stepped forward to claim the prize.

'It was me!' we admitted together. It was like a scene from *Spartacus*. Robert was quick to act and set out apologising for his actions in an effort to prove it was him. He was so convincing, I started to think it was him. This required action. I produced the tin from my pocket, and held it out for her to examine whilst Robert looked on outwitted.

'I even put a hole in the top so they could breathe, miss,' I explained. She looked at the tin and then at Robert.

'We did it together,' he said, still trying to get in on the act. She didn't believe him and sent him and the others on their way.

After waiting for the innocent to disappear into the building she stood right in front of me, our faces almost touching. I could feel her breath as she yelled as loud as she could, 'The English language is the gateway to opportunity, and don't you ever forget it, boy! Who the hell do you think you are?'

'Don't know, miss,' was all I could say. I wasn't bothered what happened next. I had proved my guilt and hit the jackpot. No more English. No more Mrs Black. Away from the dread of not being able to read in front of the lovely Lynda. The relief of it all was worth the worst punishment imaginable.

The punishment was six of the best. I was marched to the headmaster's office and made to stand outside whilst Mrs Black went in. She reappeared minutes later, completely ignored me and disappeared down the corridor without a word. I hoped I would never have to look at her again. I stood there for a couple of minutes with my back to the wall. Half of me wanted to fuck off and the other half was telling me to stay, take the punishment and get a line drawn under the whole situation. I'd just found out I didn't have to sit through another English lesson ever again and I was not about to jeopardise that! I think I was scared that if I avoided the punishment, it might give her licence to break her promise.

Mr Jenkin appeared with a perturbed expression painted on the front of his grey, shaking head and spoke only one word. 'Inside!' He followed me in; I knew the procedure. I would stand in front of his desk, he would get behind it, tell me how disappointed he was in my behaviour and how he hated this part of his job. Liar! This was all run of the mill. However, on this particular occasion he told me that because I had been honest and admitted to the offence, my sentence was to be reduced from six smacks of the hands with his cane to four. This was something I had to thank him for.

Now, if you are in an unfamiliar environment here, I probably need to explain something: giving somebody the cane wasn't just some haphazard task to be performed by an unskilled idiot. Oh no, this man really knew his trade. He was an expert. He had obviously been shown by some sick bastard even more perverted than himself at his university of headmastery how to physically inflict the maximum amount of pain on a child. It wasn't the first time I had been caned by him. It had happened numerous times. It was normally an act performed on stage, during assembly, in front of the whole school. A civilised display of savagery and a deterrent to all non-conformists. The time before this, I had been on stage and been given the full six whacks for filling Henry Whittaker-Smith's motorbike helmet up with piss in the bike shed. Not something I'm proud of today but I was young, he was rich, could afford a brand-new moped, I couldn't and it was funny watching him put it on at the time.

To correctly accept the ritual of a legal and organised beating is quite a skill too. One has to maintain one's posture, know where and how to stand and it is most important you pay attention and show full respect for the rules of engagement. I was quite an expert by now. It went like this. You would stand with your hands behind your back, and face the man whose job it was to set an example to the whole school of how we should behave in life whilst he mentally warmed himself and got ready to physically abuse you. He would pace about his office swishing a long cane down hard and then back up slowly whilst grunting like a chimp. He would stomp back and forth, spinning repeatedly on his heels until he had mustered up the required level of mental stupidity needed to perform the abuse. Then he would approach you, his weapon out level at chest height.

'Hand out!' It was always the right hand first which meant spinning your body around ninety degrees to the right and stretching out a flat hand on the end of a right arm at exactly chin level. The thumb had to be on the opposite side of the hand to the abuser.

Whack! Now you would turn one hundred and eighty degrees and stretch out the left. If the hand was too low, you would feel the cane under your knuckles lifting it to the required level of the chin.

Whack! Back around for the second on the right. He would grunt with each whack. What the fuck was that about? There was little or no difference between having four or six as the first two had your hands completely numb and after that, the pain seemed to just bottom out.

Whack! The second on the right. His grunting was getting louder. He was enjoying this. About-turn.

Whack! The last one on the left. 'Get out of my sight, boy!'

I'm not sure, even all these years on, if there was anything sexual going on. Who knows what the hell was going on in his head? Or his Y-fronts? Perhaps he'd strategically reduced my sentence by two whacks knowing the sheer excitement of the situation might render him unable to reach five. Lucky me!

I still remember the exact emotions I felt as I walked out of that office that Wednesday and the strength of the overwhelming sense of relief that radiated from deep within. No more English!

The pain was always worse on the second and third days, once the fingers had gone past blue and blackened. I was lucky in that sense. I was able to rest my hands more than some. After all, I hardly needed them for writing and all the important stuff I did, like delivering my newspapers, veg and eggs, was done on my bike. Easy. I would pedal everywhere no-handed!

7

Leaving school

I got my O level metalwork and a few CSEs in the other more practical subjects. I was actually made to sit an English Comprehension exam. I remember it clearly; there were three sheets, two of which were an in-depth scientific description of how the human eyeball worked. The idea was you read it then answered questions on it. I tried my best to hack through it but it was full of words like 'enzymes' and 'conjunctiva' and it started to appear fuzzy. (Actually, the only reason I remember it so clearly is because my youngest brought it home as a test paper only a few years ago. I read it and it made me smile.) I was not a quarter of the way through the first page and running out of time so went straight to the questions. What lubricates the human eye? I ditched the first two pages and with only minutes left went to the third sheet. It read, *Write a short poem about a rabbit.* This I could do, and I did. In fact, that's all I did!

> *Sabbit the Rabbit had a very bad habbit,*
> *Of nocking on people's dors,*
> *With his pors!*

I got a FAIL. There we go! My talents as a writer were to be ignored for another forty years. Geology was another exam

I took. I thought the school had finished with me but apparently it had not. The first thing I knew about the exam was my teacher appearing on the building site at the edge of the village and shouting up to me on the scaffold, 'Get in my car now, you have an exam!' Which I did.

If I ever find myself in a situation where I need to know the difference between a lump of iron pyrite and a lump of galena in order to save my life, I would be able to survive by simply explaining that though they are both metamorphic rocks, the galena has a much higher density than the iron pyrite which is actually magnetic. That should save me!

I only took Geology as a subject because there had been talk of being sent on field trips. Escape! It was a new subject that had just been introduced. The fact the school was sitting above millions of tons of coal might have had something to do with it. Everything was about coal.

Most of the field trips that were supposed to happen did not. The teachers were having a dispute with the Thatcher government about pay; the result was an overtime ban and all off-school activities were cancelled. We only went on three. One was to our local beach, Blackhall Colliery. That was disappointing. Like spending a day in my own front garden. The second was more successful. A bus took about thirty of us to a disused quarry in the Dales and I learned how the valleys had been cut millions of years ago by glaciers and then more recently by the River Tees. It was interesting and taught me the landscape I walked on had not always been there and should probably not be taken for granted. The third trip was to an old lead mine in Cumbria. It was to be a two-day event and we were to camp overnight. On the way there the bus stopped at a quaint little village and we were informed we could have half an hour to explore. Most did. It was a big mistake. By the time we were back on the bus the gift shop and local greengrocer's must have thought they had played host to a plague of locusts. Nobody had money yet the shops had been stripped.

We went on our way but as we entered the next town a police minivan was lying in wait. Everybody was ordered from the bus. It was searched; we were made to stand in a line, turn out our pockets and all the contraband from the bus and our pockets was placed into the back of the police van. My brother Glen, who was working at the pit, had picked up on how excited I had been about going camping and given me a fifty-pence piece. My mother had also given me one. I had done my calculations and had decided I would spend half on me and half on a present for my mother. I had gone into the gift shop and bought a six-inch-high golden ornamental plastic knight with a sword and shield rearing up on an ornamental plastic horse for 60p. I was not a thief, or if I was, I was a petty one. I was certainly not someone who would have ever dared to nick a full knight in shining armour, that's for sure. Lucky for me it was in a gift bag, with a receipt inside. I had already eaten the chocolate bar I had stolen, thrown the wrapper out of the bus window and looked crispy clean. I got to keep the knight. And his horse.

The bus was made to turn around and follow the Panda car back to the scene of the crime. We were ordered off and made to line up on the street and apologise to the shopkeepers. Some kids had gone completely over the top and the minivan was full of stuff. I remember looking in the back and seeing a string bag of onions and thinking WHAT! The trip was cancelled with immediate effect and the bus brought us straight back to the school. We were all caned, on stage, under the blanket thinking of, *If we punish them all, we'll at least get the guilty ones.* It didn't bother me, I was used to the cane, but my heart went out to some of the more timid characters who had not even dared to leave the bus. One of them was a geeky boy who I think actually wanted to be a geologist. He viewed being caned as worse than the death penalty. I tried to explain to him it was no big deal but it didn't stop him pissing in his trousers when he was forced to put his hands out. Anyway, no lead mine or camping for us. Pity, I might have learned something more than 'sleep with dogs, you wake with fleas'.

I got a pass in my German oral exam. I don't know how. I sat in that German classroom for three years and the only German I knew at the end was '*Ich bin hungrig*,' which translates to 'I am hungry.'

I got my interview at the pit about one week before we finished school. They took a bus load of us to the next village as our pit was already closing. They placed a piece of A4 covered in small print in front of me and asked me to read from it out loud. I couldn't, so they gave me a different form for my parents and asked me to get them to fill it in and return with it in one month. I got the newsagent I worked for to fill it in and one month later I pedalled back to the pithead. It was shut. Within the next few years, they would all be shut. The coal industry was being put to death, I couldn't read or write and the dole queue I joined the back of was standing at four and a half million souls long.

I soon realised life was all about living on your wits. About one year before I left school, I had landed myself a job as a glass collector in the village working men's club. It was only three hours per night but it paid one pound an hour. All you had to do was stroll around the club picking up empty glasses, seven nights a week, and return them to the bar. Twenty-one quid a week was not to be sniffed at and I would give this to my mother to help her with the running of the house. I still had my paper rounds and there was also an evening football paper which came out on a Saturday. This was a popular paper because people would use it to check the football results and find out if they had won the pools. Everybody I knew was trying to win the pools. Selling the football paper could be good money. On the Saturday afternoon I would wait at the newsagent's and at a quarter to six, a van would screech up and I would be issued with exactly one hundred hot copies (they were actually hot). Off I would go on my bike to get rid of what I could. I had about thirty-five customers who would have theirs delivered to the door. All of the time I was delivering on my bike I would shout out 'FOOTBALL MAIL!' at the top of my voice and people would come from their front doors and call me over to buy a paper. These people were good tippers. In today's world these people would keep their doors tightly closed and get the info needed from their phones. Progress apparently? After the street deliveries I would always be left with about forty or fifty papers in my bag and after whizzing around the tables at the community centre dance and getting rid of a good few more, the remainder would accompany me to the glass collecting shift at the working men's club at eight o'clock. It was always tight but I don't think I was ever late. Once in the club foyer I would set up my little stall with the last of the papers and do my best to man it between my glass collecting. By ten o'clock I had usually sold the lot to people coming into the club. The papers sold for 22p. Most people gave me 25p or 30p. Sometimes you would get a few drunken bastards who had been to the match, seen their team win, had a good day and wanted to read about their glorious victory. When I say drunken bastards, I mean it affectionately. They were happy drunken bastards, and would always give you a pound or 50p and walk off without waiting for their change. The newsagent got 14p for every copy sold and I got to keep the rest. Early on a Sunday morning I would report to the shop. You only paid the agent for what you had managed to sell and I would count out what I hadn't sold on his counter. Normally about forty. What the newsagent didn't realise was that every Sunday morning I would rise early, whip around the community centre to see the cleaners there and then race to the working men's club to see the cleaners there. The cleaners would have all the previous night's papers neatly stacked ready for me to put back into my bag and return to the shop. The papers I had sold, together with tips and then the papers I managed to retrieve and did not have to pay for, would usually raise about £25 or more. This money I would keep for me. My fiddle. Like I said, life was about living on your wits.

I did have one thing on my side. I was a young man and not a young woman. There were few jobs for men but there were no jobs for women. Looking back now at the education system then, all I see is a big industrial tail wagging a small village dog. I was never at any point given information that might prevent me having to go down the mine. On the contrary, I was only ever fed information needed if I was to find myself down a mine. Whilst we boys had been doing our metalwork, motor vehicle studies, woodwork and technical drawing, the girls had been busy doing needlework, childcare and cookery. Or as it was then known, 'domestic sciences'. They even taught the girls how to wash clothes, to dust, to iron and, of course, to vacuum. Unbelievable! While we young fellers were being moulded into being miners, the girls were being groomed by the system to be miners' wives. Stay at home, wash his clothes, darn his pit socks, cook for him, and if you find a spare minute, get pregnant. Who knows, you might be lucky and produce a boy, who would slot into the next generation of coal-cutting, brainwashed pitmen just like him. And me.

Each and every last one of us, girls *and* boys, denied all opportunity to grow and flower, bred for one purpose, and one purpose only. Now it seemed that very purpose had vanished. Coal was the reason my village was there, and for better or worse it was all my community had ever known. It appeared our way of life was being eradicated right there in front of our eyes.

Actually, thinking back to those days, I'm not sure who had it better. I don't suppose it matters. From what I can remember, all the girls thought the men had it good and all the men thought the girls had it good, when actually nobody did. Was going down the pit a better position to find yourself in than being prevented from going underground, by men, because you were a woman? I'll leave that one for the social scientists.

The only ones who seemed to escape were those who joined the army and half of them didn't really escape; they came back alcoholics or with mental health problems. The other half, I suppose, did manage to escape. I think. They must have. They never came back.

About six months after I'd left school, I received a letter informing me, *if you do not attend a job interview next Thursday, your benefits will cease with immediate effect*. The job interview was for a six-month Youth Opportunities Programme as a TV repair man for a national company called D.E.R. My father got quite excited about this and took me to the interview at the job centre in his van. He waited outside and I went in. There were about twenty candidates there for one job and the first thing you had to do when entering the room was write your first name on a card and pin it on the right-hand side of your chest. This was easy. I could at this stage of my life actually write my own name (if only in capitals) and I did know the difference between left and right. Some did not. They sat us at a desk each and told us not to touch the blank piece of A4 in front of us. Some turned it over. Not everybody wanted the job. The man at the front of the room explained that, on his instruction, we were to turn over the paper and then he went on to further explain what was on it.

'When I tell you to turn over the paper,' he shouted, 'you will see twenty-six dots on the page and next to each dot is a letter of the alphabet. Put the pen provided on dot A and then move it in a straight line to B and so on. When you hear this bell,' he said, ringing a little hand-held bell, 'turn the sheet back over immediately and write your name on the back, ready for collection. GO!' he shouted. I turned over my sheet. Some did not. My heart sank. I actually wanted the job, if only for my father's sake. I did not know the alphabet. I can't remember how far I got. I think because I had been trying to teach myself guitar and knew chords A to G I probably did the first seven and made it as far as G before more than likely going to Y or Z as I heard the ringing of his dreaded bell. I think the test was probably set to test a person's psychomotor skills. They needed somebody who was ready for a lifetime of soldering electronic panels. Anyway, I'd fallen at the first fence, or the second, I suppose – I'd managed the name card. After collecting the sheets in and examining them, about a dozen of us were politely told to leave. We were informed we would not be needed any more and we would receive a letter within a week telling us we had not been successful. I was disappointed. Most were delighted.

My father was sat outside in his van with a glow of expectation on his face.

'How did it go?' he asked.

'Not sure, they said they will let us know by letter in the next few days.' I didn't have the heart to tell him the truth. I was never scared of my father but I *was* scared of disappointing him. When the letter came through a few days later I could see the disappointment in his eyes.

'As long as you tried your best, son,' I think were his words. I wasn't to know then but this was to be the first and last job interview I would have in my life.

The work on the building site on the outskirts of the village continued. I managed to charm my way into getting a very poorly paid job as a labourer. There was no such thing as a well-paid job as it always seemed there was a crowd of people standing right behind you, willing to do it for less. I was making more money selling tomatoes, eggs and veg than I was working five days a week. The massive pit building that dominated the village skyline lay idle, and the once female-dominated, busy dynamic of the high street had changed; groups of men would stand chatting on the street corners whilst some men scurried around on their own looking lost. There had been over one and a half thousand miners working that hole and now there were fifteen. They maintained the pumps and stopped it flooding. My father was one of those fifteen and was in charge of the cage that carried the men and equipment up or down the shaft.

The pitheads that sat proud on the clifftops and followed the Durham coastline for its entirety were actually linked underground. This meant you could go down one mine and come up from another twenty miles away, but you could not flood one without flooding the next. Their heads were only yards from the beach yet once underground the men would travel some eight miles under the North Sea and cut millions of tons of coal. The Miners' Union paid for an independent survey to be commissioned in a bid to try and save our pit. It concluded that, based on the most up-to-date geological reports and at modern-day extraction rates, the pit could produce coal for another three hundred and twenty-five years. The report was delivered by hand by people who were my close friends to the front door of Number 10. It was never heard of again.

I don't think it was possible to work in a mine or know someone who did and not realise what was happening. My father told of how he had spent weeks taking four huge Rolls Royce pumps down the shaft, each one larger than a family car.

They had been ordered by the colliery management at a cost of millions of pounds and had no purpose at all. They were dropped to the bottom of the shaft by a team of men, transported to a disused stable area where the pit ponies had once lived, dug into the sidings and are still down there today, unconnected. A few months later the government produced a report to say that despite spending millions on modern technology it was no longer financially viable to keep the mine open.

Its days were numbered and my father, recognising it was a piece of history that might just be about to disappear for ever, became desperate for me to witness what it was like down there.

On Saturday mornings my mother would often give me a pound note which was to be slid down my sock and an old newspaper that would be hidden under my jumper. I would be given the job of pedalling to the fish shop, buying fish, chips and mushy peas (with plenty of salt and vinegar on) before taking them to the pithead for my father. After leaving the fish shop, I would give the parcel a few more layers of insulation with the old newspaper, knowing it could be a while before he got to open his lunch. I was rarely challenged as I cycled through the pit yard before leaving my bike by the manager's office and running over the metal bridge that would carry me over the railway tracks and into the pithead buildings. Perhaps I did have an honest face. If I *was* challenged, I would simply explain who my father was, what I was doing there and I would be allowed to get on my way. There were two shafts: the north shaft, which was the man-rider, was capable of carrying ninety-four men and this was where I would go. The south shaft was for the extraction of coal only. The mine's electricity bill for winding the cage down fifteen hundred feet and back up again in 1982 was £187; a lot of money then. I would open the cage doors, place the fish, chips and mushy peas (with plenty of salt and vinegar on) in the centre of the huge steel floor. After closing the doors, I would send the cage down with the lever. This involved pushing down on the rapping lever which was in a metal box to the side of the shaft twice. Two raps meant, 'Take it down.' Pushing down on the lever would set off a loud buzzing bell. It was linked to a bell deep down at the bottom of the shaft where my hungry dad would be expecting its ring. Standing up above, I could only imagine how my father's surroundings might appear. He would immediately engage with me and rap back twice. This meant, 'Did you mean, twice?' I would then rap back two times more to indicate that, yes, I had meant twice and all was good to go. He would then rap the winding house directly five times and instruct them to drop the cage. The cage would then drop like a stone, the winding house delivering its deep electronic hum across the village rooftops as its cargo made it down to the bottom of the hole. For some reason the one-pound bag of fish and chips (with plenty of salt and vinegar on) getting such an elaborate send-off amused me. And still does today.

On two occasions my father asked me to bring his fish 'n' chips as normal but informed me there would be a man called Terry waiting for me. He would give me a hat, boots and orange overalls and I was to get in the cage with the fish 'n' chips. Terry would rap the meal and me down. When I got to the bottom, my father was going to give me a guided tour. I was very excited but sadly on both occasions, Mr Crane, a bow-legged under-manager, came out of the manager's office, put on his pit helmet and slowly followed me across the bridge with his head on a spring and his arms tight behind his back. Bastard! My father hated Mr Crane. Not long after the war he had been hit on the head with a deputy's pit lamp and it had smashed his skull. The deputy (underground foreman) who had purposely hit him with the lamp had been my father's brother,

Ray. Mr Crane had pressed charges but it appeared that Uncle Ray was one step ahead. He was already on bail for poaching two rabbits from the coal owner's land and had gone on the run. Probably a good idea as the coal owner and the judge were the same man. Anyway, on both occasions, Terry clocked the bastard from the corner of his eye, staring down at us from a steel gantry. He took the fish 'n' chips from me, apologised through the side of his mouth and had to send me on my way. What a shame. A few weeks later my father was to ride the very last cage up, over eighty years after his father had ridden the very first cage down. I would have to only imagine the horror.

Uncle Ray made a good job of doing a runner. He got a £10 ticket to Australia in 1951, sent for his wife in 1958, became very wealthy and never came home again.

One good thing happened. The bricklayers I laboured for liked me and would sometimes let me lay bricks. At the time, most houses in the village still had outside toilets at the bottom of the yard and an incentive put forward by the previous Labour government was still in place. Money had been given to local authorities up north and they had been instructed to bring their communities into the next century in the form of a grant system. If you were still having to travel to the bottom of the yard for a piss or if you were still using a tin bath to clean your family, you could apply for a grant and, if successful, get a bathroom extension built on the back of your house. However, it wasn't quite that simple. Nobody knew how to do the paperwork or the drawings needed. What was actually happening was everybody wanted a bathroom extension built on the back of their house, the money was there, all the builders wanted to build them but nobody was capable of chopping through the red tape.

I told my eldest brother, Tony, of this situation and his ears pricked up. Tony had been to grammar school and was now a station officer at the local fire station, he was clever and had quite a lot of time on his hands. Within a few weeks he had started a small building company, had employed the bricklayers I worked for and I was now properly employed on a six-month Youth Training Scheme. I was told that if I kept my nose clean, I might go on to do a bricklaying apprenticeship. I was on £27.88 per week, three pounds more than I got on the dole. It came in the form of a Giro cheque through the door every Thursday. Plus, of course, cash for the two newspaper rounds, my fortnightly window cleaning, my football paper scam, egg money, tomatoes and veg money when they were in season and, of course, my night shifts glass collecting.

Lots of boys had been put on six-month Youth Training Schemes (YTS). In fact, I had been given one in a local sawmill just after I had left school. I had only gone for a week or so and then skipped it when the bricklaying opportunity had cropped up. Robert Chance was there and hated it but his father had told him he must stick at it, in the hope of getting a full-time job. It never happened; as soon as your six months was over and the government cheques stopped, you got dumped back onto the 4.5 million-long dole queue. Everybody knew the routine. The employers were never going to start paying you out of their own pockets when they could replace you with another sucker for nothing from the massive pool of desperately unemployed.

I only knew one girl who got put on a scheme. Her job was to be a cleaner in a doctor's house in Durham. It cost her more to get there on the bus than she earned. However, when the doctor developed a habit of trying to drag her into his bedroom after sending his wife out shopping and she packed it in, her dole was stopped. Another boy, one of the staring-out-of-the-window crew in my English class, got a YTS on a farm and was crushed by a tractor. He is still in a wheelchair today.

Thatcher was at the height of popularity having just taken the credit for taking back the Falklands despite not putting on a pair of boots or leaving London. She viewed the miners as a thorn in her side, but nobody could have known the extreme measures she was just about to take in order to completely eradicate our way of life. Government documents had been leaked exposing a massive implementation of pit closures, yet she would stand in front of the cameras and deny it all. The cameras were hers; the newspapers were hers; the BBC was hers; the radio waves were hers; the whole gullible country was hers. It was David against Goliath, and at seventeen I found myself part of a community who had just declared war on its own government.

8

The 1984–5 strike

Arthur Scargill, the National Union of Mineworkers' (NUM) leader, was on a campaign to inform the country of what Thatcher and her mob were up to. I'm not sure to this day if the rest of the country were simply uninterested, gullible or susceptible to being ill-informed. Perhaps the noise Arthur made was stifled, but whatever happened, it soon became apparent to us that the few ears it might have reached were deaf ones.

There were unfounded smear campaigns released from the Tory-controlled media machine about how Arthur was uneducated and how he had been caught with his hand in the union till or how the house he lived in he had stolen from the NUM. There were libel cases settled and most of these smears were to be apologised for years later. They were found to have come from the very top, but it was too late then, the damage had been done; the pits had gone and most had given up caring.

Arthur came to my village and we held the first of many meetings in the community centre. I attended that first meeting with my father and two of my brothers. The whole community was under threat, and the worries carried in by over a thousand men, combined with the electric tension in the hall, seemed to have left the air so dense there was no room for sound. All meetings were a closed shop. They had to be. The whole country was against us and letting Thatcher know our next move would have been political suicide. Once everybody was quiet a union official would ask everybody to look to their left and right and if you didn't recognise the person next to you, you would be asked to stand and point him out so he could be identified. This never happened; we all knew one other and I don't think there was a stranger alive on planet earth daft enough or brave enough to go into a room with over one thousand pent-up miners to spy on them. I honestly believe if somebody in that room had been identified as working for British Coal management or the government, they would have been killed and disposed of right there and then, with little regret.

There had been government documents describing how the pit closure programme was to be implemented. They had been leaked from Whitehall months before the closures had started. It had the dates when certain mines were meant to close and the methods used to close them. Their plans were already some-way through by now and my father had already witnessed, first-hand, some of it being implemented. A government official would visit the pit and close down its most efficient coal faces. Miners would clock in as normal for their around-the-clock shifts only to be paid to lie idle and wonder why they were not permitted to cut coal. Six months later it would be announced the pit was making huge losses before its death sentence would be handed down. Our pit had already ceased production, been mothballed and the dates in the documents tallied perfectly with its recent demise. It read that within five years every pit would have vanished. Arthur went on to say, 'Thatcher is no Edward Heath; she is very astute and had already been import-ing and stockpiling coal on a massive scale in anticipation of a long, bitter strike. This is not like 1972 and we are in a very weak position.'

'Why don't we ask the dockers not to take the coal from the ships?' somebody asked.

'Because in the last eight months she has rushed through legislation and has changed the laws of our land, my son, and any docker who comes out in sympathy for the miners will lose his job today and his pension tomorrow and we can't be asking men to do that. She's got us backed into a corner, lads, and she is boxing very, very clever.' He then went on to say, 'Personally, I think a strike will not only be futile but it will actually be playing into Thatcher's hands and might speed up her closure programme, but that is merely my opinion and it's my job to tour the coal fields and deliver the gloomy facts'.

'Come March, the vote is yours,' he said, 'and I don't envy you all. You have two choices. To strike or to take it lying down, and whatever the outcome, I promise to represent you the best I can.' He sounded broken. He was. Everybody was. What I remember most about that day was the quiet. As everyone left the hall, all I could hear was the sound of thousands of shuffling pit boots. Nobody spoke. I didn't realise at this point why, but soon found out. It was anger and every last one of them was going home to fix bayonets and get ready for a bloody civil war.

Watching the TV was surreal. What was really going on and what was being reported were at the opposite ends of the spectrum. The very politicians who had orchestrated the whole affair and were now busy making sure every last detail of their plan was being carefully implemented would appear smiling on TV and completely deny all knowledge of it. I remember watching Michael Heseltine refer to Scargill as a deluded conspiracy theorist on the *Ten O'Clock News*. It made me realise just how powerful these lying bastards were and just how far they were prepared to go. For what, it made me wonder?

Self-preservation? In 1972 the miners had brought the government to its knees and forced a general election and Thatcher, Heseltine, Tebbit, Lawson, Britton and all they stood with were not about to let that happen again. As soon as Thatcher got the top job in 1979 she had set about making changes to ensure her survival. The whole rotten lot wanted as long as they could at the top and they were proving to me, right there and then, live on TV, they would say and do absolutely anything to achieve it. We were doomed.

I had been beaten with a slipper and a stick at school but this was worse. This time they were beating everything that was dear to me. Everybody I knew, my community, my friends, my brothers, and because they were beating my father, they were also beating my mother. I could do nothing about it. We protested about unemployment and were told by Tebbit to get on our bikes and go and look for a job. Punk rock was about. I liked that. I was angry and so was it. It was ignorant, stupid and vulgar and I was all of that. It was anti-establishment and how could I be anything but? I was left with no other option but to put on tight tartan trousers, an old biker's jacket, stick my hair up, dye it rainbow colours, and hate them from the very bottom of my heart. *That will sort them out!* I must have thought.

I joined the Labour Party Young Socialists. It was a faction of the National Labour Party and we had our own branch which was only one of over five hundred. East Durham Branch, I think we called ourselves. I enjoyed the monthly meetings; there were only about twenty of us, but it gave me a chance to beat my drum with like-minded militant victims of oppression. I suppose I thought we were going to do something. A revolution perhaps. Everybody who could afford to (not many could) would pay a fee of £1 at each meeting. This money would be saved up and every three months or so the secretary would have a box of flyers for us to distribute. We would grab a pile each and hand them out in town centres, railway stations and the like. I would stand on a bridge in Durham City dressed like Johnny Rotten, hand out all my leaflets and when I made my way back to the bus station across the city, I would see all the leaflets I had given out, flapping around, littering the cobbles. Probably more a distribution of pollution than a revolution, but I was sure I was doing my bit.

All branches were invited to a young socialists' summer camp in Wales. I and four others decided to go. The train fare was far away from our reach so we clubbed together and bought a sky-blue Mini that somebody had taken to the village scrapyard because its bodywork had rotted. It cost a tenner. We travelled the three hundred miles or more to South Wales in it. In the back was Jonny, a hippy who looked like a young Michael Foot in a blond wig. Next to him was a friend of mine called Eric. Eric was staring redundancy in the face from his job as an electrician at a nearby colliery at the age of twenty. Next to him was a mate called Ronny who had just been thrown on the dole after finishing a six-month Youth Training Scheme cutting grass at a local caravan park. In the front was my brother Calum and next to him in the driving seat was me. I was not quite seventeen and had never driven a motorcar on a road before. However, from what I can remember, I think I started to get the hang of it as we passed Manchester.

We had little or no money. We were off camping yet had no tent. We got there and it was basically a field full of hippies in parkas milling about being very nice to one another. There were speeches. There was a beer tent full of live music. Billy Bragg topped the bill if I remember rightly. There were people from every corner of the UK. There were those from affluent areas of the country and from wealthy families who were socialists. Posh young people with posh accents exclaiming, 'Daddy is a doctor,' or, 'Daddy is a collage lecturer.' This was something I hadn't realised existed. I suppose because of where I was from, I had assumed somebody who had decided to be an active socialist must have done so because they had been dealt a raw deal in life. A personal battle against oppression. If not, why would you ever think like that? If you had money, you must be a Tory!

For the first time in my life, I pondered on whether perhaps a person having socialist tendencies might not always be sparked from a reaction to being wronged, but perhaps might be a personality trait? Perhaps until that summer camp I had thought I was involved in a peasants' revolt. I didn't know why, but I couldn't trust people who had money. Even when they realised where we were from, and insisted they paid for all we ate and drank, I think I still resented them. I might have felt patronised, or perhaps I was just young, naive and had never met someone affluent before.

There was a lot of heated debate but we must have sorted out our differences because I remember sleeping with three different girls in forty-eight hours. I woke up in the morning with all three. Perhaps this was socialism! Perhaps this was the revolution I had been looking for. Perhaps I was a communist. I was certainly sharing all I had. I drove the 300 miles back without incident, patched and painted up the Mini and sold it for thirty-five quid more than I'd paid for it. Maybe I was a capitalist. Confusing times.

A few months later ten of us went to a young socialists' conference in Liverpool in an ice cream van. We sat on beer crates in the back for five hours. The conference was interesting but sadly it was the beginning of the end. The left of the Labour Party was suddenly becoming less popular. Neil Kinnock had not long delivered his famous Bournemouth speech, damning us. The party stopped the use of the word socialist; Kinnock had taken a dislike to us and within a year the five hundred branches were fifty. The green shoots of 'New Labour' were starting to sprout and after being told by our local Labour Party we were no longer to conduct our monthly meetings in the local community centre, our revolution seemed to lose steam before dying with a sigh and a hiss. I am still friends with most of my comrades from the ice cream van today, and the lad who drove it. He lost his job as an ice cream man on his return because he had taken it without the owner's consent. He had also allowed us to eat four boxes of Cadbury's flakes. I think he was being a good socialist, sharing what little he had in the name of the revolution.

I finished my six-month scheme and was given an apprenticeship and kept on. This was rare. I didn't know another person who had completed a YTS scheme that had led to full-time employment. The fact my brother was my boss and was scared of my father could have had an influence, of course. I had to go to college one day a week which was ten miles away. Tommy Robins stepped up to the mark. He had been sacked by British Rail for never being where he was supposed to be, bought a couple of London taxis and spent some time trying to get his own taxi company off the ground. He had probably been ten years ahead of his time; people had no money and would rather walk. So when his new enterprise failed, he took a job for the local council as a rodent officer, or 'rat catcher', as he preferred to be called. His office was next to the college. He delivered and picked me up from college for two years. Because companies could now get YTS people to work for nothing, I was the first apprentice they had seen for four years and the only one there.

The course was easy, I didn't need to read or write. Sixty per cent got you a pass and seventy-five per cent of your marks came from your practical ability.

I was eighteen and two years into my apprenticeship when the miners voted to strike. These were hard bastards who were getting a raw deal and were never in a thousand years about to take anything lying down. After one month the village I lived in was under police siege. There were vans packed with policemen on every street corner. I was now, like everybody around me, viewed as an enemy of the state.

The hundreds of police in our village had obviously been ordered not to communicate with the locals. They had been drafted in from the south of England and had been indoctrinated and fully believed we were scum. I know this because a good friend of mine's sister had years previously moved to London and had married a policeman. Her husband had got wind of the massive financial bonuses being given to the coppers who were being sent north and had asked for a transfer. He was interviewed and asked if he had any connection to the North. Knowing it would be detrimental to his goal, he had lied and answered no, not telling them his wife's father and his brother-in-law were on strike. Two days later he was interrogated by the Secret Service and though they were satisfied he was not trying to infiltrate the force with left-wing thinking, he was suspended without pay for one month for not coming clean.

I soon realised, if I tried to fire up a conversation with a copper on a street corner, they would, like the Queen's Guard, stare straight ahead and refuse to look me in the eye. Even when you persisted with the pleasantries and pretended to be on their side: 'It's about time these lazy bastards got back to work, I reckon!' It didn't matter, they would continue to stare ahead before threating to arrest me. They'd obviously been told we were an underclass who could not be trusted as we had the black of dirty coal running through our veins.

The system the Conservative government had carefully constructed and quietly slipped in place to get rid of the miners was ingenious. The press had spent the last few years ridiculing the miners' cause and dehumanising my people. Where I lived had become a ghetto. The outsiders brought in to do the dirty police work had been fully convinced they were better people than us and they believed this from the very bottom of their wallets. The huge financial bonuses they were being showered with worked perfectly, successfully preventing their moral compasses steering them off course towards anywhere near decency. The southern coppers would taunt us when we were face to face with one another on the picket lines and let us know a one-week wage plus overtime for them could buy one of our houses.

Thatcher had rushed a few more pieces of legislation through parliament. Only six people were now allowed on a picket line at one time. If you were not one of the official six and you were caught on the picket line, you could now be prosecuted as a flying picket and sacked. When found guilty you would lose not only your job but all rights to your redundancy and pension. The laws that were implemented that summer ran roughshod over hundreds of years of legislation fought for by the working classes and were so radical even some Tories had the decency to abstain. It didn't matter; she got the majority needed and pushed on with her agenda.

Her new laws were ignored by us and almost everybody I knew attended the protests, but the police were always there ready. There were secret codes used when organising a protest. If there was a meeting at our pit (Blackhall), we would say when talking on the phone, 'I'll see you at Easington in the morning.' Every pit had paired up and secretly swapped its name with another to confuse the enemy. These codes would be swapped on a weekly basis as to confuse them more. It wasn't hard to find out how they collected their intelligence; it was quite common when picking up the phone to hear a couple of coppers chatting away to one another on the other end of the line. The picket lines were thousands of men strong.

The trick was, if the police made a run and grabbed some-one from the crowd, we would make sure they grabbed a dummy. Someone like me who didn't work at the pit. You would be dragged away, beaten, arrested and interviewed and when it came apparent you were not a pitman, they would beat you up again and release you without charge.

I didn't mind the beatings, it only happened three or four times. I was young, fit and the coppers were soft southerners and weren't much good at it. I could tell hitting somebody didn't come natural to them and I drew the conclusion they had been taught later as adults how to fight. When they came to my cell to beat me, they would always be in a group of three and one of them would be trying to show off in front of the others. It was a strange ritual; the ring leader would punch at me softly in the ribs and then they would all stare to see my reaction. When there was no reaction, he might have a few more digs before the rest would plead to the frustrated abuser to stop before they would all leave the cell looking like their experi-ment had failed. I must admit, it did cross my mind when they came in and shut the door that if I danced about quickly, I could probably take three out. After all, I'd probably had much more practice fighting than these fellers, but even at that young age, I had the sense to realise it wouldn't get me out of the building. Actually, thinking about those times now, I don't remember hating them enough to attack and as strange as it might sound, because of their nervous behaviour, I think I actually harboured an element of pity towards them.

The strike intensified and I imagine it was not unlike living under a state of emergency. It wasn't out of the ordinary to look out of your living room window and see a copper staring through the glass at you and your family inside. They had started erecting tripods with cameras on and taking photos whilst we were busy protesting on the picket lines. After gathering intelligence and identifying who was on their photos, they would conduct dawn raids. Men would be dragged from their homes and beaten. Later they would receive a letter informing them they were to be charged under the terrorism act, were no longer a miner and due to the severity of their crime, their pension funds had been revoked with immediate effect.

Men swapped houses in order to confuse the arresting officers but it was only a short-term escape. With an officer on every street corner, it wouldn't be long before they would be picked up. The *Sun* newspaper ran an article about 'Wife Swapping Pitmen' and how the police had discovered, in these small communities, families shared their houses and men slept with one another's wives. Men wore balaclavas on the picket lines to stop them being identified and the *Sun* did a front-page cover showing a group of masked miners under the headline of 'Terrorist Scum'. All the miners wanted was to keep working and maintain their way of life but the powers above had set out to dehumanise us and were succeeding. You only have to ask the people affected by Hillsborough about how all that works; they had it worse and for much longer than us.

In September 1984 I completed the second year of my apprenticeship and my wages jumped to £66 a week, £33 of which I would drop straight into the strike fund. My father worked a five-day week maintaining pumps and donated fifty per cent of his wage to his striking comrades. There were a few people, like my friend Tommy Robins, who lived in the village but didn't work down the mine and these people were very generous, especially Tommy. He at the age of fifty-five had just qualified for receiving his miner's pension whilst continuing to work as a rat catcher for the local authority. He would draw his pit pension from the post office every week, cross the street and drop the full amount into the community centre for his striking ex-comrades. I remember asking why his miner's pension was so generous and him explaining that because his two years' national service in the navy had been classed as continuous service to the King, he had done a full twenty years down the pit.

'But you said you left the pit after your accident at the age of thirty-three!' I challenged.

'I did. I left the pit at thirty-three, after twenty years of being underground,' he truthfully explained. Tell that to the kids of today! Tell that to the thirty-three-year-olds!

Soup kitchens were organised from churches and community centres with their long untidy queues spewing onto the streets. At this time of my life, it seemed the blood of my tribe ran thicker than the water of my nation. My community became my close family. I gave my newspaper rounds to my friend Phil. He needed the £3.10 more than me. My glass collecting career ended because nobody could afford 42p for a pint of bitter. The football paper scam died; nobody had 22p. My egg round became an egg donation round and the veg I produced was either dropped in at the soup kitchens or used to keep my friends and their kids from going to bed hungry. Christmas came and my chickens were necked, plucked and dropped at the community centre to be given to the most needy.

There was not a rabbit, hare or deer alive within a ten-mile radius of my village. There would be no turkey this Christmas.

There was only one man who broke the strike in our village. A SCAB! These days we might say he had learning difficulties, but these were different days and people had different names for things then. He was well known in the village and though in his late thirties, still lived with his mother. His mother, desperate for money and not fully understanding the consequences of her actions, ordered him back to work and he went. The police cordoned off his house and its surrounding streets and at exactly six a.m. every morning a black police van would race into his cul-de-sac. The three-deep line of riot police would open up and let the van through. Once the vehicle was outside the house the van's back doors would be kicked open by a couple of coppers inside and the scab would run out to a huge roar of abuse from the maddening crowd and dive into the back. The doors would be slammed shut and off they would race to the pithead to battle through the next mob of pickets. Apart from trying to dent the miners' morale, the exercise was pointless. One man could never fire up a pit, start extracting coal and successfully export it around the world whilst his thousands of work colleagues refused to report for duty. I later heard all he did was play billiards in the manager's office with lots of policemen.

Phil, my good friend, had a brilliant idea. He and another three miners stole a van from a police compound in Durham and the next day they flew around the corner at 5.55 a.m. The police let them through, the scab ran from his house and dived into the back, the coppers shut the doors from the outside, only for him to look up and see three masked miners staring down at him. They took him down to the beach and not only did he not get to work that day but never worked down the pit again. That day, it felt like we had achieved something, won a small battle in a war I think we were just starting to realise we might be losing. Today when I look back, all I see is a bunch of working-class men fighting a working-class man, which probably only served to amuse those who stared down from up above.

The next day someone wrote 'NO SCABS IN BLACKHALL' in six-foot letters on a gable end right in the centre of my village. The artist's house was raided the day after and he lost everything. His job. His entitlement to redundancy. His pension.

There is one other incident that holds no regret and hangs more fondly in my picture gallery of memories. It must have been the middle of summer because it was hot. We had been on the picket line all day in the heat and the police were calling us peasants and baiting us. One particular copper with a cockney accent went just one step too far. He took a handful of twenties from his uniform pocket, made them into the shape of a fan and waved them in full view.

'How long since you saw anything like these, ya fucking daft fuckers?' He laughed. 'Overtime, boys, that's what that is, fucking overtime!' he went on, whilst waving the notes. Phil, my mate, tapped me on the shoulder and winked before getting down low under the rail of the barrier that separated us from the police, like he was on the blocks of a hundred-metre sprint, waiting for the starting pistol to crack! I goaded the copper and asked him if I could have a smell of the notes because I had forgotten just how nice they smelled. He fell for it and moved closer. Phil waited for his moment and sprang from between me and the next man's legs like a young gazelle and grabbed at the bunch of notes. He spun around, we opened up, he skipped the barrier and was back in the safety of the crowd within a second. The copper thought for a moment about trying to follow him into the crowd but, realising it would be suicidal, did nothing whilst being ribbed by his colleagues. Phil had managed to grab six twenty-pound notes; it doesn't sound a lot today but believe me, it was a million dollars to us then. We went back to the working men's club, held a meeting and talked of how the money should be split and taken home and given to the women ... before we drank the lot. There were forty or fifty men there and we probably only got three or four pints each before the money ran out and the glasses ran dry but right up to that day, or indeed the present day, it was by far the coolest beer I have ever tasted and the sweetest that has ever passed my lips.

Life was hard but I still look back on those years as the best. Why, I'm not sure. Perhaps it was the camaraderie or the solidarity or the unconditional trust people placed in me while I placed it in them. I'm bonded to those people now. For ever! It wasn't far from love. In fact, I think it was love. Perhaps I'm love sick and that's why I miss those times. They had stripped us of everything we owned but they could not strip away our love for one another. I suppose we were the lucky ones: we survived and still own that love today.

The Durham miners have a gala every year. Miners from each and every village meet in Durham City and march proudly through its streets under their individual banners and to the sound of their colliery brass bands. In 1984 the authorities cancelled the gala but it went ahead anyway. The police put out a statement and said anybody found unlawfully making their way to Durham that day would be arrested and prosecuted. We all went and I marched through the city streets, under a banner reading *Coal Not Dole*. The year before we had marched with a young, fresh-faced and upcoming politician called Tony Blair but this year we were on our own. There were many arrests followed by dawn raids. All arrested were prosecuted for minor offences, sacked, lost their right to redundancy and pensions. My friend Phil was one.

The strike ran from March 84 to March 85. It could not be

won. Arthur Scargill had been right: the whole concept of the miners temporarily suspending their labour as a protest to a government who wanted to see their labour suspended permanently was a strategy that by its very nature was flawed. Apart from making a stand it had been hopeless and could never have succeeded. The power stations and steel industry were ticking over nicely on Polish and Colombian coal. It was cheaper. Of course it was, the Colombians spent nothing on safety, worked for one dollar per day and there was no competing with that. The Miners' Union had been cleverly split in two and the Nottingham miners had been offered jobs for life and large financial incentives to return to their pits that only madmen would have ignored.

We travelled down to Nottingham to protest but it was futile. We stood on picket lines there only to be heavily outnumbered by police who weren't even police. It was common for the men I was stood with to be confronted by their brothers or cousins in police uniforms even though they were meant to be serving in the British army. The odds were stacked against us and it was like we were living under a state of emergency that had not been officially declared and only we knew about. It didn't matter how hard we protested, we were an echo chamber and all the points we made and all the political statements we put out were heard by nobody but ourselves. The only hope we had was that the citizens of Britain found out what was really happening; but such was the strength of the bulletproof media screen erected by the Thatcher-led government, the truth would not be revealed for another twenty-five years. Long enough for everybody to have forgotten, died, or simply got tired and stopped giving a fuck. In October 2020 the Scottish parliament provided a collective and posthumous pardon to hundreds of Scottish miners who had been convicted in the 1984–5 strike. The independent report read, the miners were unjustly and disproportionately punished for the most minor of crimes by a politically motivated police force. Nowt like that from this government here!

The good woman I am married to today had a very affluent middle-class upbringing in Surrey and remembers the strike.

'I remember my father commenting at the dinner table that he thought those bloody miners should shut up, get back to work and be thankful for small mercies,' she told me.

'What did you say?' I asked her.

'I asked him if he would go down a mine,' she replied.

'Of course not, my dear, but that's not the point,' he had replied.

'But Daddy, surely you should not expect people to do something you would not?' she commented.

'What did your father say to that?' I asked.

'I was sent up to my room without pudding,' was her reply.

I think this pretty much echoed the wider public opinion of that time. He sat at his polished dining table in Surrey and wanted us to shut up and get back to cutting coal. We wanted to shut up and get back to cutting coal. The government was not allowing us to cut coal, yet he and the rest of the country saw us as the problem.

In July 1984 Thatcher changed the laws of our land making a strike without a national ballot illegal. She then shuffled some more laws which later allowed the government to seize the miners' pension fund. The fund stands at billions and is actually one of the largest pension funds on the planet. It is still held by the government today despite the average retired miner receiving less than £60 per week. The government has raped the fund of over twenty-seven billion pounds over the last twenty-five years. They helped themselves to £4.6 billion last year.

There has been a 'the miners' pension fund is a very complicated matter' rhetoric served up by our MPs more recently. The miners' pension fund is not a complicated matter, nor is it hard to find out who it belongs to. There's a clue in the fund's title. It's very clear. It belongs to the people who put into it. The miners! It's as simple as that! I wonder if they are suffering the same traumatic plight in a quest to find out who the MPs' pension fund belongs to?

I know ex-miners who live in caravans on allotments today because they can't afford a home. They are good, hardworking people and some of them are my closest friends. Tony Blair said the miners being stripped of their pension fund was a 'disgrace' and if he ever became prime minister, he would return it to them straight away. He didn't.

Colonel Gaddafi of Libya helped us out. He hated Thatcher almost as much as we did and had a soft spot for a working-class struggle. His help came in the form of shoeboxes full of neatly stacked twenty-pound notes that would be delivered to the community centre and evenly distributed to every miner on a weekly basis. Ironic, as a few years later, British-led aggression under Thatcher's disciple David Cameron would have Gaddafi bombed out, stripped of his power and executed by his own people.

Twenty quid a week was a lifeline but not enough to live on. Everybody was tired, hungry and though the wartime spirit was fantastically strong, for every man who held his chin up high there was a man next to him who was allowing his to drop. It became the same as all wars, I suppose. The same in the sense that those who were suffering the most wanted to see an end to the conflict the most. For the people we were fighting, this was just a game played from a cosy Westminster office, a safe distance back from the front line. They were well fed and comfortable, and experiencing the complete opposite to the suffering that to us had become the norm. Our enemy had soldiers to do their fighting. We did our own and we were losing.

On 3 March 1985 over 142,000 men marched behind their brass bands and under their banners and went back to work exhausted and defeated. Among the ones who did not return that day were five lads who had been killed and over two hundred miners who were in jail for being terrorists, twenty-one of whom were from my village. Twelve of that twenty-one had been found guilty of theft after being caught digging coal dust (duff) from a local British Railway embankment and taking it home to use it on their fires in an attempt to keep their families warm. There had been 11,291 arrests resulting in 8,392 being charged, sacked and told that not only did they not have a job but they had been stripped of their redundancies and pensions. There were 2,899 who had been arrested but released without charge. They had committed the very same crime, but there was nothing to be gained from prosecuting them because this was never about upholding the law but about persecuting miners, and these people were not miners. People like me. The pieces played by the brass bands that day were slow and solemn and I learned then, even big hard men cry. Everybody cried. The war was over, we had given it our all but had been beaten.

I kept few visual memories of that day. These weren't the sort of images you want etching on your brain. And anyway, that would have made me as sick as those newspaper people sitting on the hill with their police protection and real cameras. The same people who not long after would think it fine to stick their cameras into the faces of grieving parents at the funerals of the victims of the Hillsborough disaster. It was grief, I suppose. Grief in the sense that you look forward to the images fading because they hurt.

Thatcher lavished in her victory. Scargill had been right and she celebrated by speeding up the pit closure programme. She didn't even have the decency to keep her promise to the Nottingham miners who had shown her such loyalty and returned to work when she had asked. Their shafts filled in at the same time as ours. In 1983 there were 174 working coal mines. Today there are none.

9

Lucky breaks or theft?

Things up north got grim. The shipyards and railway wagon works employing tens of thousands seemed to disappear overnight, followed quickly by the steelworks that relied so heavily on them. The dole queue got longer and wages became so heavily suppressed the working man was no better off than the man on the dole. The only way a man could get enough money to feed his family was to sign on at the dole office every two weeks and have a secret job paying cash on the side. Everybody lived like this. Vans full of benefit officers would pull onto the building sites where I worked and just about everybody but myself would run for their lives. It was no way to live yet the only way to survive. The men who were caught and prosecuted for 'fiddling the system' would be suspended from signing on before being given heavy fines that would be mathematically impossible to pay. They would have no option but to leave their families behind and do the jail. The criminal record acquired would then prevent them getting a future job and thus the two ends of the boa constrictor of persecution would surround the victim, join up and squeeze the life out of him and his family.

Madonna was still pretending she was 'like a virgin'. It had been nineteen years since my birth, forty years since the end of the war, Band Aid were asking, 'Do they know it's Christmas?'

Talking Heads were singing about 'a road to nowhere', which I was certain was right there under my feet and it was sixteen years since Neil Armstrong had walked on the moon, yet the world around me appeared to be becoming less and less developed. But here came my first lucky break.

One of my older brothers, Glen, was still a welder at Easington pit and nicked me a nice new pair of work boots. His colliery was the last to go and survived until 1991. The history books will tell you that it closed in '93 but it was ordered to not produce coal some time before that, long enough for the government to release the figures and demonstrate just how much the pit had lost. The boots, stolen from the stores, were the type with the steel toecap on the outside, shining-black and the envy of the whole building site. Everybody wanted a pair. So, I got everybody a pair. My brother would raid the stores and I would pay him £5 a pair and sell them for £10. The only problem I had was I couldn't get enough; the demand was high but it seemed there was a bottleneck choking the supply chain. This called for action. I took a gamble and called in at Billy the storeman's house.

Now, before I go any further let me tell you about Billy. If my village had a chief, that chief was Billy. He was massive and handy with it. He was an undefeated ex-boxer, had the silhouette of a yeti and if, in the middle of summer, Billy said it was Christmas, you sang fuckin' 'Jingle Bells'. The meeting went well. He let it be known some closed pits still had full storerooms that he could gain full access to and went on to say there was nothing to stop him ordering more. We struck up a deal at £2 a pair and a beautiful relationship was born.

Within two weeks we had a routine. I would pull up at midnight on a Thursday, around the back of the pit stores in my newly acquired transit van, and load it to the roof. It was not just boots, there was everything. Tape measures, spirit levels, spanners, hand saws, pliers, expensive welding equipment, you name it, he had access to it. A pot of gold. An understanding financial relationship soon developed between Big Chief Billy and me. It worked like this: you could *not* owe him money, everything had to be paid for upfront and if you did ever find yourself in a position where he owed you money, it would be written off there and then! I think this 'take but no give' system had developed naturally due to a mutual understanding that I would not dare ask for it. He was a man monster.

Once I had managed to successfully open up the supply chain my problem was now the demand, and with slowly shuffling dole queues not being the perfect environment for wearing out pit boots, I had to think outside the box.

London! That's where the boot wearers were. The city was booming. Thousands of sacked and redundant miners had left the North to work there and it sounded like the streets were paved with gold. They were. Canary Wharf, the surrounding docklands and railways were just starting to be developed. I would fill the van, pick up Tommy Robins, head south and in ten hours the back of the van would be emptied and the glovebox filled with cash. The boots were bought for £2 and sold for £15. The tools were bought for pennies and swapped for nice new crispy banknotes.

I even had a punky, Goth clothes shop in Camden that bought all the size six boots. The size six boots were a nuisance but I had to take them because Big Chief Billy said so. There were not many men working on building sites whose feet could fit into a pair of size six boots, yet the young female Goths, tourists and punks of Camden couldn't get enough of them.

The shop would pay me £20 a pair and display them on spooky Goth dummies in their windows with a tag hanging from their laces reading £69.99. I had never seen such extravagance; I had to lay bricks for five days if I wanted to see such cash. The owner of the shop was a tall, thin, scruffy punk of a man called Mitch with a blue Mohawk like mine and a wild East End accent. I gifted him a pair of size twelves that looked like they could only be too big for him but after watching him try them on, I realised they were not. Every time I called into his shop, he would be sitting with his feet on the counter whilst smoking a massive grass joint and wearing the very same boots. Even after a year or so they were still in mint condition and I asked him how this was so.

'Army fuckin' training, boy!' he revealed, standing to attention, saluting and keeping his right hand ridged on his temple. 'When I joined the army, our sergeant major told us some of us would succeed and some of us would fail but there would be two things we would all take away from the army that we would never forget! One, your rank, name and number,' Mitch shouted as he yelped out his rank, name and number so fast it was incomprehensible. 'And two, you will always polish your boots,' he announced, standing at ease before sitting back down and crossing his outstretched thin tartan-clad legs as he clunked his feet back on the counter.

'Well?' I asked.

'Well what?' he asked, screwing up his face as if I had just walked into the conversation and had never set eyes on me before.

'Did you succeed? Or did you fail?'

'What d'*you* fuckin think, Geordie?' he laughed before sucking hard at his joint.

Mitch would always pay with £50 notes. I had never seen one till then. And here lies the problem. I would work five days a week laying bricks and then disappear on a Friday night with a fully stocked van and return to the village on Sunday afternoon with an empty van and thousands of pounds. What's the problem with that, I hear you say? Well, the problem was, the only man in the village who had money was me and I stuck out like a sore thumb. If you had more than twenty pounds in your pocket, people wanted to know where it had come from. If you had a fifty-pound note, they would call for a public inquiry. A fifty-pound note could not be spent in the North East of England. Still can't today actually. Nobody is prepared to take the risk of it being a forgery. I would call into every service station south of Watford Gap and use a fifty-pound note to put a fiver's worth of diesel in the tank just so I could change my money into a currency that would be acceptable where I lived.

I recall on one visit to London Tommy couldn't come and I was with my brother Glen. The van was crammed with stolen contraband and we were driving through the built-up area of Millwall. A police car passed us, going in the opposite direction and the two coppers stared at us, hard.

'Did you see that?' asked Glen.

'I fuckin did!' I said, looking in the wing mirror. 'And they're trying to turn around,' I said as I put my foot to the floor and sped off. The road was clear and there was a natural bend that quickly got me out of sight of the police. I took a sharp left and flew down a concrete ramp and into a basement car park under a block of flats. I took a left again and tucked the van between a line of parked cars and a row of metal garage doors. We waited. Nothing. We gave it ten minutes. Nothing.

'What do ya reckon?' I asked Glen.

'I think we should give it an hour. If we get pulled with this lot, we're fucked.' Glen was still working at the pit and if he was convicted for any crime, he knew he'd lose everything.

'I've got an idea,' I said, jumping out of the van. 'Let's try those garage doors.' The first one I tried opened. There was a small fibre-glass boat inside.

'Right,' I said. 'Put everything from the van into this boat and let's drive out of here empty. If we get pulled, we'll be laughing and we'll come back and get the gear when it's all clear.' We worked quickly; the boots were in brown paper sacks containing five pairs in each and were easy to move fast. The tools were in small hessian bags and in no time at all most of the stuff was in the boat.

'That'll do,' said Glen. He had everything to lose and was a nervous wreck.

'No, let's get the lot,' I insisted as the police car pulled up right next to us. We had been rumbled.

'What have we here?' said the bigger of the two coppers.

'Boots, Officer. Would you like a pair?' I asked him.

'And what are you doing with all these boots?' he asked, splitting a bag open and examining a pair of size nines closely.

'Selling them on the building sites,' I explained.

'Have you got a receipt?' he quizzed.

'Receipt for what?' I asked.

'A receipt to prove you have bought these boots,' he explained whilst still curiously examining a pair.

'Certainly, Officer,' I said, walking to the van. Glen looked confused. I pulled a receipt from the dash of the van and handed it to him. I had been to an auction some weeks before and bought a huge wooden chest of second-hand Cowboy boots for six pounds fifty and despite not even picking up the boots, had made sure I had paid for them and got the paperwork. I had asked a girlfriend of mine to change the £6.50 to £650.00 plus VAT. He read it, nodded his head and gave it back.

'Where are they from?' he asked.

'I bought them from an auction, Officer. There's loads of them in the auctions up north. I think they're probably from the coal mines that have been closed down. I don't know if you're aware but they have shut all the pits up north?'

121

'So why are you trying to hide them?' he asked.

'Because I've heard you have to hold a street licence to sell on the sites in London and I haven't bothered to get one . . . with it just being a one-off.' I smiled.

'What do you think?' he turned and asked his partner.

'I can't understand a word the fecking filthy Geordie bastard is saying,' came the answer.

'Careful, my mother is from Newcastle,' he smiled whilst getting in his car. 'It's your lucky day, boys. If those boots are kosher, I'll eat hay with a feckin' donkey but we are off shift in half an hour so goodbye and good luck,' he said as they sped off.

If things had gone the other way that day and those two coppers had decided to put that little bit more energy into finding out more about us and our van full of gear, if they had not been so close to the end of their shift or if one of their mothers had not been from Newcastle and we had wound up in front of a judge, there would have been no doubt we were villains. If all the facts had been laid bare, there wasn't a jury in the land who could have possibly returned a verdict of 'not guilty'. With the amounts of money involved plus the forgery of the receipt we might have got three or four years behind bars. Glen would have lost his job and pension. Technically, I suppose, we *were* criminals. Thieves. But ask yourself this. Who was the victim? The National Coal Board? I hope so, but think not. I've told you all about myself. Am I a bad man? Was Big Chief Billy a bad man? Margaret Thatcher had taken away his pension fund. Had he not then decided this was a game where everybody could play dirty, and was he not just getting back what was his? Topping up his pot? Living on his wits? Would we have been so busy trying to beat the system if the system had not been so busy trying to beat us? I'll let you decide.

That day we made more than ever and split it fifty-fifty.

Getting rid of the money was becoming a problem. I put a deposit on my first house and took out a small mortgage to cover my tracks. I bought a second-hand car. I didn't dare buy a new one. The police had put a young policeman on the beat in the village in an effort to repair the damage done by the strike. His name was Tim and he would knock on my door and constantly ask how I could afford to be out every night, have a van, a car and a house. I put the van in my mate Phil's name and tried to convince him I was in masses of debt. I think he knew better.

I once returned from London with a stack of cash. I had a lock-up in an allotment in the next village and would stash the cash there. It was good I did. When I returned to my house the police were lying in wait; it had been raided by the drug squad. They thought I was a drug dealer! I had four thousand pounds hidden in a hollowed-out mock distribution board in the electric meter cupboard and they hadn't found it. I had about twelve hundred pounds under my bed and they took it and reported they had found nothing. They had taken up every floorboard in all three bedrooms and not replaced them.

As the last of the pits closed, the supply of boots and tools got thin, then suddenly Big Chief Billy died of a bleed on the brain in his sleep. He was fifty years old. After a few months the cash dried up. I thought then my money problems might be over. I was wrong. My money problems were just about to get a whole lot worse. Or better. It depends on which angle it's viewed from, I suppose.

10

Black money

Coal was still big business at this point but British coal was history. Despite the death of the mines, the power stations, the remaining steelworks and most domestic dwellings were still addicted to the filthy stuff. Now that supply was kept less than demand, the price per ton had more than doubled and if you could get your dirty hands on dirty coal, you could find yourself in possession of a lot of 'dirty money'. It was black gold.

The modern-day dynamic of the North East of England had switched. Instead of the coal coming out of the ground and travelling a short distance to the power stations or to the docks to be loaded onto ships for export, the coal was now coming *into* the docks from halfway around the world, being unloaded *from* ships, stored in massive coal yards and then sold to the highest bidder. All this, whilst billions of tons of the stuff lay dormant under the feet of thousands of stunned miners as they moped around idle, learning how to sign on the dole.

All I had to do was stand at the head of the blackened beach tops on the grey mountain of slag that now replaced the once massive grand structure of our village pithead, one thousand feet above millions of tons of unwanted coal – and I could see all of what was going on. If I turned my head south, I could see the town of Hartlepool surrounding its dockyards, only eight miles from my village with its filthy man-made mountain range of coal dominating its skyline. I could see the orange and red glow of the steelworks' blast furnaces and coke works, burning twenty-four/seven with their colossal clouds of yellow poisonous gases stretching up miles into the heavens. I wondered, *if there is a God, maybe Thatcher is trying to smoke him out? Then she would have full control.* That's how it looked. But if there was a God, surely he would never allow the world to look like this, would he? I worked right in the middle of it.

If I turned my head north, you could see Sunderland and the city of Newcastle with their tall, redundant shipyard cranes reaching high into the sky. It was the same picture. Like an L. S. Lowry painting but smudged. Black and greys all running into one another.

If I was to look straight ahead, there were ships. Hundreds of them, each one as big and as long as the next, sitting like ducks on a poisoned pond. Some had travelled from South America and were full of coal. Some were laden with steel and were about to take it around the world. Apparently, it was more efficient to get our ships built overseas and there was not much need for British steel here any more.

If I tipped my head forward, I would see the yellow of the beach. Not yellow because of sand. Oh no! This was sulphur, beautiful yellow sulphur. A waste by-product dumped into the sea for almost a century only to be washed back onto our shores and kill every living creature that dared try to live there.

If I was to lift my head and spin around, I would see my village clinging to the hills, crippled with the new terminal illness of alcoholism, divorce and depravation that was spreading like a cancer through its red-brick numbered streets, closing down its shops and eating its way into its schools, churches and the very bones of community life. Little was I to know then, this was just the start.

Hartlepool was beginning to take on a very lunar and volcanic look. It would have made a grand setting for a 1970s *Planet of the Apes* blockbuster. Somebody somewhere had decided the coal yards had to be hidden from the public eye and money was being released by local authorities in the form of grants to build huge red-brick walls around each and every yard in an attempt to hide them from view. I was right in the middle of it, building the walls. It was a bad place to be. It was dirty and it was Baltic; the walls were straight, vast and boring to build and though there was a huge amount of money being flashed about and swapping hands, very little of it was coming anywhere near poor old me. I hated the place.

There was one particular coal yard that was massive. It had taken almost one year for about twenty bricklayers to build a wall around it. Being the apprentice, I had been left there to finish the job whilst everybody else had moved on to pastures new. I don't know to this day why they trusted me to be left alone. Perhaps Tommy wasn't taking the piss and I did have an honest face?

It all came about by accident at first. I was in my own little world, at the very bottom of the yard which was more than half a mile long. My job was putting coping stone after coping stone on the top of the walls. I was startled by somebody shouting my name. I looked down. It was Phil, my good friend, and he was driving his ex-army wagon, laden with a full load of heavy sea coal. The beaches up north had been left in a terrible mess by the coal industry. However, a lot of this mess was coal in the form of dust. The sea coal men would back their ex-army lorries into the waves, wade out chest-deep into the freezing water and shovel the coal from under the water and onto their wagons. It wasn't a job for the faint-hearted. I had given it a go once with Phil. He had tempted me there with the lure of cash, just before Christmas one year, but after having to jump chest-deep into the North Sea in the dead of night and then being expected to shovel non-stop until the ten-ton wagon was full, I had come to the conclusion that perhaps laying bricks was not such a bad job after all. The men who did that job were the hardest I'd ever known.

I climbed down from the scaffolding and Phil got down from his wagon and we talked for a while. Suddenly Phil stopped me halfway through a healthy piece of gossip and asked, 'You don't happen to have the keys for those gates, do you?' I said I did and his eyes lit up. The gates were permanently locked but I had borrowed the spare keys from one of the coal yard owners, explaining the access was better for me to get my building materials closer to where they needed to be. I had been walking around for months with them in my pocket. He quickly explained his thinking.

'Let me out that gate, I'll go around the corner and sell this load to the next coal yard and then you let me back in empty, I'll drive back up to the weighbridge at the top of the yard, they'll think I've tipped it in here, they'll weigh me off empty and bingo! I get paid twice for the same load.'

'How much is it worth?' I asked him.

'Well . . .' He thought for a bit. 'I normally get about £350 for a load like that, so I'll get £700 instead.'

'No! I mean, how much is it worth to me?' I pushed.

'Hundred quid all right?' He was back in less than ten minutes; the gate was locked and I had earned more in ten minutes than in a seven-day week. Imagine the buzz. It wasn't long before I had approached most of the sea coalers from my village and was doing more than ten loads per day. Some of the lads would bring in three loads a day and wanted to do it with every load but I insisted every wagon could only do it once a day. My thinking being, like the bottles of milk stolen from the steps on my paper round, if I kept the amount of loads moderate, I might just get away with it. The men would get nasty but I would stand my ground and explain calmly, if they didn't stop being so cheeky, they would be let out with no loads per day. One big nasty bastard called 'Ned the Bear' shouted at me, 'How about I come up that ladder, take the key out of your pocket and throw you off that fuckin' scaffold?'

'Good idea,' I said, standing at the top of the ladder swinging a three-foot metal spirit level about. 'Up you come,' I smiled, holding the level like a cricket bat, whilst not letting on I was almost shitting myself. He drove off. I still see Ned the Bear around the village today. He is stooped and old and still laughs and calls me a cheeky young bastard. I'm fifty-five. If he only knew just how scared of him I was. Ah well, I guess life is a battle of wits and I won that one.

Keeping it moderate was difficult if not impossible. Phil was doing three loads a day and getting double paid for them all. Word had got out about the favouritism and it was not going down well. The number of loads had crept up and was probably averaging over fifteen loads a day. I was getting £86 a week for a six-day week for my bricklaying and over £1,500 a day (£10,000 a week) for being in possession of a magic key. Sleeping became impossible as I couldn't help worrying that perhaps I was taking too much milk from one step. I discussed things with Tommy and we agreed all good things must come to an end and it would be better for me if I stopped on my terms than if I was caught. It was up to me; all he could do was to advise and to help hide some of the loot.

The two brothers who owned the coal yard were gangsters and Tommy knew them well. They owned lots of the nightclubs and pubs in the North of England and they didn't like anybody; in fact, they didn't even like each other. They had separate identical offices in separate identical buildings in the same yard and though in business together, had not spoken to one another for over ten years. They had sawn-off shotguns on their desks. Tommy told me how they operated. He told me how he'd known people who had stood up to them in the past who had mysteriously disappeared thereafter and let me know how worried I should be. I knew, if caught, I would have likely been tortured, murdered and got rid of without a trace, probably in the blast furnaces just across the street, yet stopping was still to this day one of the hardest things I've ever had to do. Casting my mind back today makes me wonder, was I braver then? Perhaps it was a greed or a hunger I no longer possess? Or was I just fucking stupid?

I had to stop. I got about two months into it and I could not string the bricklaying job out any longer. It was too much of a good thing to just give up overnight and handing the key back was just too hard to do. Like a near-dead junky staring into the bathroom mirror, knowing it would be better for their wellbeing to flush the drugs down the sink before injecting themselves, I was addicted to a situation which could only end in self-destruction.

After a further couple of weeks, I was too far gone and needed desperately to wean myself off my habit. Tommy, scared for my life, came up with a plan. We drove forty miles to a locksmith's shop where Tommy knew the owner from his time in the navy. He was a very dodgy locksmith, or to be completely honest, he was a safecracker, and we got twenty-five keys cut for £100. I sold them for £250 each. It was a clever solution because once the keys were sold, I was redundant; cured, clean and free. I took the original key back to the office and handed it back to Cyril, the oldest of the two brothers. He was sat at his desk, smoking a cigar; his shotgun was surrounded by tall stacks of bank notes. This guy had almost as much money as me! He had two Rottweilers sat like bookends on the floor, one at each end of his desk. It was like a scene from the film *Scarface*.

'The keys for the bottom gate, Cyril,' I said, throwing them in among the towers of cash. 'I forgot I still had them!' I lied.

'Ah, yes, Pip,' he said to me, as he stood up smiling and displaying a row of brown teeth, apart from the gold ones. 'I've been wanting to catch up with you for a while.' My hull started to glug in water. I concentrated on keeping my keel upright and steady whilst hoping if I appeared confident, he might remain oblivious to how close I was to capsizing.

'You've done a good job here and I've been watching you very, very closely,' he smiled. 'The thing is,' he growled before pausing to suck on his cigar, 'I need you to build a porch on the front of my new house.'

Surely Tommy *was* telling the truth? I did have an honest face.

11

London

One year on

I finished my apprenticeship on a Friday afternoon at 3.30 p.m., grabbed a lift from Tommy and was stood on the side of the A1 with two friends, Phil and Ronny, both sacked miners, hitching a ride to London at 6 p.m. I had been getting £86 a week up north and started work on the Monday in the centre of London on £120 per day. Every Friday I thought I'd won the lottery but nothing could have prepared me for the reaction I'd receive from the people there. I was in my own capital city but I was viewed as an outcast. The community of builders I was now a part of was made up of predominately Irish men who hated anything English, a few locals who hated northerners for taking their jobs and a scattering of Scottish who had been taught to hate us more than the Irish did. I was shocked. The Scottish had just had the poll tax thrown at them. I'm not sure whose idea it was to try the poll tax experiment out in Scotland first but it was a perfect example of just how out of touch the English elite were, and still are. The Irish, as we all know, have had their problems but I certainly hadn't expected to land in London and have to take the blame for it all.

I suppose everybody hating me came as such a shock because I felt just as distant and disconnected from the political elite as they did. After all, I'd just spent a year on the picket lines taking regular beatings and fighting like hell against everything they despised. There had been a lot of negative press about the Irish. The TV and tabloids had the average Englishman thinking that every Irishman was an explosives expert and out to get them. However, when it came to us northerners the reports meant nothing. We had also been depicted as terrorists and we were more than aware of the breadth of the chasm that hung between what appeared in the press and the truth. What struck me most was, we were all victims in our own right and us squabbling amongst ourselves was probably something that amused those at the very top and was almost certainly purposely contrived. However, because we were English, we were viewed as ambassadors of Thatcher, so not to be trusted and not liked.

Individually, I could break a man down. After working with a person for a while he would realise I was no better or worse than him. I remember one angry young Belfast man eventually letting his guard down and explaining how the British soldiers would come into his house and make his whole family lie face down on the floor whilst they would laugh and go through his sisters' and mother's knickers. They would pull out and empty the contents of the girls' knicker drawers onto the back of his father's head as he laid face down with his kids, on his own hard kitchen floor. To him this was a war. I told him a few stories of my war, the miners' strike, and of how the police had become carried away with their authority and how they too had used violence and intimidation to oppress us. His attitude towards me changed and his anger seemed to drain away.

Phil would tell them straight. He would tell them they were spoiled rotten and he was a bigger victim of the political elite than they could ever be. He had been sacked for being on a protest, been stripped of his redundancy, pension, put in jail for nothing and given a criminal record in an attempt to prevent him from ever working again. When we first arrived, Phil worked with two bricklayers who had attended the same college in Ireland but lived on different sides of the same town. They had known one another for five years but had never spoken because of their political and religious differences. This amused Phil and he ribbed them constantly.

'You don't like each other. You don't like me. You say you love your country yet you can't afford to live in it. There's no work for you in the country you think is so great. If there was, you would be earning a fraction of what you get here and your government would be taking forty-five per cent tax off. You need to live the life I have,' he would say. 'At least I'm not brainwashed and know I'm from a shithole. At least I know those who rule over *me* are bastards. The sooner you lot stop squabbling with one another and turn your attentions to your real enemies, the better for you all.' Phil's raw deal in life seemed to have left him with an ability to say anything to anybody and they would listen. Within a week the two Irish lads and Phil were the best of friends, a partnership that lasted years. Phil took the lads up north a few times and they actually got to see the shithole he was from for themselves. The Irish lads married one another's sisters. Bet that created a stir back home. Phil was best man on both occasions. Perhaps he should have done a little work on the Israel and Palestine problem.

I didn't blame the southerners for not liking us. We were cheaper to employ; we were happy with our £120 per day when the southerners cost £180, so we *were* nicking their jobs. It was worse than that. We would start a new job and as soon as they realised how fast and efficient we were they would instruct the locals to take their tools home that night and not come back. This would leave us feeling awkward at times but what could we do? It was probably true they were using us to suppress wages and to keep the locals on their toes, but we needed the money, and after all, this was supposedly *our* country too.

It didn't take me long to realise all the hatred and prejudices were spawned from nothing other than naivety, ignorance or a mixture of both. Somebody would land on the building site from Ireland, Scotland, the Caribbean, or anywhere. They would keep themselves to themselves and be very defensive for a week or so, before looking up one day only to realise everybody around them was just like them. Some of the older men couldn't be cracked. They were too far gone. Steeped in historical hate. Some of the old Irish men would not only refuse to recognise my existence but would try and dissuade anybody young and Irish that did. I've since read about this, now that I can. It's called 'cognitive denial'.

An American professor performed studies on people who had been drawn into cults. He found some disciples had believed absolutely everything their leader had preached. Some had handed their messiah every dollar they owned, their life savings. Some had sold their houses for the cause. He even found some had donated their children.

Eventually, when their guru was led away in handcuffs for wrongly predicting Armageddon for the twenty-third time, or being outed for being the pervert and thief he was, he found the victims would be left stunned.

He studied these people. He found the cult members who had not invested so much money and time would simply walk off, realising they had been hoodwinked. Yet the disciples who'd put in the most time and dollars would mill around for weeks and sometimes months in a state of disbelief. He found the amount invested correlated directly to the amount of time it took them to wake up and admit they'd been swindled. Some who'd invested all they had would never wake up. They would shut themselves off from the facts and all advice given by the authorities, and in some cases they would quickly join a new cult.

Perhaps our brains have a self-preservation mechanism that activates when we might wind up with too much egg on our faces or dying of embarrassment. Most of Hitler's henchmen/women went to the gallows professing no regret. Perhaps this built-in mechanism clicks in because it would be catastrophic to the person's wellbeing to face reality. Could they function successfully if confronted by their evil? Could they stand tall, converse or nourish themselves if they allowed the horrors to seep in?

Probably not! 'Cognitive denial', interesting! I'll talk of this more later.

It wasn't that I was on a moral crusade to rid the city of all prejudice but after what we had been through up north, I was quite intrigued when realising we were not welcome, trusted or even liked. Anyway, with over one million Jocks, Caribbeans, Paddies, Geordies, plus the Indians who had been chased out of Uganda by Idi Amin because their skin was brown and not black, and God knows who else cramming themselves into the inner-city melting pot each working day, I might have had a bit of a job on my hands.

I remember going to a comedy night in Hammersmith and a big fat cockney geezer taking to the stage. He complimented Thatcher on her work and the audience clapped and cheered. I thought I'd been landed on the moon. I wondered if he knew that if he tried the same act three hundred miles north of here, he would be lynched. I hadn't seen anything like it. He called the Jocks greedy bastards and said they had only started coming down to London because the heroin was cheaper. He asked if there was anybody from Sunderland in the crowd and like an idiot I stood up, shouted out and waved. He pointed at me.

'Somebody's getting a cheap extension built!' he joked. Don't get me wrong, he was funny and I suppose he was only doing his job. He was doing it well. Two thousand people laughed and only one man looked the fool. However, it was the first time this fool had actually looked hard at what and who he was. It was the first time this fool realised life was a postcode lottery. I suppose I had what religious people might describe as a revelation. I saw the light!

On 28 December 1879 in Dundee, Scotland, a train went into the River Tay with a great loss of life. The stone and iron bridge had collapsed and there were few survivors. Bodies were being washed up for days and not all were found. Nobody knows how many died. But what I do know is my great-grandfather's body was recovered from the water and identified. He was uninsured and the breadwinner and within three years his widow and their six-year-old boy had been evicted from their house near Fife and were living in squalor in a workhouse in the North East of England. My father's father was that boy. If you needed workers then, you could go to a workhouse and pay the owner for the labour you required for that day. After eight years of living in the workhouse and at the grand old age of fourteen, my grandfather got a job with a team of sinkers. These were the men who sunk deep shafts into the crust of the earth in search of new minerals needed to quench the thirst and to feed that hungry monster we now recognise as the Industrial Revolution. He would be picked up at dawn, travel by horse-drawn cart to a digging site where they would be lowered, in large wooden buckets, by rope down shafts and told to dig. The tubs of waste that came up would be laid out on the surrounding landscape for geologists to scrutinise before the men and boys would be taken back to the workhouse at dusk. The men were told that if they struck gold, the fortunes would be theirs. This never happened but it made them dig hard.

My grandfather promised my great-grandmother that if he struck gold, he would use his fortune to remove her from the hell she was living. They did strike gold, only black gold. Those crushed ancient rainforests of yesteryear were a thousand feet down but it was too late. His mother died at the age of thirty-six in Easington's workhouse and he was rewarded for his hard work with a lifetime of getting dirty black coal from under the ground.

Once the coal was discovered there was mayhem. No planning permission needed then. You didn't even have to ask the King. Industry was king. Whole towns and villages with their cobbled streets, bellowing chimneys, churches, schools, shops, pubs and rows upon rows of cottages to house the miners and their huge families replaced the once lush green farmlands and forests. Hundreds of thousands of families crammed into small cottages and encouraged by their churches to breed, the only contraception exhaustion, illness and death. The earth's crust turned inside out and set alight on a mass scale.

So, there I was sitting listening to a fat cockney geezer spouting off whilst undergoing a revelation and thinking, *I exist because of coal yet those shafts are capped off now and here I am, one of thousands of migrant builders in London and I'm here because I have little choice. A victim of circumstance.*

Ah well, the money was good and the craic was almighty. It was a rat race and hard to get paid sometimes. We always got our money but a lot of men didn't. On one particular occasion we got ourselves into a situation where we were owed three weeks' wages and I found myself with my foot on the foreman's neck whilst Phil emptied his pockets and got our wages – and a little more. Like I said, we always got ours.

If, when I had left school, I had the reading age of a six-or seven-year-old boy, at this stage of my life it had reduced to zero. Mentally, I'd had a fight with reading and put it in the bin. Filed under junk. At this stage of my life, it had been over six years since I had finished school and I had convinced myself I would get on fine in life without all that embarrassing reading and writing stuff. It was a mild disability and a form of blindness I had decided I would have to live with. Now I *can* read, I realise how much we do read. Walking down a high street in a very foreign country is probably a good example of what it's like to not be able to read. Go to some obscure little town in Asia and try to shop and that's how it feels. You stop trying to read the adverts and logos because you know they don't mean anything. You have to walk into a shop to see if it has got what you are looking for and walk back out when you realise it doesn't stock what you need and you've got it all wrong.

If a blind person wants a cup of tea and find themselves confronted by three decanters, one displaying the word COFFEE, another displaying the word TEA and the third SUGAR, what would they do? Just like me at that time of my life, that person doesn't know what's inside each container. Their sense of touch that they have relied on so heavily and therefore has become more sensitive could have them recognising its contents by its weight. They might give it a shake and let their finely tuned ears in on the act. Sugar would behave and sound different to teabags. Finally, if all is not conclusive, the nose would settle the argument for good, the distinctive aroma of coffee a thousand miles from the earthy smell of tea, or the odourless sugar. To me, it would be a similar process of elimination but I would be using only sight. I would pick up one at random, remove the lid, look inside and go from there. If it wasn't what I was looking for, then I would simply try the next. That's what living with a disability was to me.

Those close to me knew of my weakness but I didn't like it when the news spread to somebody new. I think this was probably the first time that cracks began to appear. We hear heroic people who have been blind from birth say that their lives don't feel difficult, because it is the only life they know. Though I feel uncomfortable comparing blindness with illiteracy, I believe they are related. Very distant cousins perhaps. Not being able to read is a blindness people are blind of. Perhaps if Robert Chance, my non-reading companion from my English class, had been born with no sight, he might have been given more help, allowed to move at a different pace and lived a fuller life. A life I'll discuss shortly. Who knows?

I felt a change in myself. All the time I spent on my own, of which there was plenty, I would try to read. Perhaps it had started to dawn on me that I didn't *have* to live the rest of my life in darkness. At first, I would pick up newspapers on trains and stare at them for hours, trying to make sense of their ink. The next step was to buy a newspaper, sit on a train and pretend to read it and enjoy looking normal. I would look at the pictures for clues to what the words might say. It wasn't going well, and for the first time in my life, I started to recognise I might need help.

12

Running away

After a couple of years in the city, what was once exciting had become the everyday norm. At first, I would reluctantly travel up north on visits and could not wait to get back south, but as time moved on my visits home got more frequent and driving south got harder. I met a girl up north too. That might have had something to do with the pull of magnetic north. Not sure if it was the pull of the northern girl or the blow of the southern rat race but before I knew what was happening, I was living in the flat I had bought with the dirty coal money and working back up north. I was working twenty-nine hours a day, eight days a week and doing my very best to make a go of it. I don't know how I found the time but before I knew what was happening there was a baby on the way.

It would be an understatement to say having a baby had not featured heavily in my life plan. I was still far too selfish, and knew it. When you grow up in a place like that, moving away for a better life has to feature strongly at the forefront of your thoughts or your lack of optimism for your future wellbeing might get you down. Like a release date making a prison stretch more bearable. I could tell from people's reactions to the news that they did not think it was a good idea. Just about everybody I knew would burst out laughing. Everybody except my parents, of course. The due date drew closer and the relationship I was in started to melt in the heat. There was love there but I hated what was happening. I am not about to try and rewrite history because as I have already said, at that stage of my life I was unbelievably selfish and that I admit. I ran away from all that resembled responsibility and even though I will later describe how it all worked out fine in the end, I could not have possibly known that then. The baby was born on the first day of January, only one and a half hours into 1989. I visited mother and baby in hospital, said my goodbyes and ran away to the south coast of England the very next day.

One of my many brothers was working as a civil engineer for BP on an oil plant near Bournemouth and he made some phone calls and found me a job working on site with a bricklaying contractor. He was up north visiting my parents for New Year and on 2 January we travelled down in his car together. The job was good, the money was good and given the situation I was in, it seemed to provide me with the fresh start my brain thought it needed at that particular time of my life.

BP had needed accommodation for its oil workers and had commandeered a local Pontins holiday park in Weymouth some twenty miles from the oil plant. It was perfect. They had kept the park staff on and we were well looked after. I had a very nice chalet of my own. A hearty breakfast in the dining hall would be served every morning and a very nice meal was supplied for all on a night. They even laid on coaches to and from the oil plant. There were pubs and entertainment in the show bar for everybody who wanted it. My brother was the master of ceremonies and would arrange the acts and compere in the evenings. Perfect! Perfect, except for one thing. No women allowed on site! The oil workers knew nothing else. They had spent their working lives offshore. But to the young me it was unbearable and it seemed like I was back in the school yard, staring through wrought-iron bars at the girls on the other side of the fence.

It wasn't long before I was in trouble. I would leave the park by the security gate in my brother's car, babble some nonsense to the security guys about where the nearest supermarket or post office might be because I needed some first-class stamps before nipping down into Weymouth town centre. An hour or two later I would return with no shopping or stamps but a girl hidden in the boot. Yes! A girl in the boot. Thinking back, I must have had something then I haven't got now. I must have either been very attractive to the opposite sex or had a massive spate of good luck. I would talk to a girl for a while and casually explain I was working on the oil plant. I would then tell of how unfortunately we would not be able to get to know one another better as girls were not allowed on the camp site. It wouldn't take long for the idea of hiding in the boot to be hatched. I can't remember if it was always my idea or theirs but I don't recall any girl ever saying no. It didn't matter, we were just young people having a night of fun, but it would become a problem in the morning. I would leave for work at 5.30 a.m. and they would almost always insist on staying in bed. Hours later, and often still in their evening attire, they would wander up to the park gates and ask the security guards for a ride into town. The guards were gunning for me but lacked proof. They would interrogate the girls and ask them for the name of the man who had smuggled them in. This would confuse them as they would get a different name every time. By the time I was finally caught by some jealous bastard of a security guard who had taken it upon himself to hide in the car park one dark night with a disposable camera and collect snaps of a girl entering my chalet, I had almost run out of names. Time to move on.

Actually, it wasn't so much as 'time to move on' as me being kicked out. And not just me; my brother had been in the car with me on this particular night and he was evicted with me. It didn't matter. Our jobs were safe and we rented two bedrooms in a dormer bungalow in a quaint little village just two miles from the oil plant. The owners, a middle-aged couple who lived downstairs, were heavy drinkers and quite eccentric. Having had no children, they had plugged the gap by purchasing two massive St Bernard puppy dogs before convincing one another they had actually conceived them.

They had a number of house rules and rule number one was never leave the side gate open as the dogs might get out onto the busy road. Somebody did and one of their beloved dogs was hit by a car. It wasn't me but I came in from work and got the blame. I tried to explain I hadn't been home that night but they were a little tipsy and had already decided it was me. He approached me as soon as I entered the door, him yelling with her behind screaming, and he slapped me hard across the face. Not something you should do to a northerner. It was one of those quick slaps that stings because you don't get a chance to close your eye. I instinctively cracked him back and knocked him out. An ambulance was called. Kicked out again. We had been there for less than one month.

We hired a static caravan for a week but it was very expensive. The following weekend we visited a cousin of ours in Portsmouth and he came up with the answer to our prayers. He had a small touring caravan on his drive that he rarely used and said we could borrow it. Off we went with our new home attached to the back of my brother's car. We pitched it only half a mile from the oil plant. Perfect! This was to be our home for the foreseeable.

Life was good. Winter vanished in a drunken haze and as spring turned into summer the caravan site and nearby town came to life. When sober, I would be haunted by what I was running from and because of this I drank heavily every night. Being drunk and getting lots of attention from females seemed to help but as anybody who has tried it knows, it only ever serves as a short-term solution. As soon as each morning arrived, I would be back to a tormented reality. I partied harder but nothing changed with how I felt. It never does. To all around I was having fun. Jack the lad. I suppose there was no denying that, but behind the facade of the carefree life was a young man vexed.

Any time spent alone and not under the influence was spent wondering what was happening with my child. What did he look like? Was he healthy? What colour was his hair? Would I ever see him? What was going through his mother's mind? Being abandoned like that and having to cope with a baby on her own, what the hell must she be going through? Yet still I drank and still I buried my head, chasing the next good time in an effort to shake off the bad.

The caravan was tiny and very old. It had a double bed at one end and a single at the other. Each night we would toss a coin and the loser got the single. It had a little fridge, a little two-ringed hob, a little sink, a little wardrobe for my brother's suits (being a civil engineer, he had to attend meetings twice a week) and a bucket for a toilet. I got a better job with better money and gave up working at the oil plant. My brother would get picked up every morning by the company minibus and off he would go to work. Everybody on the bus would laugh and jeer as he would appear from the shack we lived in immaculately dressed. They must have wondered how the hell he did it. I did! I would shoot off to work in his car, get home before him and make us both a meal. He worked longer hours and together with me thinking I was the better cook, it seemed to make the perfect marriage. We would eat our meal, shower in the communal shower block and go straight to the pub. Every night.

Summers on the south coast were a lot hotter and longer than I was used to but before I knew it, the long hot days had galloped on by and autumn had taken hold. The caravan became cold. I bought a gas bottle and got the heater working. It was bearable. We got a call from our cousin. He needed the caravan as he was going on holiday. We promised we would drop it off the following weekend and discussed our next move. A bigger caravan seemed to be the best answer as the winter rates for pitching on a site were very cheap and after all, we needed all the money we could get for drink. We looked in the local evening paper, there were a few for sale and we arranged to view one the very next morning.

Brilliant! We emptied the caravan into a friend's garage, cleaned it out and off we went to return it. We spent the night with him and set off early in the morning to pick up our new home. We found the address but the man who was selling the caravan apologised and explained that somebody had just beaten us to it. We could not afford hotels or B&Bs as it would have soon eaten into the money we had clubbed together for a caravan.

Time for plan B. I was seeing a girl called Bev and she had just bought a big army tent. She had bought it for her and a couple of her brothers to go to a festival in the summer and it was lying idle. We would borrow the tent, put it on the caravan pitch that was already paid for and sleep in that for a couple of nights. Just until the new evening paper came out on the Tuesday night and then we could go and get a new caravan. A good plan B.

You can imagine the reaction of my brother's work colleagues when the minibus pulled up on Monday morning. Everyone spilled out of the bus and circled the tent in hysterics.

He emerged immaculately dressed, joined his friends and off he went. Shortly after, I jumped in the car and set off to work. The car needed oil. On the way home from the pub the night before a warning light had come on whilst we were racing down a country road knocking down rabbits and stopping to collect them. He had bought a can of oil at the service station and before he left for work, he had told me to check the oil before I even thought of starting the engine. I didn't. I got about a mile down the road and the engine went BANG! I parked it up and got a lift back to the tent. The friend who had agreed to store our belongings in his garage turned up with our stuff expecting to see a new caravan. I explained we hadn't managed to buy one yet and he dumped everything we owned on the grass and left laughing.

I sat in the front of the tent and watched the minibus, filled with muffled laughter, drop my brother off. It was raining and I had taken cover inside on one of two camp chairs.

'What's for tea?' he asked, getting out of the rain and joining me in the tent on the other chair.

'Those two rabbits we got last night, but the fire is fighting with the rain and I think they're still a bit raw,' I explained. He looked around at our belongings that had been dropped off.

'Where are my suits?' he asked.

'There,' I explained, pointing to his suits hanging in a tree only a few metres away. 'I've put bin liners over them to keep them dry,' I reassured him.

'Thanks,' he said. 'I'm starving.'

'They might be cooked now, we'll try them,' I said. I got the two rabbits and put one on each of two plastic plates with a few slices of bread. I handed him his and sat back down. He bit into it. It was raw.

'Where's the car?' he asked, scowling.

146

'I forgot to put the oil in and blew the engine, it's parked up in town,' I admitted.

He spat his raw rabbit out onto the grass and stared at his suits hanging in the rain. He spoke and I'll never forget his words: 'Pip, the time has arrived for me and you to part company,' he said.

Nigel had to do four months of each year in his company's head office as part of his training and because of this, and me, he disappeared quickly to London. I bought another caravan and decided to stick out the autumn and winter on the south coast. I remember this particular time of my life as being emotionally quite difficult. Perhaps having my brother there had kept my mind away from my little boy and my responsibilities. That's what brothers do, I suppose. If it *had* been his intention to help his younger brother out by assisting him with taking his mind off things, he had certainly gone over and above. Probably just got out in time. If we'd stayed together longer, I'm not sure what might have come after the tent. The gutter perhaps.

13

The great cock and dole swindle

I'd had enough of drinking but it felt better than being sober.
I'd had enough of one-night stands but it felt better than waking
up alone. The campsite manager knocked on my door early one
Friday morning and gave me a letter that had been delivered to
reception but was addressed to me. He also collected the ground
rent and informed me there had been a number of complaints
made about me. A few female residents had got together and
complained about some of the girls who had been staying over
in my caravan. Apparently, some of them had been a bit too
noisy! I told him how it was difficult and how I was in a no-win
situation.

'If I don't give the girls my full attention, I get complaints
from inside the caravan and if I do give them my full attention,
I get complaints from outside the caravan!' He looked confused. 'What am I supposed to do?' I asked him, as if in despair.
He didn't get me, and stared back blankly, before counting the
cash I had just handed him and informing me that if it happened again, I would be kicked off site immediately. The
following morning, I was kicked off site. I tried to argue my
point but it was useless. The man had no compassion or understanding of what it was like to have to deal with such an
addiction. It seemed I had no option but to move my home to

another campsite ... two miles down the road. Well, not so much move as be kicked off, I suppose. The new campsite was good: it was closer to town, a little cheaper and there were no restrictions on noise levels which allowed the girls who stayed over to comfortably reach as many decibels as they liked.

The letter that had been delivered to the campsite was from my mother and contained a photo of my little boy and his mother. He was about nine months old; they looked well dressed, happy and they were smiling at the camera. I still have that photo today. I got a girlfriend to read out the letter. It went on to say everything I was running away from was not going to go away. You might think any fool would know that anyway but at that particular time of my life, despite all the hurt and pain suffered, I had still not managed to suss out something so simple. Mother and child were living in my house. My mother had stepped in and sorted things out. The letter went on to explain, my mother had taken her to the social services where she had filled out the forms for claiming housing benefit. On one of the papers, she had to declare she didn't know who the father of her child was. She had filled it out, signed it and been so humiliated, she cried all the way home.

This was another tool in the box commonly used to beat the system. Everybody was at it. If somebody had a child, she would fill out the forms, declaring she didn't know who the father was. The rent would then be given directly to the mother for her to give to her landlord and she would keep it because the landlord was the father. This was perfect for all concerned as it meant the system could not chase the fathers for child maintenance because they didn't have a name. This loophole in a fractured system worked well, the winner of course the innocent child. The mother claimed rent but had no landlord to pay. She got her dole money plus child benefit and, in most cases, the father got to keep all of his dole. And if mother or father could pick up a bit of cash doing fiddle work on the black market, it was a win-win. Another child being brought up just above the breadline and escaping a lower level of poverty that would be difficult for people who were not involved to ever imagine. The only downside was the social services were onto it and would do regular spot checks on the mothers' houses. This meant no men's clothes, shoes, toothbrushes, razors, photos or anything indicating the presence of a father could be kept at the family home and the men would have to live out of a suitcase at their parents' or a friend's house. If the father was caught being there, he would pretend he was the new boyfriend before making a quick exit. This loophole in the system was commonly and affectionately known to all who were involved as 'the great cock and dole swindle', and believe me, it still goes on today.

There was lots of time to reflect on what I had run away from, but it didn't matter how much I weighed up the pros and cons, going back north was still not an option for me. I probably thought returning home meant personal failure. In my mind the place was a deprived dead end and if I returned, people might think I'd been chasing rainbows or I was the dead end. I would stare at the photo for hours as if I was suddenly about to see something new. I got a girlfriend to help me write a letter to my mother, enclosed some money and acknowledged that burying my head in the sand was not making things any better and agreed to go home for Christmas and talk. I think this was the first time in my life that I actually lifted my foot off the accelerator. Even if it was just a small amount. I began to spend more time on my own before starting to see more of one girl, Bev, the owner of the tent; but not for long.

My brother Glen had been made redundant from the pit and had been to university. He was training to be a school teacher and was halfway through his one year of teacher training in a school only two miles away from our village up north. He landed on my caravan doorstep and announced he had seven weeks off for his summer holiday. I got him a job with a contracting company as a carpenter on the building site where I worked. We tossed a coin for the big bed every night and life was good. He had been getting paid £650 a month for being a teacher and was now receiving £800 a week for being a carpenter.

I packed in bricklaying and started working alongside him. The skills he'd acquired as a welder at the mine whilst working on shaft maintenance were rare and ideally suited for tall buildings. We were the lift shaft team. We were building an eleven-storey American bank and were put in charge of forming the timber moulds that would be filled with concrete to form its huge lift shafts and stairwells that connected all its floors. The job had stood still for some time before our arrival because of a lack of expertise. Within a fortnight the American managers had spotted the leap in progress and the reason for it and they wanted to see us. A meeting was held in their offices. They asked where we had come from. What were we doing there. How we had acquired such skills. And how long we planned to work in the area. Glen told them the truth. He had worked as a welder for British Coal, had worked on construction sites since his redundancy and had then done a degree in education and was just here to earn some extra money during his summer holidays. I told some lies. I said we had worked down the mine together, that I also had been made redundant, I had done a college course in joinery and had been working on shafts ever since.

The only thing these people could not afford was to lose us. In true American style they doubled our wages, told us to take our pick of who we wanted from the men on site, bring in whoever else we needed, build a team of men and make some progress fast. We stayed there five months, finished ahead of schedule and earned more money than we could have dreamed of. They asked us to do the next multi-storey for them in Swindon and off we went. I was twenty-two years old, it was 1989 and I was getting £1,200 a week. Not bad, I thought, for somebody who still couldn't read or write. My brother never stood in a classroom again.

Now let me explain. If Nigel had been a carefree idiot, Glen was an eccentric lunatic. To put things into perspective, Glen today is sixty years old, runs the pub in the village, is over twenty stone, drives a motorbike and side car the same age as himself, has long grey hair and is also something of a stand-up comedian. Though he finds it hard to stand upright for any length of time these days. If my foot had lifted off the gas a little, it was now well and truly fully back down. There were times when I would be asked to read or write and Glen, being the only one in on my little secret, would step in and rescue me. At one point I was asked to write the daily weather reports and justify any man-hours lost due to poor weather. Glen had a word with the manager. He sweet-talked him and suggested it might be better done by somebody with too much time on their hands, as I was too valuable as a foot soldier and needed on site at all times. Phew!

As planned, we travelled home for Christmas. I had not been home for fifty-one weeks. The visit was good and bad. Bad in the sense that I talked to the mother of my child and realised our relationship was not going to be. And good in the sense that the conversation was adult and constructive. We talked about how we would deal with the future because the boy was beautiful. She was a better woman than I was a man and probably still is. She explained she would be moving out of the house in the new year. I argued she would be financially much better off if she was to remain and I didn't mind her living there while I paid the mortgage but she wasn't having any of it. She said she needed to start working again for her own sanity and if she was doing this on her own, she needed to be a free agent and not somebody's ex. She told me I would always be his father and she would never get in the way of that and if I felt the need to help out financially, I could, and she assured me that all the money given would be allocated to his needs. She displayed more maturity in those few meetings than I have ever shown in my life. I got to spend time with my boy over the Christmas period and it was wonderful. It didn't last long enough and before I knew it, we were heading back down south to work.

We arrived in Swindon, rented an unbelievably cheap flat in the centre of town and as night came in, we realised why it was so cheap. It was smack bang in the middle of the red-light district. It didn't really bother us. In fact, if the landlord had come clean and told us the truth, we would have probably still taken it. We were never in. If we were not ten floors up on a scaffold, we were in the pub and if we were not in the pub or on a scaffold, we were in bed, so it met our needs.

I was away from my boy yet due to the honesty of his mother, the torment seemed to have been lifted and my behaviour, though remaining selfish and lacking any true direction, might have just – at that point – started showing the first signs of levelling out.

I had a few flings, probably taking advantage of the 'new kid in town' syndrome. There was the odd barmaid and a couple of girls I'd met in the pubs around town, a few students who had got into the habit of bringing me food and talking to me through the building site fence on their way to classes, the girl who sold flowers in the kiosk outside the railway station, one of the girls from the on-site canteen who had just separated from her husband and the lady on the reception in the railway museum who was at least twice my age and very attractive. I had visited the museum one Sunday morning in an effort to stay out of trouble. I asked her to read something I was interested in but couldn't and ended up in bed with her that afternoon. Oh, nearly forgot about the on-site nurse who I had not met until she removed a small fragment of concrete from my eye . . . and then there was Bev. Okay, so perhaps it doesn't sound like I was starting to level out my behaviour, but believe me, things were happening at a slower pace than before and for the first time I found I was actually capable of enjoying my own company. To me, at that time, I couldn't see any harm in what I was doing. Just young people having fun. And a museum curator. Thinking back now, I had probably been used to spice up her dead marriage or save it. Hope it worked for her. See, I was spreading good. And as for Bev, who was now one hundred miles away, I suppose my thinking was what she didn't know, couldn't hurt her. Not yet!

It was a long drive for Bev to come and see me but she did it regularly. I think she loved me. Poor Bev. We would speak most days on the landline we'd had installed in our flat. I would enjoy the calls and look forward to her weekend visits every two weeks or so. But they didn't last long. I had a little book full of girlfriends' names and numbers and Glen got his hands on it when I was out. He thought he'd have some fun and rang them all. He invited each and every one of them to the same pub at the same time . . . at the place I was meeting Bev that evening for a meal. He could get away with it because his tone of voice and accent was exactly the same as mine. I thought it was a bit strange when I spotted my brother sitting at the bar with a bunch of our work colleagues but put it down to coincidence. Bev arrived, we ordered food, the food arrived and then it started. Within twenty minutes I had been confronted eight times and as the ninth queued behind the eighth to deliver me a piece of her mind Bev got up and walked out. I never saw her again. I gave her a few days to cool off and rang her but I could hear the distaste for me in her voice. My loss. It was a true example of not knowing what you have until it's gone and a huge lesson in life.

We stayed in Swindon for eight months and again we completed the building ahead of time. Those eight months were different. We worked harder and played less. The next job the company wanted us to do was in the city of London. There was a gap of six weeks between one job finishing and the new job starting and I took some time out to think. I landed back up north and was surprised how much the place saddened me. The same sad bastards sitting in the same sad seats telling me how lucky I was to be in the position I was. Lucky! Really!

I enjoyed my parents. I'd forgotten how funny they were. I hadn't seen them for almost a year and was greeted by my father grinning whilst shouting over the neighbours' fence.

'Try not kicking it, Bob. See what happens when you stop kicking it!' I knew exactly what and who he was laughing at. Bob next door had a Jack Russell and the Jack Russell hated Bob. They'd lived there since we'd moved in and I had grown up to the muffled sound of Bob from next door letting the dog out into the backyard and then spending all day noisily trying to get the dog back in. If he tried to pick the dog up, it would attempt to strip the flesh from his fingers and if he tried to move it with his foot, the dog would quickly latch onto his shoe. This would always result in Bob trying to football the animal through the back door. When he had been a little younger, he had scored some crackin' free kicks, but as he'd got older this would almost always result in the dog hanging on to his foot whilst he shouted, 'Bastard thing! Bastard thing!' whilst hopping backwards into the house with a dog on his foot.

It was a great spectacle and it wasn't until that particular moment I realised I actually missed its ritualistic sound and splendour.

I visited my son and enjoyed time with him. He loved books and would constantly jump on my knee and ask me to read to him. This stirred something in me and moved my gremlins to the forefront of my mind. I bought a Walkman and some cassette tapes. Whenever travelling or on my own I would take the card from the cassette box and follow the written words as the song played in my ears. Poetic music was simple because it was more spoken and the key words that rhymed gave clues to the logic of language. It fascinated me how one word that was spelled completely different to the next could also sound so similar. Leonard Cohen's music was perfect and I owned everything he ever wrote. What a teacher!

We left Swindon; I flew to Thailand for a month. On my return, I rang Nigel, who was living in south London, and asked if Glen and I could stay with him for a week or so just until we found somewhere to stay close to our new place of work in the city. He agreed. We got a train to London and realised we had to change from train to tube to reach the city centre before again travelling south. We crossed the platform, got on the tube and sat down. I was not to know but my life was just a split second away from taking on a whole new direction and becoming a completely different story.

14

West Ruislip tube station, north London
6.15 p.m., 28 May 1990

So, I'm sitting on the tube watching a small man help his girl-friend from the train. She is a large lady and is pushing to get off. Her boyfriend is holding her arm and helping her. She successfully but awkwardly steps down from the train before readjusting her tight white leggings. They make their way across the platform. It is a strange scene. I'm probably smirking. I look straight ahead and there is a woman sitting directly opposite. She is sharing my amusement. She looks like the blonde from ABBA (not the one with the beard, I might add) but is dressed more like Debbie Harry.

The doors suck shut and the train starts to move. I'm looking at her as much as I dare without coming across as a creep. She's wearing a tight pink boob-tube, ripped jeans and a denim jacket. She is reading a book and has a Walkman plugged into her ears. At this particular point of my life, I couldn't possibly have known that thirty years later this woman would be my wife. These trains run every two minutes. If I had been two minutes earlier or two minutes later, I might have sat there totally oblivious, an empty seat in front of me. She would have gone on her way, only minutes away from me, and had two sons with someone else.

At our wedding some ten years after, she made a speech. Not very traditional, I suppose, the bride making a speech but neither is your children being there on your big day. She said, 'We met on a train, it was love at first sight, and then some three years later he had fallen in love with me.' I'll never know why she thinks that! When we first met she slipped the book she was reading into her bag, turned up her Walkman (remember them?) and looked at me. I could hear a tinny sound leaking from her headphones and recognised it as Leonard Cohen. I spoke.

'Sorry,' she said, removing her headphones. She said later that she didn't normally talk to strangers on the tube but for me she would make an exception. Believe that if you can.

'What ya liznen to?' I asked. It took a few goes. 'What ya liznen to? . . . What ya liznen to?' She told me later in our relationship she had thought I might be Russian or perhaps Norwegian. She always jokes she hadn't realised at this point that I was even more foreign than that. A northerner!

'Leonard Cohen,' she eventually answered. Conscious of my accent, I spoke slowly in pidgin English explaining I had every Leonard Cohen album ever made. I asked where she was going and she told me she was on her way to a friend's house to meet a bunch of girls before going to see a band. She kept talking. She was the poshest person I had ever encountered. I'm not telling this because it is a love story, though I suppose it is. I'm telling this because this woman was so opposite and different to me that it changed my way of thinking from that moment on. Within minutes she'd told me she was an accident and emergency nurse and after another minute or so her life story. It felt very comfortable. The train stopped. It was her stop but not mine. I was travelling into the city. She stood; I'd only known her for ten minutes but already it seemed awkward for us to part.

'Could I walk you to your friend's house?' I asked.

I walked her to her friend's house and she took me inside. She introduced me as Pip, the stranger she'd only just met on a train. I could see in her friend's eyes they thought she'd gone mad. She had. We both had. She still didn't even know my real name. I tried to explain that all northerners have nicknames just to confuse things and my real name was Christopher but I couldn't tell if she understood. We had drinks and I had the decency to feel awkward first. I told the girls how I had been working on the south coast but was now about to start on a new building project in the city and how I was staying in temporary accommodation in Croydon. Feeling out of my comfort zone, I suggested perhaps it might be a good idea if they went off to enjoy their girly night and maybe we might catch up with one another at a later date. They agreed and Wendy walked me to the door. We stood outside and kissed. She wrote her number on a piece of paper for the landline of the house she shared with three other nurses in Harrow and we said our goodbyes.

As I walked down the path she smiled and said, 'give me a ring on that number and you might get more than just a kiss!' I didn't ring her for three weeks and when I did, she screamed with delight down the phone and almost burst my eardrum. I explained I had been busy for a few weeks working and tying up a few loose ends and we arranged to meet the following Saturday at her friend's twenty-first birthday party in a wine bar in Harrow on the Hill.

The night went well. I was a little late. Two hours actually, but I got there. The place seemed full of disappointed men. Disappointed because I had turned up. The conversation flowed, or so I thought. She told me later she couldn't really understand what I'd been saying but whatever it was, it sounded nice and it sounded complimentary. She laughed when I did, I thought I was funny and the vibe was electric. I could understand her perfectly; she sounded like she was reading the news on BBC Radio 4. I discovered her father was a retired architect, she had a younger sister and her mother had lost her battle with cancer two years previously. I was honest, and explained the loose ends I had been tying up were called Paula, Susan and Lynn. The wine bar closed at midnight and the taxi was almost an hour late. She was desperate for a wee. I held her arm and looked out for her whilst she hitched up her mini-skirt and squatted between two parked cars. I was a hero. It was only our first night out together yet it seemed our relationship was now in full bloom.

A few weeks later I moved to Ealing Broadway which was only thirty minutes from where she lived and we looked forward to our weekends together. We were completely unalike. She would eat student food and always put her knife and fork in the twelve o'clock position on her plate to show she had finished eating. I ate the best foods, in all the best places, and didn't know what knives and forks were for. She was five-foot-four, petite and quite reserved. I was a six-foot, hairy-arsed male. I had a wild northern accent. She spoke very posh. She had not long graduated from nursing college. I could barely spell my own name. I was very working class, from near Newcastle, and was in London escaping the aftermath of the recent miners' strike. She was an upper-middle-class Surrey girl from Woking and in London escaping nothing. I was the youngest of six boys. She was the eldest of two girls, her sister being a concert pianist and classic oboe player at the Royal Academy of Music. My mother was a teacher. Wendy's had died. My father was a redundant miner. Her father since retiring early from being an architect was now a freeman of the city of London. She was twenty-eight and I was only twenty-three. Over half her monthly wage would disappear as rent and after she'd paid for make-up, clothes and the odd pair of seven-inch heels she would spend three and a half weeks of the month completely skint. I, on the other hand, earned more in a few days than she earned in a month.

We were poles apart but she fascinated me. She'd lost her mother but was optimistic and seemed free of strife. I'd never met somebody from Britain who was actually happy with the deal they'd been dealt. Everybody else I knew was suffering some sort of trauma or upheaval, were running from something and were not doing what they were doing because of choice. That was the difference, I suppose, though I was probably having difficulty putting my finger on it then. I'd had little or no choice; I'd been born in my village and when the mine shut, I had to get out. Nothing to lose. Yet here was this person who had been wrapped in cotton wool but had spat out the silver spoon and flown the nest as soon as possible. This, to me, was new! How things should be, I suppose, but to me, at that point it seemed strange. I hadn't known of it.

She said she was in London escaping nothing but I think her being there had, in fact, been a deliberate effort to get herself some life experience and for the moment, I was it. She'd left home at eighteen to attend nursing college and after qualifying and specialising in paediatric trauma and securing a position in the busy accident and emergency department in Northwick Park General Hospital, life experience was definitely what she was getting. She would some days go out on the ambulances and believe me, she was dealing with things that a nice girl from Surrey should never see.

There was a large community of us northerners living in

Ealing Broadway and we didn't need showing by anybody how to enjoy ourselves. We even had certain takeaway restaurants where we could get gravy on our chips. Work hard, play hard was the motto. The weekends were 'life in the fast lane', and the fast lane was great fun. Wendy found out from the northern girls who were working as nurses in the city that I had a two-year-old boy up north. Probably should have heard it from me but as I explained, I hadn't wanted to chase her away with baggage. We got on with things.

I got to meet her sister, Caroline. She came across London to us with her new boyfriend. He was a very tweedy, five-foot-one-inch opera singer called Rupert. I'd never met a Rupert before! It was a lot for a northerner to take in. Thinking back to those days now, I think Wendy should have perhaps been more worried about scaring *me* off with *her* baggage. I met her father and grandmother and I was the perfect gentleman. I think! I wasn't the first man she had taken home. Some years before she had been dating a junior doctor. Apparently, he had been quite upper class. The whole family were very impressed by him and her mother and grandmother had advised that it might be a good idea to marry him.

'No, I can't!' she had said.

'Why on earth not, dear?' they asked.

'Because he will become a consultant and I will become a consultant's unfaithful wife,' she told them.

Christmas came and went. I took a trip up north to spend time with my family and my little boy (Lee). His mother was in a relationship and everything was settled and cool. I returned south. However, the office block I was working on in the centre of the city was almost built. The economy had slowed dramatically and the company I worked for advised I should look for work elsewhere. There was no well-paid work about. I had travelled to where the money was but it seemed it had dried up.

I couldn't go back up north; there was definitely no money there. Time to think outside the box. And I did.

I walked into Australia House, got myself a work visa, bought an aeroplane ticket to Sydney and explained what I had done to Wendy. She was devastated. I left her in tears early one morning and headed for Heathrow. I landed in Sydney six weeks later almost penniless having travelled through Asia. Sydney was a disaster; the global depression had hit down under harder than it had hit the UK and realising there was no chance of work, I jumped on a train and headed a thousand kilometres north to Brisbane.

After staying in a youth hostel for a couple of weeks I found work. Things were going well. I moved out of the city into a farmhouse in a small village and became their local builder. After six months I spoke to Wendy and asked if she would like to come and spend some time with me in sunny Oz. She landed the following week. It was very hot and steamy when she arrived and the weather was fine.

Unless Wendy had actually got herself shot into space, this was geographically and culturally as far as she could ever be from the city of London yet she shocked me. It seemed she had never been so at peace with herself. I was building a house for somebody I had met in the pub. I told Wendy I would have to work for a couple of weeks to finish it and then I would take some time off. I think she was a little bored in the farmhouse during the day when I wasn't around. It was very isolated. She couldn't drive so I taught her in my truck on the field at the front of the house. The lesson was about one hour long and that was it, she was on her way. I would go to work and she would drive around the Gold Coast, trying her utmost not to kill herself or anybody who got in the way.

The weekend arrived and I suggested she should pack a little bag and it might be a good idea to get away for a few days. She

163

was already as away as a girl could get but she did confess she was quite excited at the prospect of talking to some human beings instead of the noisy family of possums who lived in my roof. Who knew? We might even reach civilisation. We jumped in the truck and drove. And drove. And drove. And drove some more. We rented a beach hut that had wild turkeys nesting on its roof. I took some metal spikes and a whole load of fishing tackle. I would walk down the beach in the early hours of the morning, knock the baited metal spikes into the sand and when we sat around the barbecue in the morning, the tide would retract and our breakfast would be there flapping around in the wash of small waves. The nearest Wendy got to meeting somebody civilised, and I include myself in this equation, was the large family of kangaroos who would sit with us on a night. We roasted potatoes in the fire for them. However, they were not very good at waiting or sharing and would try and grab them from the hot coals. I would smack their hands with a stick and shout at them and they would actually do what I said. We would eat the potatoes and they would get the skins. One particular young Joey had a real taste for dairy products and one night hopped off with a whole block of cheese. He was the cutest thief. It was a pleasure to be robbed.

After a few days we said our goodbyes to the kangaroo family and I drove some more. And some more. And some more. Wendy had a map and would comment that this place or that place might be worth looking at and I would immediately change direction and head towards where she said. After another few days she started to ask questions. Reasonable questions, I suppose, like 'Where are we going?' and 'How long are we going for?' to which the answers were 'Haven't got a clue but I thought we would have a couple of months at it.' All of her money, clothes and possessions, including her contraceptive pills, were now two thousand kilometres away.

So, I'm sitting in a rust-eaten truck going across the Simpson Desert and my girlfriend is complaining she is down to her last pair of clean knickers. She still talks about this time of her life today. She calls it her 'reference point'. She says that, when one of her friends is complaining about the standard of a hotel or having to wait in an airport for a few hours or about their husbands generally, she always secretly drifts off to this point. She will listen to them whinging, smile and appear concerned but what she is really thinking is, *You need a fortnight with Pip, that would shut you up!*

We drove. And we drove. And we drove. Some days Wendy drove. It wasn't as if she could crash into somebody or something. There was nobody and nothing there. We found a town but it was not what we could recognise as civilisation. It was actually called Longreach because it took so long to reach. It rained while we were there. It was the first rain they'd seen for eight years. The school let the children outside to get wet. They'd never seen water coming from the clouds before. We watched from a cafe across the street as the children screamed with delight and thanked the sky for the warm shower. The rain didn't stop and by early afternoon flood warnings were issued as the whole town got busy transporting anything valuable to higher ground. Wendy managed to get to a charity shop and grab some knickers and a few other items of clothing. Actually, thinking back now, it probably wasn't a charity shop at all. It was probably Longreach's answer to a high fashion outlet. I don't think the stuff was second-hand; I think it had just hung there for years being bleached by the sun whilst slowly going out of fashion. The till must have taken more that day than it had in the last decade, helped only by me and the desperate situation my girlfriend was in. We ran, in the rain, to another shop which was half chemist and half hunting equipment. It wasn't an elephant gun or a colt 45 she needed but make-up and contraceptive pills and a very understanding lady sensed her panic and gave her a one-month supply without her having to see a doctor. She popped a pill, we jumped in the truck and fled before we were drowned. We headed north-east and as she drove, she asked me if I could read. She had sussed me out.

I explained that at school I had been given the basics but as all the men in my village were expected to be miners, the basics they had given me were in metalwork. Unfortunately for me the very year I'd left school was the very year of the implementation of a massive pit closure programme. Surprisingly she announced she was pleased this had happened, for if I *had* gone down that pit, I wouldn't have been on that train.

When it came to reading, I knew the basics and if shown a word, I could eventually read it, but the sentences didn't seem to flow. Wendy started me off on newspapers. She had also picked up a few books from the charity shop. One was George Orwell's *Animal Farm* and she helped me read it as we crossed back over the desert. If I struggled with a piece, she would grab the book and read it out loud before passing it back and making me read it again. After a few days, I thanked her and informed her it was the first book I'd read.

This was, I believe, a turning point in my life and that particular book, I believe, is the reason I can read today. Its pages set my mind spinning. Politically, it made me question all I'd ever thought, been taught and fought for. It was also the first time I realised that left-wing policies could create tyranny. I suddenly realised I'd grown up under the misapprehension that there had only ever been one tyrant and my dad had helped get the bastard: Adolf Hitler. Due to this book and the revelation it stirred in me, I became obsessed with the Russian Revolution.

We talked for long hours and this is when I discovered for the first time that my very English girlfriend had always held a genuine empathy for the miners, even long before we had met. This was the first time she told me of that incident when she had been quite young and her father had commented at the dining table that the striking miners should be thankful for small mercies and should be forced back to work. She described to me how the exchange had suddenly become quite heated, making her sister cry and resulting in herself being sent up to her room without pudding for having socialist views. She spoke of how her parents would laugh about her and refer to her as 'the red from under the bed'.

'No wonder I moved out at eighteen,' she laughed.

A few days later we landed in a large town and I think I had started feeling sorry for the city girl. I could sense her desperation for the bare essentials so did the decent thing and booked us into a two-star hotel. She took full advantage of its running cold water tap and the postage stamp mirror in its telephone-box-sized bathroom before we went out for the evening.

We visited a rum factory and sampled its many different styles of the spirit. This night was the first night we had actually argued with one another. She shouted at me in the street and I shouted at her in return and the next morning neither of us could remember what all the shouting had been about. We had breakfast and laughed. We went to a bookshop and she managed to get her hands on some books on the Russian Revolution for me. Not knowing how long it would be until she might see another, she made full use of the cold tap and mirror and off we went north. She drove and I read.

The Russians wanted socialist equality. They murdered

Nicholas the Second. Lenin came back from exile and stirred up the Bolsheviks, the leading Marxist political party. The Bolsheviks, following the writings of Karl Marx, promised all citizens peace, land and bread. They abolished land ownership, arrested and evicted hundreds of thousands of farmers who were now labelled as enemies of the state. The farmers, who were mostly peasants and had worked their lands since time began, were forcibly transported to the cold north with their families to starve and freeze to death. Because of who they were! Nobody knew how to work the farms and one hundred and twenty million people perished. I was fascinated.

I also noticed the similarities to this and Cambodia. Not the Cambodia of centuries gone by but the Cambodia of the here and now. This was 1990 and it was all over the news about Pol Pot and the Khmer Rouge. The media in Australia covered Asia more than it covered Europe and there was little escape from the images of the genocide that was taking place. Naively, I tried to get my hand on some books about what was going on there but was advised that, as it was still happening, I should probably read the papers. I did. The situation was horrendous.

Call it Leninism. Call it Marxism. Call it socialism. Call it communism. It was left-wing, it was what I had always believed in and it didn't work. I read about Russia during the Second World War.

Stalin took the helm and between twenty-seven million and twenty-nine million souls perished. They didn't even bother to keep an accurate tally of victims. This hadn't occurred one thousand years ago; this was only twenty years before I was born. One of the chapters in the book I was reading was about China. Chairman Mao, the Chinese communist leader, murdered between fifty and sixty million of his own people between

1958 and 1962, because of who they were! Only four years before I was born.

The tyranny created by the right is well documented and so it should be. If you haven't been to Auschwitz and Birkenau, you should go. If you haven't taken your children, you should. I have. It is an unbelievably horrendous atrocity and it's good that it is preserved as a monument to 'what can happen'. The Nazis eradicated over six million men, women and children. Because of who they were! My mind boggled.

The tour continued for another month or so. I rang my father from a phone box and got contact details for my auntie who had outlived his brother and we went to visit her. Her house was less than one hundred kilometres from where I had been living. We arrived and her house was full of their friends, mainly ex-pats, waiting to meet the 'English couple'. They loved the sound of Wendy's voice and would crowd around her. It must have reminded them of home. A great friendship and some strong connections were made. We stayed the night and left in the morning before eventually landing back at the farmhouse.

We'd had the time of our lives. We'd spent a small fortune and I had got to know my girlfriend a lot better. Australia and the Australians suited Wendy. Like her, the place and its people had suffered little strife and I think this was when I first started to recognise why we were so different. She respects everybody. To me, people have to earn respect. I trust nobody; she trusts all. Like a pampered dog that's never been kicked she jumps up at everybody. I think because of having to live on my wits to protect what little I had, I'd developed armour, where she'd made do with the very soft and very well looked after skin she'd been born in. Why wouldn't she trust someone? Everybody she'd ever known had been lovely and lacked motive when it came to ripping someone off. We had both been moulded by our surroundings, but I think this might have been when I first started to realise that her way was probably the better way to approach life.

I started to work again. However, it wasn't going well; she was distracting me from my work and I was feeling guilty leaving her alone in the house. I only worked basic hours as I felt an obligation to be around. This left me with less money to pay for two. 'A tuppenny pie was costing fourpence!' as my mother would say. I suggested it might be a good idea for her to return to London and I would join her four months later when my visa ran out.

She got on the plane in tears. I spent a lot of time reflecting on what the hell I was doing and why I was on the bottom of the planet. Was I running away from something or was I out there trying to find something? If that pit was still open, on top of the world, I would most certainly be down it now. When it closed, lots of the men in my village had started commuting to London. It was a common sight in the village high street to see men crowding onto National Express coaches late on Sundays and spewing from them again on Friday evenings before running into the pubs. It looked exciting and made me want to go. That and the disparity in lifestyle that existed between those that went and those that didn't. To me, £86 or £600 per week had not been a gamble or even a choice but an obvious step forward. However, London had been one step but this had been a little further. Where next – the moon?

Thinking back now, my father's elusive brother, Ray, disappearing down under and dying there some six years before my arrival probably had a bigger influence on me than I had realised. Before my birth he'd smashed a pit lamp over the head of everything that was wrong with post-war Britain and disappeared overnight. I was mystified by the intrigue he'd left behind.

'They reckon he's a millionaire! Don't blame him for not coming back here!' the locals back home in the village would say.

I started to ring my parents more often and the more I spoke to them, the more distant they sounded. I received a handwritten letter from my father. He never wrote letters. It was difficult to read, but helped by my recent lessons and fuelled by a sheer desperation to find out what he had to say, I chopped my way through it. I was shocked. It read that there was nothing for me in the north of England, the world was a big place and I would be a fool to come back. He wanted his son to make something of himself but I'm not sure to this day if the letter was a subconscious act of reverse psychology or if he meant what he said. What I do remember is an overwhelming feeling of rejection. The letter was two and a half pages long and had a newspaper cutting wrapped up in it. It went on to fill me in on bits of village gossip. I couldn't tell if he was showing me how trivial, insignificant and unimportant the village and life there was, but I found myself hanging on to each and every word in a desperate effort to feel what it might be like to be back there. I'll never know if he wrote the last line because he wanted me home but if he did, it worked. It read:

Stay safe. Your dad. P.S. Bob next door died yesterday; the dog was pleased!

This was a lightbulb moment for me. To live your life without humour is to not live at all. I gave the background story of Bob and the dog and tried to share the humour with my so-called friends in Australia but they couldn't get it. They ribbed

171

me and thought the humour in the letter came from my father telling me not to come home. I read the newspaper cutting. It was from the deaths column of the local newspaper. My best friend Phil had fallen asleep at the wheel whilst travelling north from London. He'd got within seven miles of his front door and crashed. He was twenty-six. I didn't just want to be home. I wanted to be back in my mother's womb.

15

Back to Blighty

Nine months later I was thrown out of Australia for overstaying my welcome. It wasn't that I'd wanted to be there particularly, as much as that because I had become the local builder, I had become committed to finishing a lot of work I had started.

I took a slight detour to Papua New Guinea to see a man who had known and worked with my uncle Ray. I had an urge to find out for myself exactly what had kept him from ever returning to England. I found out! It was the most colourful and exciting yet undeveloped place I had ever seen. Undeveloped, in the sense that the British had landed some years previously, built a parliament, set up a government, yet 95 per cent of the country's population had no idea of the government's existence.

I also got an inkling of what a respected man my uncle had been. He'd been dead for about six years yet I was treated like a king because I was his nephew. I was given a very nice three-bedroomed villa for the time of my stay. I had a maid, a gardener and a chef. *Not bad for a bricklayer from Blackhall Colliery*, I thought as my housemaid poured my morning coffee into a fine china cup on the veranda, as I sat on the edge of a tropical rainforest and looked over Port Moresby harbour. It very quickly got more interesting.

A few nights after my arrival I could hear gunshots from my villa and the next morning I asked what had been going on. The British had set up a makeshift government consisting of a few local tribal leaders and had told them to get ready for their first elections. They were calling it independence. The British government had some months previously shipped over two Daimler limousines to be used as presidential vehicles as sweeteners. One for the prime minister and one for the deputy prime minister. Unfortunately, they had taken the cars from their wooden shipping crates and without reading the paperwork, had driven them straight away. Each luxury car had a can of gearbox oil in its boot that was supposed to be put in before the cars were fired up. Both gearboxes had ceased. The British asked them to put the cars back in their crates, ship them back and they would have the problem sorted.

The prime minister and the deputy prime minister lived in what was known locally as the presidential palace and the crates had been thrown out of the back gates and into the back streets by the palace staff. When the palace staff went to retrieve the crates, they found both had been adapted and were being used as family homes. The staff were ordered to evict the crate squatters and return with the crates. They tried, failed and reported they had been met with violence and one of the staff had been stabbed with a spear and had died.

The prime minister's reaction was to send in the army to get the crates, which they did but, as a result, eight locals were shot dead. These were the shots I'd heard from my veranda. Unbelievable.

I was taken into the bush by a Welshman called Blyth to spend two very different nights with two very different tribes. Papua New Guinea hosts 750 different tribes that speak 750 different languages. It was amazing. The first night we stayed in what I can only describe as beach huts with a very friendly tribe who fed themselves mainly from the ocean. They would wade into the shallow waves with long sharp sticks and bob around spearing fish from under their feet. I had a go. The clear blue water was no more than four or five feet deep, wherever I walked. After about two hours and wading about half a mile from the beach I'd caught nothing. I noticed the locals had collected a dozen fish each on their sticks and were laughing at my hopeless attempts and lack of success. I stared into the water and tightened my concentration. Suddenly I was cloaked by an overbearing shadow and turned around sharply. To my surprise there was a massive oil tanker passing within thirty metres. It looked surreal. I was standing in four feet of sea yet right there, passing with very little sound, was a ship the size of an island. We swam back on the breaks created by the iron monster.

I explained to Blyth what I had seen. He laughed and explained that there was a sheer underwater rift about five hundred metres from the beach.

'How high is the cliff?' I asked.

'Ah, about two or three miles,' he casually announced.

This tribe occupied a sandy bay no more than two miles long and the forest behind it that stretched about one mile deep. It didn't stop there, but the tribe's territory did. There was a stream and that stream could not be crossed. It was explained to me by one of our hosts, in a theatrical display backed by a spit of pidgin English, that the land on the other side of the water belonged to the next tribe and trespassers would be killed by spear. I didn't need to see the other side of the valley *that* much.

After our fish supper, I realised that all the men were seven foot tall and their women were not far behind. I put this to Blyth. 'They're waders,' he explained.

This took some digesting. These people had been there since the beginning of their time and had grown into their environment. For millions of years, they had stayed put, having no thoughts of the wider world. This probably made me think deeper than I had ever thought before. I had been naive and had first thought, *These people have nothing*, yet it suddenly started to dawn on me, they had everything. I couldn't help but wonder how long their isolation from the rest of the world could last. They were sitting on great mineral wealth that had the rest of the world rubbing their hands because they were coming to get it and these people didn't know. Man has never found a reservoir of minerals and then decided to leave it well alone, apart from under my village back home. It almost always comes out.

That evening Blyth explained that my uncle had been the first white man this tribe had seen and how after living with them for a while and teaching them pidgin English, he had taken him there and introduced him to their elders. To my surprise, when Blyth informed them of my uncle's death, they became quite upset. Blyth pointed at me and told them of my family connection to 'Mister Ray'.

'Yim big pello (man) belong Mister Ray,' he told them. They immediately became noticeably warmer and more affectionate towards me. I felt truly honoured to be associated with his memory. Strange, I suppose. We'd never met.

In the morning we were served a seafood breakfast and got ready to leave. I couldn't go without seeing the underwater cliff and quickly returned to the beach. Much to the amusement of the locals I put on a pair of plastic goggles Blyth had found in his Jeep and waded out to sea. Standing on the edge of that cliff was an unbelievable sensation. I was teetering over a magnificent drop yet couldn't fall. Peering down, I could see about two hundred metres deep and then it went black. There were large fish, deep down, feeding from the side of the sheer ridge. Sharks, I think! I swam off and on that cliff again and again. I returned and we said our goodbyes and left.

We drove up the side of a mountain for two hours via a makeshift grass track. I got to see the morning clouds, first from the underside before peering down at them from above. The track came to a stop. We were surrounded by dense rainforest. Blyth switched off the engine and whispered that we must wait. We did and within two minutes, about twenty tribesmen's black faces popped from the bush and stared at us, hard. One of them approached the Jeep and to my astonishment spoke to Blyth in pidgin English about 'Mister Ray'. Blyth explained to the naked tribesman that Mister Ray was no longer with us and the man's breathing became heavy as he became noticeably distressed. Blyth pointed at me and explained who I was.

From that moment on I was treated like a king. The trek to their village, of stick-built huts, was a rugged half hour and was up steep rocky terrain under a canopy of thick forest. We were fed, with what might have been pork and little cakes that tasted nutty. There wasn't an allergy disclaimer sign anywhere and I felt at peace. We spent the day with them and they showed us how they cooked before we helped them with some large ornamental carvings that looked like they must have been being worked on for a while. I watched the locals busying around in front of us. The men had legs like tree trunks and none had grown anywhere near five feet tall. Evening came, they gave me a hut of my own and offered me a girl for the night. Her mother and sisters had painted her up and her father presented her to me. He and his daughter smiled wildly. I accepted the shelter and politely declined the girl. I was definitely learning.

We sat outside our hut and talked over a bottle of red wine that Blyth had the good foresight to bring. I watched the locals interacting with one another. They used timber and basket-woven drag-carts that performed like a stretcher might with nobody manning the rear. We were fed with the meat of I'm not sure what, and as night fell, Blyth put on his battery-powered radio and we listened to the BBC World Service. The Cambodian war looked like it might be near to reaching a settlement. We listened some more, the newsreader's perfect BBC tone sounding weird and out of place. The Americans had launched the Hubble Telescope into space and we were informed how the satellite could, on a clear night, be seen with the naked eye. I looked at our hosts with their drag-carts and I looked into the clear night sky. I took a deep breath.

'That's nothing, son,' laughed Blyth. 'I sat here twenty-odd years ago with your uncle under a full moon and found out that Neil Armstrong was walking about on it; and look!' He smiled. 'These fellers here still haven't got around to inventing the wheel.' This point in my life is still a very poignant one. I'm not sure why. Perhaps I was struck by the two extremities of human endeavour; or I had just witnessed the birth of my own learning; or perhaps I was simply coming to terms with the fact that the highest level of escapism I would ever achieve had just been reached.

We left early in the morning and on the way down the mountain Blyth told me what he had been doing for the last thirty years. He had arrived in New Guinea in the sixties and my uncle was already well established there. At the end of the war the Japanese navy had scuttled a fleet of warships in the capital's port and my uncle had won the government contract to remove them. There were about ten ships, laid on their sides, half submerged and choking up the harbour. Since the war the country had been crawling with prospectors. Copper, zinc, silver and even gold, not to mention oil had been discovered in abundance; however, until the port was cleared nothing could be plundered. Some of the large oil and mining corporations, that I won't name, had given the government money to get it sorted. Uncle Ray had been a deputy at my village mine and the deputies handled explosives. He had arrived in New Guinea with his explosives licence and promised the government he could blow their troubles away. He did and made himself a very rich man.

Later that evening we met at the yacht club and Blyth gave me a tour of the empty lounge. The place was like a shrine to my uncle. There were photos of the Japanese warships and of him posing in his diving gear in what looked like blazing sun. He looked like my father, with a ten-year beard. On the other side of the room the walls were covered with more black and white stills of the ships being blown to pieces, each one show-ing tall sprays of white ocean leaping into the sky.

Blyth stared at the photos of Ray. He explained how he had grown up in Wales without a father and how Ray had taken him under his wing when he had first arrived in New Guinea.

'I only came here for a fortnight and because of him,' he said, still staring at a picture of my uncle, 'I've now been here most of my life.' He became distressed, I felt awkward and we retired to the bar.

'Your uncle built this club and then donated it to the com-munity,' Blyth informed me, as I returned with the pints. He then went on to describe in detail what my uncle had been up to. He told of how he had become a mediator between the local tribes and some multinational companies. Ray had spent years living in the mountains and had built up some very close and useful relationships that were of great interest to these compan-ies. He had imported heavy plant machinery and made roads which only he knew, connecting previously unreachable and remote areas.

He told me of how dangerous his work had been and an incident my uncle had been caught up in.

'One tribe had gone to war with a neighbouring tribe over a missing pig and approached Ray wanting to use one of his diggers to help them win their war.'

'Did he give them it?' I asked. He laughed.

'Of course not, but they didn't like his answer and returned later that evening and beat him badly.' He then put his laugh away before becoming more serious and going on to describe how a mob of angry tribesmen had dragged him from his house, thrown him into a pit and stoned him with large rocks. 'He played dead as they took the keys from his pocket but they failed to start the digger anyway,' said Blyth, looking concerned.

'Was he badly hurt?' I asked.

'He had a broken skull, was taken to Australia by plane where he spent three months in hospital. He didn't come back to New Guinea for a year. His wife never came back at all,' he said, rubbing his face.

He also told me of a more pleasant trip into the jungle he and my uncle had taken. Blyth glowed as he explained how flattered he'd been after being invited along. An executive from an oil giant had arrived and wanted somebody to take him into the mountains and help him negotiate with a tribe.

'The rock that made up their mountain had a high copper content,' he explained. He described how happy the elders of the tribe were to see my uncle. He had taken a bucket of cheap plastic jewellery and as they arrived, he distributed the multi-coloured, beaded necklaces and bracelets to each excited local. They probably got a dozen pieces each. Plastic had just been discovered as an unwanted by-product from the process of refining oil and at this point nobody had decided what it could possibly be used for. They were given a hut each and as the three sat with the locals and ate, their hosts celebrated and decorated themselves with their pretty new gifts. Ray explained to the company executive that negotiations might be better left until morning. They retired to their huts and slept.

'Eat your breakfast or they will be insulted,' Ray instructed the executive.

'What is it?' he frowned.

'It doesn't matter. Eat it or you'll get no copper,' Ray smiled. They watched him eat whatever it was and Ray started the talks. What the executive wanted to do was move the tribe of about four hundred men, women and children from the mountain where they had lived for hundreds if not thousands of years. His aim was to put them into purpose-built concrete huts at the foot of the mountain whilst he took their mountain away and, after two years, put them back on the wasteland where their homes had once been.

Ray put this to their chief and a group of elders in pidgin English. He translated the truth and waited for their reaction.

'How much?' asked the chief.

'How much do you need?' asked Ray. The elders whispered among themselves before the chief spoke.

'One million pounds!' he smiled. This was in the mid-sixties. Ray looked at the executive with raised eyebrows.

'That's okay,' he nodded.

'Wait!' said Ray before addressing the chief.

'Where would you put your one million pounds?' The chief pointed to his hut.

'I'll put it in there,' he said. Blyth showed me how Ray looked down at the floor and started slowly shaking his head.

'No, no, no. If you have one million pounds, it makes a big stack. Pound notes will fill all the huts here. Too many pounds. Need more huts!' The elders chatted amongst themselves and looked concerned.

'One thousand pounds!' The chief smiled, holding out his hand for the executive to shake.

The deal was done.

Blyth explained to me that for attending that meeting Mister Ray gave him a bonus.

'That bonus paid to build my first house. It had eight bedrooms and a swimming pool,' he smiled. Suddenly Blyth became straight-faced.

'How long have you got left here in New Guinea?' he asked.

'Eight days,' I replied. He moved forward in his seat and looked more serious than ever.

'Now listen,' he said. 'There's an election here in two weeks and it can go one of two ways. One, the New Guinea Party will win. In which case I'll be moving down to Australia for good; and two, the party we have set up and paid for will win and then I will need you to work for me.'

'Doing what?' I asked.

'Taking over where your uncle left off. There are still tribes out there that have never seen a white face,' he said. 'I've been watching you. You have no fear. When your uncle first took me into the mountains, I was terrified. You were not!'

It all sounded very exciting and I think I was flattered. The next day he took me to his offices and his secretary cashed in my return Qantas ticket for £700 and had the money telexed to my bank. She then booked me a return flight with Yugoslavia Airways for two days after the election.

'When we win the election, we'll cancel that one as well!' she smiled.

I waited the two weeks. It was a pleasant two weeks and life was good. The election happened and the newly formed New Guinea Party won by a narrow margin. Everybody involved in the plundering of the country's mineral wealth panicked, said their goodbyes and fled. Funny how life takes its turns. Looking back at my path in life it often seems like a bobsleigh ride. Everybody running behind me, pushing hard to get me off to a good start, then suddenly you're on your own.

I took the flight, popped across to see a brother in Abu Dhabi for a few weeks before trying to fly to Russia to do the Trans-Siberian Express train journey from Moscow to Beijing. What I hadn't realised was that the cheap Yugoslavian Airlines tickets Blyth had bought had been cheap for a reason. By the time I'd left Abu Dhabi and was in the air, Yugoslavia had erupted into civil war, the airline was bankrupt, had ordered all its planes home and within six hours I was stranded in a war-torn Belgrade. It hadn't been Blyth's fault. It wasn't that the news of the troubles in Europe or Yugoslavia had not made the news in New Guinea. It was more like news of any description didn't find New Guinea.

The British embassy sent an ambassador to the airport and we were told to sit tight and they should get us back to Heathrow within a week. I made it clear I was on my way to Moscow but was told that I was now going to the UK and for that I should be very grateful.

After a day or so of being stuck in the airport I was bored. I tried to get out of the main entrance but there were armed guards who were having none of it. One of the guards spoke a little English and I tried my best to sweet-talk him into letting me out for a look around town.

'I go to cafe and have coffee with local people,' I smiled.

He laughed and we joked and he told me, in broken English, there was a war on and how me wanting to go outside the airport building was nothing short of madness.

After a while I noticed the only people who were allowed in and out unchecked were the airport staff. They wore bright orange trousers and coats with hoods. Like watching ants on the floor and slowly learning where their nest is, I would watch them disappearing and then reappearing shortly after from the same unmarked door. It got to about midday and I approached and opened the door. Inside I found a long corridor with what looked like a mess room door at the bottom and lots of bright orange clothes hanging on pegs down both sides. Bingo! Within a minute I was walking around the airport building dressed in orange. I was careful to walk with purpose. I walked past the main entrance a couple of times and from the corner of my eye noticed they paid me no attention. I went for a third walk past, and noticed the group of heavily armed guards were busy sharing a box of cigarettes and a lighter. I took a sharp turn past them and walked straight outside. Conscious they might be watching, I took a left, put my head down and headed across the car park and up a steep hill. I looked up and the area ahead of me appeared built up. It looked like I might be heading into town. I was, and within minutes I found myself in a rather grand high street with shops on either side yet there was not a soul around. I kept on walking, came to a T-junction and looked right and left. I took a left, crossed the street, stopped and looked around. Not only was there not a soul around, there were no cars. The shops were closed and most were boarded up. I could see through the windows of the odd shop that hadn't been cladded in metal or wooden sheets and could see they contained nothing. I don't know how but I could feel that only days before, the pavement where I was stood had been buzzing with shoppers, its roads gridlocked with frustrated motorists and its shops filled with goods, sellers and buyers. I looked up at the traffic lights above my head. Dead!

Where had all the people gone? I crossed the street and looked over the shops' roofs into the backdrop of forest that stretched up the steep hills as far as the eye could see. I could see smoke from hundreds of small campfires bellowing from the treetops. It dawned on me that the locals had taken to the hills. I looked around the street again, the only movement a few flapping pigeons, the only witless creatures stupid enough to have not picked up on the danger and fled. Suddenly, I heard the roar of a larger-than-life diesel engine coming up the main street. I knew I only had seconds before whatever it was appeared over the brow of the road. The pigeons took to the air as I ran as fast as I could back across the street and down a narrow alley. Realising I might not get to the bottom of the alleyway before whatever was making that terrifying sound passed on the main street, I jumped into a doorway. Whatever had panicked this town was now panicking me. I had come to my senses. My heart thumped in my neck as the loud rumbling sound passed slowly by. I will never know what made that roar but I can still hear it now. It sounded like the monster was running on tracks rather than tyres. Could have been a lorry, could have been a tank. I didn't want to know.

I don't know how much time passed until I made my next move. Long enough to be sure it had definitely gone, I suppose, but I do remember going back down that hill one hundred times faster than I had come up.

I crashed through the airport entrance doors and was confronted by the guard I had been joking with earlier.

'There's a war on out there!' I informed him, as I gave him my orange coat and trousers. 'Shouldn't be needing them any more!' I smiled.

I sat in that airport and reflected on what was going on in the world. Perhaps I wasn't learning at all. I suppose I had thought things like that only happened in places like Cambodia or Russia or China, and not in so-called developed Europe. How silly I still was. In the history of the world there had only been two world wars and both their epicentres had been in the heart of the so-called civilised developed western world. The heart of Europe! Here! And in Britain. My own father had been involved yet it still seemed it had taken this very personal jolt to drive this home.

I think the Yugoslavian conflict probably affected me more than any other on three counts. One, I was not studying history. This was now! Two, I hadn't read about it or seen it on a TV screen. I had touched it, heard it and smelled the fear first-hand. And three, the place didn't look like Asia or black and white images of historical Russia. It looked familiar, like my country. Closer to home and more real. The sudden breakdown in communication and misunderstanding of one another was more akin to striking miners and Thatcher's police.

Four days later I landed in Heathrow. Wendy commented on the fact I was wearing exactly the same clothes I had departed in almost two years previously. This was true, I had left Britain in a thick woollen jumper and jeans, landed somewhere hot, bought a holdall and some summer clothes, put my winter clothes into the bottom of the bag and had not needed them again until I landed back in England. It was fuckin' freezing! At least I'd progressed to owning luggage. My Trans-Siberian jaunt was put on the back burner. It's still there now. I was twenty-five.

16

London

The work situation in London was dire. I rang a few old contacts but the global depression had infected the crowded city and the money I was being offered was half of what I had been receiving before Australia. Realising there was little option, I eventually took a job in the heart of the city moving walls and ceramic tiling in the kitchens of the Waldorf Hotel. The wages were shite and it cost a small fortune in travel. Because of this I would nick a few pieces of silver each day and on Saturday mornings I would visit my local pawnbroker's with a builder's bucket of saucers, cutlery, serving spoons, milk jugs and all, weigh it in and supplement my meagre wage. Double it actually. It came as a shock when I realised just how much the stuff was worth. I was surprised to discover a small silver spoon could bag me as much as thirty-five quid but I suppose, coming where I'd come from, my specialised chosen subject could never have been silver spoons. Living on your wits from 1966 to the present day could have left me with a high score, I suppose. Thirty years on, I still have a silver teapot with matching milk jug. Perhaps if my writing ever takes me that way, I could get my wife to slip them from her handbag and back onto a table whilst we enjoy a cream tea. Perhaps not. Don't want them spotting us and asking where the rest is! Anyway, back to the plot . . .

Wendy had moved into a fourth-storey flat of her own so we could be together on my return and I moved in. She'd done her best and thought it was 'lovely'. I had been living on a five-acre farm surrounded by tropical rainforest and thought it was concrete, cramped, expensive and definitely temporary but kept my feelings to myself. She continued to work at the hospital and did extra shifts for an agency. It certainly wasn't life in the fast lane but we were together and together was good. But not for long.

She got a job offer from the agency. It was a one-year contract as a nurse on the *QE2* cruise ship. Before I knew it she was gone and I was in a London flat on my own whilst she sailed the high seas. She'd been gone two weeks and I'd heard nothing when a friend rang and told me to put on the TV and watch the news. The *QE2* had run aground and all the passengers had been taken off. I rang Cunard, the owners, and they assured me there had been no casualties and the ship was on its way to Boston to be put into dry dock so the damage to her hull could be properly assessed. I rang again after a few more days and I was informed there was to be a temporary repair done in Boston before she was to be sailed to Hamburg for permanent fix. She'd gone away for a year and five weeks later arrived back in London, disappointed. I never did find out why the ship could not undergo a permanent repair in Boston. And I don't know again why it could not be fixed where it had been built, in Britain. They probably rang Britain but nobody answered the phone.

She started working at the hospital again but things had changed. Having matrons and sisters in charge had become old hat and had been replaced by a system where one manager ruled over several wards and Wendy complained continually about how this didn't work. This was a new initiative unfolded in her absence by the Thatcher government and basically the idea was that the NHS had to be more businesslike and more efficient.

The new managers had been carefully selected from industrial and retail backgrounds. The idea was, they might bring new thinking and fresh ideas with them and at the same time the newly demoted and demoralised matrons and sisters would have more time to be hands-on with patients whilst being lectured to and scrutinised by somebody that once ran a tyre and exhaust centre or supermarket. I don't blame her for complaining – her new boss had once managed a Wimpy hamburger outlet.

The effect on the hospital staff's morale and my girlfriend's wellbeing was catastrophic and every time she finished work and walked through the door, she would be in tears.

I had already suffered Thatcher's wrath and as a result had developed a very thick skin and a laid-back attitude to work. If I didn't like where I was or the money wasn't right, I would instantly walk away and find work elsewhere. The reason I was not surprised and believed instantly she was being mistreated whilst trying to save lives was because I'd already had a run-in with the Iron Lady and her cronies and was completely aware that her evil had no boundaries. Wendy, on the other hand, never experiencing this first-hand, couldn't quite bring herself to believe that somebody could be so purposely destructive. She viewed the situation like it must be some sort of accidental breakdown in communications between the very top and the working people. Eventually, after attending a few meetings where she was advised to shut up and get on with the changes, and being informed the fundamental right of withdrawing your labour if you were unhappy with the way you were being treated had been made illegal, she started to come around to my way of thinking. I advised her to throw the towel in. She was to spend the next year selling children's jewellery.

I took her up north for Christmas. My God, it was bleak! I hadn't told her how cold and run-down it was. Not on purpose; I'm not sure if I had become numb to how bleak it was or if it had actually got worse. My parents were away, and she wouldn't get to meet them for some time yet.

We spent all our time in a huge, red-brick pub in the centre of the village called the Hardwick Hotel, and Wendy commented that all the men were massive and looked like they'd just taken the Falkland Islands back and the only women she saw, of which there were very few, were pulling pints behind the bar.

'Welcome to the North, lass!' I told her.

We returned south; winter turned to spring. I broke my leg jumping over a wall and after a few weeks I had taken it upon myself to saw the plaster off and had gone back to work. My southern nurse didn't like that. Summer came and my brother Glen, who worked in Egypt, rang. He was up north visiting my parents and rang to say that the Hardwick Hotel was going to be demolished to make way for a supermarket. He wanted me to go into partnership with him, buy it, rescue it and run it.

So, I'm sitting in a transit van with my southern nurse and everything we own, heading north up the M1. She finally met my parents at their house. It was handy Wendy was a nurse because after an hour of wine flowing, she was stitching my mother's forehead after picking her up from the hearth. It was a little different to visiting her father's house.

We bought and saved the village pub and were heroes in the community. We still own it today. We lived upstairs in one of its massive bedrooms. Glen and his wife Jeana lived in the room next door. Jeana was Filipino; Glen had met her in Egypt.

Her English was poor; she had lived in a rainforest and had not lived with electric until landing in Egypt. The whole thing was mad. After a few months I started a building company with my eldest brother Tony, and Wendy was working four shifts a week in a care home. Life was one big party. What must her father have thought? If her mother had been around, I think she might have hired a couple of heavies to kidnap her and take her back south, thinking perhaps she'd been sucked into some strange, party-mad cult that celebrated and worshipped nothing but the fact that they were alive. She missed her mother. Her death had been tragic but all I could do was do my best to cheer her up. And anyway, there was no time for grieving. Not in the Hardwick Hotel. Upside-down smiles were not in fashion and if you were caught wearing one, you could be knocked down and trampled into the dirt by the stampede of partygoers, as the herd made its way from one good time to the next.

She would ring her sister every Sunday morning. I would listen in and would hear her describe how different families were up here. 'Most of the families are big up here but not in the same sense as southern families with all their extra step-parents and step-kids and the like; they have the same parents but there are just lots of them,' I heard her explaining. She would try her best to describe how it was up north but they were worlds apart. I think her sister probably couldn't comprehend most of what she told her and the bits she did grasp I think she probably thought could only be lies. Life was mad. I once heard her describing her life as like 'living above a fairground carousel'. It didn't matter what time of day or night it was, there was a continuous bizarre and lunatic party in full swing downstairs, right there in our front room.' She was right; you could jump on it for the ride whenever it took your fancy and jump back off again when you'd had your fill. Nobody ever came to the Hardwick Hotel for a quiet few pints or a small tipple. Every customer who walked in staggered out much later. Sometimes days later.

It must have been a lot for her to take in. I knew everyone; she knew nobody. She was a city girl and alien to being part of a village community. I watched her struggle as each new person she met seemed to be connected in some way to the last. It didn't take her long before she learned to listen before she spoke and I think she discovered the true meaning of the phrase 'never judge a book by its cover'. I can remember her going into the village butcher's for the first time, only to be told by the jolly, red-faced shopkeeper behind the counter she was wasting her time and she had been beaten to it by me. I had finished work early and had decided to make tea and had only just left the shop. The butcher informed her she was having minted lamb chops and roasted potatoes for dinner. I can clearly remember her bursting through the door and confronting me.

'Not only does the local butcher that I have never met before know who I am, but he even knows what I'm having for my fuckin' dinner before I do! It's like living in a fuckin' goldfish bowl!' she complained. Much to her frustration I found her reaction hilarious. It took her years to realise why. There was no escape, even when we were off the beaten track and away from the village, people still knew who we were. We could travel twenty miles into Durham, go ten miles south to Hartlepool or north to Newcastle and people would still call me by name. I remember standing among a crowd watching a bagpiper busking on a bridge somewhere in Northumberland only for him to finish his piece, put down his pipes and make a beeline for me. It was somebody I hadn't seen in years. This was strange for a city girl and I suppose difficult for her to get her head around. We got pulled by the police one day on the way back from a shopping trip. As I wound down the window the copper said, 'Pip, put ya seat belt on, mate, or I will have to fine ya!' before jumping back in his car and driving off. It was normal to me. People in cafes, people in shops, receptionists, even the cashier in the bank, but to her it was bizarre. Until only a few years ago Wendy shopped in that main street every Saturday morning and it would take for ever. When I asked her why it had taken her so long, she would explain who she had been talking to before filling me in on all the local gossip. I'm not sure if she is aware that she has become part of it.

There was a big difference between the village girls and Wendy. They were a funny bunch and I don't think they could fully understand her. She was, when we first landed, in her early thirties and as she didn't have a child people made the assumption that it was because we couldn't have children. It was rare not to have a kid before you were twenty around here and there wasn't a young woman she had got to know who had a career. Some had jobs, not careers, and because of the low wages these were treated like hobbies. Due to the high unemployment in the area, the difference, financially, between somebody who worked and somebody who didn't was miniscule and therefore getting a job seemed unimportant. Most women got benefits and family allowance for their children and would do a bit of work on the black market for cash in an effort to beat the system and survive.

Life was mad. Life was fast. There was lots of drink and there were drugs. Speed replaced dope and then speed gave way to ecstasy. Leah Betts, a young girl from Essex, died after taking an ecstasy tablet and then shortly after a girl from the village did exactly the same and also died. She was only fifteen and her parents drank in our pub. Wendy had not lived in a tight-knit community before as it dealt with unexpected death. There were no police needed; there was an unofficial meeting held by the men; the drug dealers were beaten, stripped of all assets and chased out of town before the girl was buried.

We had a couple of trips down south. One was for her grandmother's funeral. She was ninety-six. The other was for her sister's wedding. She married David, a match made in heaven. She was now head of music in a large private school and he had moved more towards making music for TV and film. Her father had met a very nice lady called Jill at art classes and after enjoying one another's company for a while, she had moved into their family home. Separate bedrooms, of course! Separate everything actually. She, like Wendy's father, had been widowed. Jill had brought all of her possessions with her. There was a TV at each end of the lounge with different channels displayed loudly on each. There were two washing machines, two microwaves, Jill's stacked on top of her father's, two kettles sitting side by side. There were even four taps on the kitchen sink. She had a plumber take her taps from her old house to the new because she liked water from them. It might have been easier to have chopped the house in half and let them live in one half each. However, they provided one another with company and it wasn't my place to acknowledge the lunacy.

After a few years my building company had grown arms and legs and employed lots of men from the village. My little boy, Lee, was around. He was six when we first moved up north and lived quite near the pub. He would call in from time to time and everything was good. However, his mother's boy-friend got a job in the Midlands and after a few months of having him around they had moved away and he had gone. This affected me, probably more than I let show. Wendy got a job as a drugs rep for an American pharmaceutical giant. The company car was very nice and the money was cool. She travelled a lot. Life was good but as time moved on, I think she started to wonder just how long this party could last. She wanted a child, was letting her feelings be known, but we were at loggerheads. Things got nasty and we agreed to have some time apart. Wendy flew to Australia for a one-month holiday and to catch up with some friends she had there. I naively hoped this might rid her of her maternal madness. It didn't and when I picked her up from the airport four weeks later, she explained that our relationship had reached a point and it was now my decision: all or nothing. I think the conversation was a bit one-sided and went along the lines of, 'Pip, if we have a baby, I promise I will do everything, you won't even know you have one.'

I remember those words exactly and every time I take our boys out to football, boxing training or motorbiking or whatever, and I leave the house so she can enjoy a bit of 'me time', I will mimic her voice and remind her of those exact words on my way out of the door.

So, I'm sitting in Wendy's company car, travelling to London to break the news to her father and sister that she is pregnant. They were pleased. I think. You can never tell with the southerners; they are just too bloody polite. Being the red from under the bed, I don't ever think her father expected her to do things the correct way around. She was never going to marry a banker, move into an Edwardian townhouse and then produce two point two children. Though actually, she could have married a banker. She was always attracted to a bastard. There was no excitement shown over the pregnancy. I should have probably expected that. They don't do excitement down there. Her father lived his life like he was for ever in a library. A very gentle man who might wear the same face for winning the lottery as he would for accepting a kick in the balls. If anyone is old enough to remember *Butterflies*, the sitcom from the 1970s, that was them. It was filmed just around the corner and represented just what their life was like. Her mother, I think, had been the Wendy Craig and was a very bad cook, a talent Wendy inherited and has her barred from our kitchen still today. I'm talking burning-the-house-down bad.

17

USA

The baby was starting to show and, staring into the shackled abyss of parenthood again, I suggested we took a 'small holiday' before we became anchored. A last gasp of clean air before the thick mist of fatherhood descended. At this particular stage of my snail pace development towards adulthood, I don't actually believe I was dreading having a baby. After all, she'd promised to look after it and I wouldn't know I had one and I was still at such a primitive stage, I believed that possible.

So, I'm sitting on an aeroplane, Wendy is five months pregnant and we have got return flights to San Francisco. It was fantastic. We did all the Haight-Ashbury, hippy stuff for a few days, which she loved because she is one. She just dresses a little finer. We hired a car and off we went travelling, slowly down the Californian coast as her belly grew bigger. We passed LA and headed on to San Diego, booking hotels on the way. It was good to have Wendy to myself again. I'd forgotten just how funny she could be. The roller blading women on the Californian coast were too good-looking and fit for a pregnant woman's eyes and I think she was pleased when we turned east onto Route 66 towards the Grand Canyon. It was a four- or five-day drive and as we made our way across the Arizona deserts it got more and more and more barren. She drove and got me reading again. I think she probably saw my illiteracy, or at this point poor reading ability, as more of a problem than I did.

A month or so previously whilst on our way to London with the baby news, I had asked her not to tell her father I couldn't read so well. She nodded yet ignored me and later told me I should not live a lie. Whilst sitting at her father's dinner table she explained the whole thing to him, right there in front of me. However, she explained the situation from an angle from which I had never seen it before. I suppose I thought the reason I couldn't read was because I was thick. That's what I had been told. But as an outsider she told it as a story of a failed education system and one of lack of opportunity. I listened to her describing me to her father as the most intelligent uneducated person she had ever met. I suppose me hearing it from that angle gave me the confidence to face my gremlins and give it another go.

Wendy picked up a couple of books from a Californian charity shop and helped me as I worked my way through them. One of them was a dusty old copy of John Steinbeck's *The Grapes of Wrath*. This book was, I believe, the reason I write today. Perhaps it helped being there, right where the book was set, making it feel real, but even without that, the author, with very few words, had me knowing the characters better than my own family. For the first time since Australia, I could not put a book down. Wendy laughed and said it had been years since she had seen such wonder in my eyes.

The cities turned into towns and then the towns turned into villages and as the villages disappeared behind us, we were left with the odd motel, farm or roadhouse. We reached the Grand Canyon, put a dollar into one of those clifftop telescopes and viewed the base two miles down. The journey to the base was six and a half hours by donkey. Wendy pointed out that the donkeys were dusty, they stank and explained that in no uncertain terms was she putting one between her legs.

Still not being mature enough, I pointed out the canyon *was* one of the seven natural wonders of the world and it would be a shame to have travelled this far and not see it from all angles.

'If I manage to survive that trek without giving birth in the saddle, I'll classify *myself* as the eighth wonder of the world. It's not fuckin' happening!' I think were her words.

So, we are sitting in the car heading for the civilisation she craved. I didn't really know what to expect from Las Vegas. I had seen bits on TV, but TV screens, I have learned, rarely do anything or any place justice. All of a sudden, after weeks of glaring at flat desert and the odd giant hole in the ground, we hit the city. The tallest structure we had seen in the last few weeks had been the occasional wigwam or cactus and here we were suddenly dwarfed by hundreds of brightly illuminated skyscrapers. It was spectacular.

We found a hotel and went out for a walk around the city. Every time we turned we seemed to be confronted by a little makeshift church. Christian churches, Gospel churches, rock 'n' roll churches and, of course, Elvis churches. There were couples being married everywhere. I only found out later she'd assumed we had gone there to tie the knot. Don't know where she got that idea. After all, we'd only been together then for eight years. Perhaps she thought I'd grown up overnight or got the wrong idea because of her belly expanding daily due to a physical commitment we seemed to have made.

What I did find out was that a pregnant English woman should stay away from Las Vegas. She found it all very sad. It might have had something to do with the thousands of vodka-drenched old widows cladded in thick make-up, sitting on rows and rows of tall bar stools in front of bright, flashing one-armed bandits, doing their utmost to rid themselves of their life savings before the good Lord above decided it was time for them to meet their maker. And hopefully their husbands. Or perhaps it was the Japanese businessmen and bankers who would fly in, lose thousands of dollars on the roll of a dice, the spin of the wheel or the turn of a card and then fly away happy. We stood behind a group of men and watched them gamble. I explained that each red plastic chip they had in front of them was worth ten thousand dollars. They would push a high stack of these plastic chips into the centre of the table every minute or so and then casually laugh among themselves when the croupier scooped them away. She hated it and commented that there were probably enough red chips on that one table, between the whisky tumblers and ashtrays heaped with smouldering cigar butts, to build a small hospital and then pointed out the table we were looking at was only one of hundreds. Now and again, we would hear a huge celebration as someone somewhere hit the jackpot. Elegant call girls with long legs would appear from, I think, behind the skirting boards and be on hand to assist the winners if they needed help to carry their winnings back to their hotel room. I'm not sure if because, at almost six months pregnant, she had just started to realise she was now the only adult in our relationship or she just wanted a better world for our child to arrive into or if it was actually an awfully hellish, selfish sinkhole, but her shaking head and the constant look of distaste she wore didn't look like lifting anytime soon. We planned to spend a week there and left after only three days. As we headed out, she ranted that it was a plastic place where plastic people wasted plastic money. Perhaps she was just too English. Or a true hippy. I probably shouldn't knock it. I suppose not being able to understand man's greed for money is an asset I have, at times, wished I possessed. If it had been left to me at that stage of my development, we might have spent the full week there before leaving penniless and disappointed I hadn't made us millionaires.

Anyway, did we get married? No, we fuckin' didn't. Apparently, I hadn't 'picked up the vibes'. However, the childish ignorance was bliss and the reading was going well. I chopped my way through *The Grapes of Wrath*. It made me cry (nothing childish about that, probably the first sign ever of me behaving like a grown-up). What a powerful book! Set in 1930s America during the Great Depression, it made me realise that even people who sleep in the cradle of a functioning democracy today can suffer immeasurably tomorrow.

I spoke to an American veteran, in a bar, who had served in Vietnam. I felt ignorant that I didn't know enough about what had happened there. He must have picked up on my ignorance and rang his wife from the bar phone. Minutes later she turned up with a book for me, on the USA's involvement in this troubled region. I read it from front to back. It made me wonder about the left and right thing again. Communism against the free world. Even the Americans couldn't win this war and had pulled out leaving the whole area with years of unrest. Pol Pot grabbed the reigns and galloped the whole area into self-destruction, killing two million educated professionals and academics for the cause of a new socialist republic.

I enjoyed the Americans and was pleasantly surprised how well informed they were. I have been back more recently with my kids and it never ceases to amaze me just how switched on and honest the average man or woman in the street is. Individually it seems each and every one of them believes they must keep their eye on the ball as they could one day be asked to be president. No downtrodden working class there. They have a sense of belonging I admire. I admire parts of their political system too and I'll talk of this later.

We headed north, through Death Valley and out of Nevada

through Zion Park before reaching Salt Lake City. This place made me think hard about religion. I remember returning to the table in a restaurant to find Wendy talking to a waiter who had three wives. During my short absence he had managed to explain that God was the father of her unborn foetus (presuming it wasn't gay) but its mother was a sinner. She was pregnant and had not been married (nearly had). I asked him if he had ever been abroad and he explained he had never felt the need to leave the city because he felt God was there and all around him. I felt offended, or perhaps patronised, and scattered the irritating bastard like he was a wasp. An action my hippy partner didn't enjoy.

'But he might have been a really nice man!' I think were her words.

'But you've just found out he wasn't!' I think were mine.

Perhaps my time spent travelling had made the world a smaller place. It seemed to me as I toured and dipped in and out of different cultures that religion was little more than a lottery. My thinking being, if the man who had just scarpered had been born two thousand years ago in Rome, he would have most surely been worshipping the roman Gods of Apollo, Neptune and Vulcan or if he was born in war-torn Yemen today, Allah. It made me think that perhaps the common denominator that umbrellas all religious persons was merely a gullible susceptibility to believe in whatever was put in front of them before they were old enough to think, their faith predicted by geography or even postcode and not choice. After all, surely the one thing that unites all of mankind is that we were all atheists once?

We headed further north, Wendy grabbed a few more books from a second-hand shop and I read obsessively as she drove. Thinking back now to the situation of my poor reading ability, I realise how hard she worked. I think I was probably being moulded into being a better parent without knowing it. She denies this and says she wanted me to read because of what I was missing but the prospect of your child's father having the reading ability of a small boy can't have been an attractive one.

We scraped the Canadian border and dropped back down into Oregon before dropping into California from the north. My hippy loved California; I did too. No wonder the hippies built their homes there, even if they are old psychedelic-painted buses, sheds and shacks with upturned boats as roofs. It took us three or four days to get back to San Francisco and by the time we got there my English Literature teacher had let her hair down, was dressed in tie-dye and her belly was four weeks bigger. Just a small trip away? We killed three days in the city. I didn't feel guilty; it was a fantastic place for them to die. We crossed the Golden Gate Bridge a few times, looked around Alcatraz, ate the nicest of foods at the nicest of restaurants before flying back to a cold Newcastle in the North of England.

Tom was born by caesarean on 14 December 1998 and three weeks later I flew to Thailand with a few of my brothers for January after buying Wendy a washing machine for Christmas (I'm not joking). I know what you're thinking! But she didn't and amazingly she was still there when I got back. I like talking about these things because it makes me realise just how much I've evolved. Actually, I think the situation itself made me evolve. I arrived in Thailand and wondered what the hell I was doing there. I booked an early flight home and left because I didn't want to be away from my new family.

My eldest brother and his wife looked after Tom during the day and for a while it worked well, but the pub was not the place to bring up a child and when Wendy handed the baby over and went off to work, she would often park around the corner and cry. I watched her getting more and more unhappy. Small issues became big ones and she was not in a good place.

I recall I had finished work early one day and after picking up our little boy I had taken him for a haircut. It was his first haircut and she hadn't seen him all day and had wanted to be there. I was a bastard, she was devastated, and was spiralling down.

I suppose at that time this bloke couldn't see the problem. She had everything she'd always wanted. I tried to talk to her but things just seemed to be getting worse. She had her man. She had her baby. She had a brilliant career yet she had never been so sad. We had a day away. I drove us out of the village, away from the pub and up to a beautiful waterfall in Weardale. We sat the baby in the middle of a blanket and had a picnic. I asked why she was so down and asked what it was that she actually wanted. She didn't know but gave it to me from both barrels. We'd been living above the pub with the baby now for almost a year and she hated it. She wasn't enjoying motherhood; she didn't like her job or the people she worked with and she didn't like me. I think she loved me but didn't like me.

The wages and bonuses she had been getting were more than we could spend and every month she would give me a little spare money and tell me to put it to good use. You might think that strange but like I said, she's a hippy and money means nothing to her. I *had* put it to good use and we had bought a small terraced house and rented it out. I listened to what she said, told her to hand in the car and pack in work, which she did. I promised to get a manager in the pub so we could move into our house. I had new carpets fitted, the house redecorated, bought her a car and had a manager running the pub, all in two weeks. We moved in. The house was small but nice. Tom had his own bedroom but to her the damage to our relationship had already been done. I think the time I thought that was it, I had done everything she had asked and she should now get on with her life, but she was in a dark place and all that I had done appeared too little, too late.

As I've already said, I was a slow learner; we lived in the house for two weeks and every night Wendy would stay in with the baby and I would go out with Tommy to the pub. I know what you are thinking. And she did! I rang and asked when she was coming home and was surprised when she announced she wasn't. Apparently, I was a bastard because it took me three days to ring and I hadn't noticed her wardrobe was empty!

She'd driven to London, landed at her father's house and spilled her heart out to him. I later found out his reaction was, 'Well, my darling, I must admit I quite like the chap and while I hear what you are saying, I think there is an element of better the devil you know.' She was furious. This made me laugh. He was supposed to be on her side.

Her sister was no better. 'Well, sis, you've made your bed.'

Perhaps Wendy had been up north too long, because she later confessed to thinking, *These southerners are pathetic!*

After a few weeks, I travelled down south and met Wendy, her father and our baby in a motorway service station. I think she was surprised by my reaction to them. The time apart had, I think, been the steepest man-up curve I'd ever ridden and she had never seen me like this before. I was genuinely sorry and apologised for the way I had taken them for granted. I said that the door would always be open for their return and I apologised to her father for not showing her as much care as I should. Having Tom taken from my arms that day and him heading south whilst I headed north was the hardest thing I have ever suffered and provided me with the biggest lesson in life I would ever have. I was devastated and though I'm certain it had never been her intention to take her man down, she had. Looking back now, I see it as a positive, the last bit of selfishness chased out of my inner soul and replaced with the minerals needed for me to be a decent father.

So, I'm sitting in my car heading north having just learned what life is about and she is in her father's car heading south wondering if I would ever learn anything. I later discovered her journey was to be no more pleasant than mine. She told me of how the atmosphere was filled with an awkward silence. I think they were a little stunned by all the heightened emotion and my reaction. I wouldn't have wanted to be her father! She said her father knew what she was thinking and she knew what he was thinking whilst our little soldier in the back was oblivious to it all. She confessed to being desperate for some fatherly advice but I think he was clever enough to realise whatever he said would, at best, not be what his daughter wanted to hear or, at worst, be taken the wrong way. She talked to me in great detail about their journey south. She explained that after a while she found herself trying to justify *her* behaviour and realised she was the only one talking. After a few more hours of her rabbiting and throwing all of her cards on the table and telling her father more than she should have, her father eventually spoke and said, 'You must follow your heart, my darling.' She was furious!

'I knew what that meant!' she said. 'It was code for get back to Pip without actually saying it.'

To be fair, he was in a no-win situation. At the time she thought he was being a coward. I think she was probably desperate for him to explain to her the meaning of life and wash away all her woes. That never happens. I think she knows that now and realises, when it comes to love, the only person who can sort it out is the person who is in it. This is what he had meant by 'follow your heart'. Clever man, I reckon, but I would, it was in my favour and I'm a bloke!

On the way up the motorway that morning she had been in a dark place, yet whilst travelling back down there was the appearance of the first cracks and these cracks, I believe, was how the light started to get in. Her father died some five years ago but unlike her mother's situation, she did at least have the time to thank him for his wise words and for putting up with her.

I spoke to her on the phone and she agreed to bring Tom up north for his first birthday. The people up here are an old-fashioned bunch (especially my close family). Their attitude was one of 'it's a bad hen that leaves the nest', even though they didn't have a clue what had been going on behind closed doors. They didn't actually bother me but I knew they would bother her, so I instructed them to treat her well. They would have to get over it. It was us we had to work out. Was it worth working at? Yes! Had I changed? Completely! From a man who had fought not to have children, I had evolved into a doting dad. Did she like the stone cottage I had just bought on the side of a golf course about five miles away from the village and I was planning to move into? An easy one. 'Follow your heart' was all she had to go on and that is what she did.

What I didn't tell the mother of my new child was that in her absence I had been to see an old dodgy barrister friend of Tommy's. I asked him for advice on how I could get access to my child. He listened to the whole story and then informed me that as an unmarried father I had little or no jurisdiction over my baby and told me, man to man, that if I wanted to see my kid grow up, the best thing for me to do was go for the 'fresh start' approach and buy a nice little house out the way of the pub and my family. He had then gone on to say, 'As soon as you get her through the door, get her up the stick again. It takes a couple of kids to calm a good woman down.'

I have never quite worked out who on this planet are the slyest, us men or the women, or whether we are all as sly as one another for the common good of mankind, but his plan worked and after a year in the cottage, baby Jack was on his way. Things were moving fast. I asked Wendy to marry me. And, of course, she said NO!

18

The stable twenty

Jack was born in April 2002. He hated his mother and because of this I believe I realised it was probably just as important to be a husband as a father. Despite carrying him for eight months he wanted nothing to do with her. As soon as he could walk and before he could talk, he would cry at the window when I left the house and not cheer back up again until I returned. He spent his first six or seven years letting his mother and his older brother know that every day spent with them was indeed a tragedy. He thought he was twenty-six from the day he was born and when trying to teach him something new, he would remind you he had always known that anyway. He actually, at the age of eight, asked me, whilst pointing at his mother across the dinner table, 'How long has SHE been with us?' What a fiercely independent whirlwind. He is twenty now and is about halfway through a degree course in electrical engineering. He is signed up to a multinational shipping company based in Glasgow because he wants to travel the world, despite not being able to fasten his own shoelaces because he won't let anybody show him anything. He has levelled out to be a great young adult and that joint achievement between me and my wife is probably one of the things I'm most proud of. However, he is exactly like his mother and though I'm not religious, I'm sure her mother sent Jack down for her own amusement.

Wendy's sister had a boy in the middle of our two. His name is Samuel and he is of course very musical; he couldn't have been anything but. As they say up here, 'you don't get rats from mice'. He is twenty now and is studying at the London Academy of Music and has just been sponsored by the Arts Council to set up his own orchestra so he can experiment mixing traditional and contemporary music with modern jazz. It seems her sister went one way and she went the other. Her situation often reminds me of one of my jokes my wife has probably had to listen to over a thousand times over the last thirty years. It's the one where two middle-aged men meet in a supermarket and have not seen one another since their days at school. One is a pianist, has married a brass band leader and has a son who has his own rock band and a daughter who plays fiddle in the London Philharmonic. The second man goes on to explain he's just retired after a very successful career in wrestling, his wife of twenty years is a gold medallist in judo, his daughter is with Team GB training for the Olympics and is expected to win a medal in jiu jitsu and his son is a heavyweight boxer.

The men agree to keep in touch and as they part the first man says, 'You must bring your family to our house one night and we will play you a nice concerto.'

'Yes,' replies the second man. 'You must call around our house one night and we will kick your fuckin' heads in!' This just about sums up her life. Ah well, her fault for being attracted to the bastard.

The decision to have more children, I fear, was a catch-twenty-two. If I didn't, I might have been a little richer. Loads of money but full of resentment for depriving myself, of what? I would never know. If I did, then that was that. No going back and always wondering what might have been. Regrets, I have none. Looking at my boys now makes me feel like the richest man in the world and how could I regret the decisions made anyway? It wasn't me that made them. It was little more than organised chaos and if I did take direction from anywhere, it must have been from very deep within.

Life is about ups and downs and bumps and scrapes and straightening yourself up when you are knocked off balance. Learning from your mistakes delivers order; regrets cause chaos. I think Wendy was a little off balance when I asked her to marry me a second time. She must have been – she said yes. Or perhaps that dodgy old barrister friend of Tommy's had been right. It might take a couple of kids to calm a good woman down.

Me embracing fatherhood like I did was something I hadn't seen coming. Naive, I suppose, because us northerners are almost Italian when it comes to raising our kids. It's all very 'get around the table, old or young' with roast beef and Yorkshire puddings on Sundays and something I can't imagine being without. A culture I know my southern wife is now very fond of. It's strong and comes with a teaching of good family values and routine I feel every child would benefit from. I involved my kids in everything like my parents did with me. They would dig the garden with me, cook the dinner with me and as soon as they were old enough, they would come to work with me. We have dogs, chickens, pigeons and pigs and all it takes to care for them would be shared.

Now that we live up north my wife has learned when it comes to my illiteracy, I was not alone. Some of my old school friends she knows personally and lots of them can't read or write. A few years ago I bumped into Robert Chance in the supermarket. I had not seen him since my school days. Wendy walked off as he asked me if I had ever got around to reading and writing. I said I had and Robert asked me for help. Everything in his trolley had pictures on it and he explained he had to buy the expensive products as the 'Smart Price' products displayed only writing and he couldn't be sure what was inside the tins. I went back around the aisles with him and helped him swap everything. I don't think my wife fully understood what we had been doing and as I explained the situation on the way home in the car, tears welled in my eyes. The reason I think this affected me was because it scored ten on the Richter scale of somebody not getting a fair deal in life. I think my wife sensed my frustration and anger at the injustice of the situation and didn't like to talk about it or push it any further and there was an eerie silence in the car.

'Great name,' she said. 'Robert Chance! Should have been a film star with a name like that.' I didn't talk for a while.

'Should have been a lot of things but if you can't spell chance, you've got no chance,' I said. She pried no deeper.

I explained to my wife I only had one fear in life and that was a fear of my kids realising their father couldn't read and she helped me further to polish up on my act. She would supply me with books and I would read to my boys most nights. They were too young to realise I had a weakness and by the time they got old enough where they might have picked up on it, it had gone. Reading to them was important to me.

Some of the kids' books I would read to them were dross and after finishing the last page I would often say, 'Well, that wasn't very good! I reckon I could write a better book than that!' to which the kids would say, 'Why don't you, Dad?' My wife always says, I never do anything by halves. She is probably right, because before long she'd bought me a few writing pads and a pen and I was off.

The kids were still young and we had a wedding to organise! Not that I would be asked to get involved, of course. I only had one stipulation which was that I didn't want to involve God and religion. I think my actual words were 'and no men in dresses' but she knew what I meant. A guest list was drawn up and I think at this point in my fiancée's life she realised just how much things had changed. She counted her family and friends from down south. Seven. Then she counted my family and friends and the friends she had made up north. One hundred and fifty-eight. It seemed the wedding might have to be on northern soil.

It was harder than I had imagined having a wedding without inviting God. We had to attend an interview at a registry office and explain to a registrar why we didn't want him there. I startled the lady by saying God has never been to *any* wedding because just like Santa and the Easter Bunny, he is not real. This left an awkward silence in the room. She then asked what music we would like to have. There were three pieces of music and Wendy wrote them down.

'I'll have to check these out with Southampton,' she explained, sitting at her desk. And she did. She made a phone call and started speaking to somebody.

'I've got three pieces of music for you to check here,' she went on, as she read them out. One of them was a requiem that Wendy's father had played at her mother's funeral. The lady on the other end of the line had no record of it and because of this, we were allowed to use it. One was Lou Reed's 'Perfect Day'. That was allowed because it was deemed to have no religious connotations and the third was Leonard Cohen's 'Hallelujah', which was a definite no-no.

'The word Hallelujah belongs to our Lord,' the lady explained. I couldn't stop myself.

'So, let's get this straight,' I said. 'There is a person sitting by

213

the phone in an office in Southampton, whose job it is to vet music in case it upsets an imaginary man who lives in the sky. Is this what we are dealing with here today?' I got up and walked from the room laughing loudly. I was not invited to be involved in our wedding arrangements again.

Thank God!

I played the music anyway on the day and it seems nobody told God because not one person that day was struck down by a bolt of lightning or prosecuted by him for copyright thereafter; perhaps he heard the music but believes in forgiveness?

We booked an old manor house only two miles away from where we lived and organised for the disgruntled registrar to come there. The bride's dress was £200 and she asked her father for her mother's eternity ring (hippy).

The day went well, our kids called it 'our wedding' and it was a very hot September day. The one hundred and fifty-eight northerners and the seven southerners turned up and filled the room. It was a good job God didn't gatecrash; he might not have found a seat. Her father made his speech and made everybody laugh by explaining what an awkward kid she had been and how he was filled with admiration and respect for me because of what I had taken on. Wendy made a speech and told of how we had met by pure chance on that train. 'It was love at first sight,' she said, 'and then three years later he fell in love with me.' That made everybody in the room laugh and me wonder. She thanked her father for allowing her to be herself, watching her make lots of mistakes and never saying, 'I told you so,' and then she took the northerners head on. She told them they had better get used to her because she was here to stay. They gave her a standing ovation and I even saw a few big men cry. Might have been all that free wine. I made a speech but I think she had stolen my thunder. I couldn't choose who was to be best man so I had ten. The foreman of them was

Tommy. He made his speech and took the house down. Like Lou Reed said as Wendy walked down the aisle, it was a 'perfect day' and one that still crops up today as being truly memorable in people's hearts. I think she was pleased she had eventually got around to saying yes.

My wife has no mother and no father now; an orphan. I'm lucky, I don't know how that feels yet. I know how powerful an emotion grief can be. Tommy dropped dead on me halfway through a bacon butty at the age of seventy-seven. His last words, as he lifted the lid of the last half of the sandwich and stared at it, looking robbed, were, 'Is the war still on?' Then he went. The brightest light I'd ever known switched off. Not even a goodbye. It was, and still is, hard. We had been inseparable for almost as long as my memory could stretch.

I had to watch my father crumble to Alzheimer's and all that goes with that. My hero's brain gave up before his body and just like all everyday witless fools, he was fine, whilst those around suffered immeasurable grief.

My mother was eighty-eight last week and despite suffering a massive stroke shortly after losing my father, is full of fire and still the head of the family. After raising six boys she studied at university and got a degree in education before having a twenty-year career as a school teacher and then a seven-year career as headmistress. She is by far the most intelligent, hardest yet softest, steely yet funniest woman you could meet.

I'm genuinely sad I never met my mother-in-law. After her funeral all contact with their grandmother, who had once been a large part of their lives, was lost. A breakdown between her father and his mother-in-law apparently and, in true southern style, this was not to be spoken of. Her mother had a brother who had gone to Norway and married a Norwegian lady and had a family there. They would spend their summers there as children and my wife and her sister were very close to their cousins. All of this had gone with her mother's passing and as the years went on this irritated me more and more. I think the sisters felt a little disloyal to their father but I convinced my wife to search for her grandmother. She did and found she was still alive. I think her enjoying my family and now her own had made the situation of not talking to people she had once loved less acceptable. She and her sister arranged to visit their grand-mother in Brighton. It went brilliantly. She was ninety-six and died shortly after but I think they all gained something from that meeting. Closure, I suppose.

The fallout with her father had been ridiculous and hard for this northerner to grasp. From what I could understand it had been about class. Her grandmother had said she had always felt her daughter had 'married above her station'. How sad, years wasted because of some twisted interpretation of an invisible class structure. None of that up north. More of a level playing field up here, where relationships, love and family trumps all. To her grandmother's generation, class, I suppose, was all important. To them, a person had to stay in the class bracket they'd been born into and could never move up. My wife always jokes if the subject of class crops up when we are social-ising, that she used to be upper class but since the day she met me, she dropped to middle. I've also heard her say, 'I was born upper or middle and have now moved *up* to working class.' She feels a shift away from the stiff pomp of a world where family and relationships do not always come first and people marrying for reasons other than love can only be described as a shift up. Hippy!

She struggles with being down south now. I'm not surprised. Lots of people we meet down there have an annoying habit of turning the conversation around to themselves, what car they drive, money in general or house prices. It makes me laugh. At her father's funeral a friend of the family sat with us at the wake. He immediately started talking about himself, pointed outside and informed us which car was his and then went on to explain how he worked in the markets.

'Oh, how interesting,' I said. 'And what do you deal in?'

'Mainly copper, silver and zinc,' he explained.

'Wow!' butted in Wendy. 'I didn't realise people would actually go to a market on a Saturday morning and fill their shopping bags up with heavy metals.' He chewed on her comment for a while before making an excuse to politely leave and mingle in the room.

'I think he was referring to the financial markets,' I whispered.

'I know, darling, I was just getting rid of the boring bastard for you,' she laughed.

We spoke more about her Norwegian connection and I felt the need to snap straight into action.

So, we're sitting on a ferry going from Newcastle to Rotterdam. We've got a transit van with a huge caravan in tow, our two youngest boys and two Jack Russells. The dogs have passports with photos of them on the front page. Crazy! We camped on the way and drove through Holland, across the north of Germany, up through Denmark and met her cousins there. She hadn't seen them for thirty years yet they just seemed to naturally pick up where they'd left off. Like I said, hard for this northerner to grasp. What a senseless waste of years. We spent a week with her cousins. They were very patriotic, and heavy drinkers. It was their national day and boy did they know how to party. We then got a ferry across to Sweden and headed north and into Norway. We met her long-lost aunt and uncle and we spent one week there. It was *their* national day and we were forced to spend a further week drinking very strong beer and partying. Norway was actually more spectacular than I had ever imagined and helped me realise just why the Norwegians were justifiably so patriotic. Her uncle, helped by my kids, would rise early on a morning, raise the Norwegian flag in his garden and take it down each evening without fail, as did all their neighbours. I don't know why but I admired this.

After one week and just before my liver rejected me, I booked a cruise ship from Oslo to the top of Germany and we headed for home, camping in Holland on the way. What an experience. Especially for my wife. Not only had we got to travel to some fantastic places but we had kicked open the last of the doors that had been inexplicably shut tight.

I've lost count of how many times the older people from my community and my family have, whilst watching me enjoy my boys, told me, 'Cherish every moment, as it passes in a flash.' They were right. Twenty years gone like twenty months.

So that was then and this is now. I can read and I can write and I am back up north running building sites during the day and writing books by night. I've been on with this one for nearly two years now. I heard my wife talking yesterday on the phone to her sister. Her sister must have been asking about the book.

'It must be a book of fiction,' she explained loud enough for me to here. 'He's been writing about himself for over a year without using the words arrogant or opinionated.' Perhaps she was just having a bad day. However, she might be right. On the whole, I do believe planet earth would be a less complicated place to live on if more people took on a small slice of these traits but I suppose that might just be my own arrogant opinion.

Those fast twenty years I jokingly refer to as 'the boring twenty', though my wife would say the stable twenty. I suppose she's right on that one also, but making sure there's bread on the table for the jam eaters was never going to be as much fun as driving across a desert just to find out what's on the other side. Well, at least I could tell my kids while they chomped on their jam and bread, from high authority, that the world is not flat.

A typical week for me now is laying bricks for two or three days and then organising materials, men and wages the rest, whilst every night and most weekends I write obsessively. Though if it gets too late, my wife will whisper down the stairs, 'It's one o'clock!' and off I go.

'At least I'm not using my laptop at one o'clock in the morning for the same reason as most men!' I'll remind her as I climb into bed.

19

Why lay bricks?

To me, my working and the writing fuel one another. If I was to not sit at a table having my ten o'clock with twenty-five people from all walks of life and of all different ages, what the hell would I write about? Today I had a seventy-six-year-old block paver who has a side-line as a stage-act magician to my left and a sixteen-year-old apprentice joiner who's grown up on a farm and is a virgin to my right. The magician had the young boy convinced that some sixty years ago, when he was sixteen, he had sex and it was so traumatic he never bothered again. The whole table was in on it.

'Well, I forgot how awful it was and tried it again last night and I'm telling you now, that's my last!' announced one of the middle-aged plasterers with a passionate sincerity in his voice.

That to me is electric! Gold! I will probably remember that conversation for the rest of my life because to me it is remarkable. It's what the mining industry was about before they ordered all the men to the surface and filled in all the shafts.

I'd like to think my building business has in some way helped replace what was once there. Not on the same scale obviously, but in some small way perhaps. It continues to put millions of much-needed pounds every year into the beaten-up local economy whilst giving some sixty or so people purpose, I hope.

Not everything I see and then decide to put down on paper is done because I find it funny. Last Friday, Keith, a bricklayer I've worked with for the last twenty years suddenly went blind and fell over. He's had a recent cancer scare and has been receiving chemotherapy. We lifted him into the back of a transit van and rushed him to hospital. We laid him on a trolley in the reception of the A&E department and I alerted a member of staff. He explained to the triage nurse how he had suddenly gone blind and lost the use of his legs and then explained what medication he was on.

'What the hell are you doing on a building site whilst being halfway through your chemo?' she asked with anger in her tone.

To which Keith yelled, with his blind eyes open wide, 'I'm fifty-nine, I've paid tax and national insurance all my fuckin' workin' life and when I went to the dole and told them I had cancer they told me I wasn't able to fuckin' claim a penny! I've been workin' because I need to fuckin' eat!'

That's remarkable and I'll definitely remember what my good friend screamed down that corridor for the rest of my life. I don't think I live a remarkable life, but I do think the world is becoming more remarkable and if you put yourself out there, you'll see what I mean.

My business growing like it did was another thing that seems like an accident. When I first returned up north, one thing I had learned was I couldn't live well on a northern wage. Bricklaying is a simple science: the more bricks you lay, the more money you get. Using my first hand to hold a trowel and my remaining hand to pick up bricks soon made me realise how limiting this could be.

Bricklaying contractors are, on the whole, sharks. I've not met one who has ever laid a brick and they are usually Flash Harrys with big fancy cars who rarely attend site. This is nationwide. They get paid as much as they can for each brick you lay and then give you the least they can possibly get away with. Cruel, but that's how it works. The next stage seemed a very natural progression. I would cut out the contractor, take on the contract myself, employ all of my mates, give them a better deal than they would normally get whilst still making enough for myself. If I made too much, they would get a bonus. I'm not sure whether that makes me a capitalist, a socialist or some sort of co-op institution but it works. The workforce is loyal which makes my company reliable and because it is reliable the work is continuous. It's a win-win and I think, apart from a small amount of people who have quickly come and gone over the years, who have mistakenly thought the world owes them a big fat favour and just don't get it, it's a happy and sturdy ship. I have an ethos of you don't work *for* me, you work *with* me! And like I was taught by my father, I would never ask someone to do something I wouldn't or couldn't do myself. In fact, I dare write, the people who work with me are my friends first and my work colleagues second and not one of them has any desire to work elsewhere. Sorry, must go. Apparently 'It's one a.m.!'

Good afternoon. The writing world is another one I think I fell into accidentally. A couple of years ago I attended a funeral of a dear friend of mine and Tommy's. At the wake, I was approached by a Scottish man in his seventies. He was a TV scriptwriter, and after chatting for a while we realised we had met before. He had been researching for a play he'd written about the hard bastards who shovelled coal spilled on the beaches from almost a century of mining, out of the North Sea, onto their ex-army wagons, and the criminal world that surrounded them. Some of the top sea coal men would own twenty wagons and have men driving them and filling them around the clock, who they would exploit heavily for their own financial gain. This was a time when laws to tackle money laundering, modern-day slavery and proceeds of crime were in their infancy, leaving the very affluent and seedy underworld of sea coal men to flourish. There were links to illegal vending machines, bootleg spirits, prostitution and even the forging of bank notes. I grew up thinking these gangsters were the norm. It was common to see these teddy-boy-type characters driving through my village with the roofs of their brand-new Ford Zephyrs peeled back, displaying a back seat full of glamorous girls with beehives. They wouldn't wait for anybody and would drive on the pavements tooting and shouting at everybody to get out of the way. Thinking back now, they looked like a pound shop version of the American film *Grease*. No wonder my dad referred to them as 'the ten-bob millionaires'.

The scriptwriter had been to my pub some fifteen years previously researching and I had introduced him to some of the people he needed to know. He'd spent a couple of days travelling around with these men and a few nights drinking in my pub. He could remember all of it and reminded me he'd returned a few months later and left a draft of the script with my bar staff for me to read.

'Did you ever read it?' he asked. I hadn't. Because I couldn't! I was honest and told him the truth. I told him of my writing and I could sense his genuine interest.

'Anybody who's grown up in that wee shite-hole and has started writing should be listened tee!' he said. 'Have you submitted your writing tee anyone?' he asked.

'I have actually, I have just put a story I wrote into Penguin Books and the deadline for hearing back is today,' I explained. No sooner had I got the words out my mouth than my phone pinged. I pulled it from my pocket and read the email. It was a rejection from Penguin and I showed him.

'Their loss!' he winked as he gave me his card and asked me to send him my work. I did and didn't hear anything for weeks. *TV scriptwriter, my arse!* I thought. About two months later he rang and asked where I was.

'I'm in the house,' I explained.

'Good. I'm coming there reet noo!' he said. He landed, explained he'd enjoyed the book, it was better than he had hoped, and though novels were not his field he did have some contacts of people who should be interested and he gave me their details. I thanked him and as he left, he winked and said, 'Any friend of Tommy's is a friend of mine!' I closed the door and stared at the picture of Tommy I have hanging in my hall. He had been gone fifteen years but for that brief moment I was able to bring him back to life right there and then and thank him from the bottom of my heart.

The contact he gave me was for a man in Newcastle who wrote drama for radio. I met him and soon realised that when it came to working-class writing I was sitting in front of the guru. Tommy was long gone, yet from beyond the grave the old bastard had somehow managed to shoot me straight to the top. Guru man took away a hard copy of a book I'd written. It was called *Birds Up*, is set in 1984, is about three miners/pigeon fanciers who become so disgruntled with being on strike in Thatcher's Britain, they turn to crime and attempt to pull off a huge cash robbery (a bit weird, I know).

I didn't hear anything for two months. *Drama for radio, my arse!* I thought. However, the phone did eventually ring and he said he would like to meet up again. We met in a coffee shop and he said he had really enjoyed the book but then surprised me by holding it up and asking, 'What do you want me to do with it?' to which I think I said something like:

'I don't know, I'm a bricklayer that's written a fuckin' book. What would you do with the fuckin' thing if it was yours?'

Why lay bricks?

He thought for a moment before going to his bag and placing the details and a link for a working-class writing competition in Newcastle on the table in front of me. Up until this point all my writing had been done by hand. The book he was holding had been typed by one of the secretaries in my building offices.

That was it, I had to borrow a laptop and learn how to use it quick. To me, this would be the sharpest of learning curves. I got the application in on time (two weeks). It asked for a two-thousand-word sample of my writing, two hundred words about me, a piece about why I write and then last of all, 'Please could you write three hundred words to prove you are working class!' I'm not sure why but I found this last one quite insulting.

I've written about what I have seen whilst growing up on a council estate in Durham. My writing is about mining, miners' strikes, allotments, racing pigeons, ferrets, miners dying of pit lung, whippets and, like me, it must be working class. I don't know anything but.

(I'd only used up forty-six words at this stage, so I then wrote)

If the above does not qualify me as working class, then here are a few pointers about myself to consider.
1. *I do not have any friends called Pippa, Poppy or Oscar.*
2. *I do not have bottles of wine in my house that aren't being drunk that day.*
3. *I do not get out of the bath for a piss!*

I didn't hear anything for two months. *Competition, my arse!* I thought. I then got an email. I'd won!

Wendy said she would buy me a dress jacket for me accepting my award. She told me my donkey jacket just wouldn't do!

'As long as it's not one of those corduroy type with leather patches on the elbows,' I insisted. It wasn't and I accepted my award. And prize money! And bought this laptop!

Everybody I meet in the writing world is 'educated'. I often wonder what that means. I'm not knocking education. My mother and a few of my brothers have degrees. There is a mosaic of photos on my mother's living room wall showing some of her sons and grandchildren wearing mortar board hats, gowns and holding scrolls. I'm not on that wall. That was never me. I could never have been a student. Apart from my illiteracy, I would have been too busy building a wall and chasing the next pay packet to enrol. It's not that I have never been to university; I have attended Durham Uni twice. Once because a branch had blown from a tree and damaged a slate roof and the second time somebody had driven into a bollard in the car park and the block paving needed reinstating. After both visits, I graduated none the wiser. Again, I'm not knocking the value of a good education but I have, in my life, encountered dreadlocks, colourful mohawks and cloth caps that have turned out to have a far superior level of intellect sat under them than some of those who have at some time supported a mortar board. We only have to look at politics to see this.

It doesn't matter. Some people are academic and others are not. We need them all. Surely the last pandemic has shown this.

Thank you to the thinkers, but do not thank the Lord.
Good thinkers believe their thinking is thought out by
*   their own accord.*
Thank you to the zero-hour domestics who clean our
*   hospital floors.*
Thank you to the law makers who refuse to come
*   outdoors.*

Why lay bricks?

Thank you to explorers for travelling far and wide.
Thank you to the masons, we no longer live outside.

Just a little one I wrote in my head whilst building a wall this morning. Sometimes if I can't get my point across, poems seem the easy solution. It's not that bricklaying is boring; it's just like the piano man's fingers, or somebody packing box after box in a factory: in the end, you don't know you're doing it. I can go to a pile of bricks and mortar, build a wall and when the wife and kids asks me at the dinner table, 'What did you do today?' I can't remember the wall. I suppose that's what I mean about the building and the writing fuelling one another. Handy really, as I'm completely addicted to both. That and a phobia I harbour of not daring to miss a shift for fear I might miss something humorous or human to write about.

20

The organised chaos we all call life

Well, what happened there? A life, I suppose. Not that I'm ready for dying. Probably should have never been born. The odds were certainly stacked against that. My father has been gone for almost ten years now but recently somebody unexpectedly stepped into our lives from his past. One of his comrades from the 2810 Regiment contacted my mother. Despite being in his nineties he drove to my mother's house in County Durham from the Midlands in his two-seater MG sports car for tea with the family and drove back home later that day. Just before he departed, he told us something none of us knew.

Hitler was dead, the Germans had surrendered and the Second World War in Europe was being celebrated as a win. However, the Japanese were still fighting on. In reaction to this situation Lord Mountbatten had gone about setting up a special elite parachute regiment in Burma of two hundred men to hit the Japanese ground troops in Malaya. Five hundred men would volunteer, and then be selected for rapid and intensive training that would take only one month. He told us about the fierce training he had gone through with my father.

'Every Sunday morning, we'd stand on parade and be reminded, "This is a non-return mission." They would explain how we were to be dropped in the dead of night and be expected to take out as many Japanese as we could. We were to cause as much damage to their campaign as possible. Then the CO would explain again that *nobody* was coming to pick us up. "This is a non-return mission," he would repeat again and again.'

He explained to us how it was a voluntary mission and how anybody could drop out at any time. Every week about a hundred would walk from the parade ground and return to their barracks. At the end of the month there were only one hundred and sixty men left and they were fired up and ready to go.

'I was sat next to your father on the floor of a Dakota as it waited on the runway. The engines thumped loudly and the plane vibrated heavily. We had written letters to our mothers, handed them to our commanding officer, had our parachutes on our backs and all the explosives, grenades and ammunition needed between our knees. However, instead of the noise turning to a buzz and the plane humming, the thump of props and engines slowed and eventually stopped, leaving a silence as everybody looked at one another, bewildered,' he said. 'At that, one of the pilots climbed from his seat, removed his helmet and spoke. "Sorry, chaps, but the mission is to be suspended. The Americans have just dropped an atom bomb on mainland Japan and Lord Mountbatten thinks the war could now take a different direction."'

A bomb had dropped from the *Enola Gay* for forty-three seconds before its timer and trigger had detonated, firing a uranium bullet down a stainless-steel barrel into a second uranium target, setting off a nuclear chain reaction as it smashed apart solid matter, releasing unimaginable quantities of energy and vaporising seventy thousand souls in less than half a minute.

It is weird to know that before that bomb detonated, I could not have been born – *This is a non-return mission* – yet from the split second it went off, my fate as a human being was sealed. If the Yanks had decided to not tell the British or had dropped it one day later, then surely I could not now exist. It seems to me the only truly predictable part of life is the chaotic unpredictability of life itself. I now feel I have taken on a more personal connection to the Hiroshima bomb; an empathy, perhaps, to the thousands who perished. Even an ownership I didn't know before. That's something I hadn't realised I'd ever own. How could I? Six days later, and two days after the detonation of the Nagasaki bomb causing unimaginable devastation, the Second World War was over.

Not sure if I was born in the wrong place at the wrong time or the right place at the right time, but whatever it was, it happened. Could have been worse. I could have lived one of my grandfathers' lives. Down the pit for fifty-something years before spending your retirement in a chair with no legs then dead soon after. Or my father's life. Seventeen when war broke out, blown up and then running around efficiently killing humans until he became tired of it. I say 'efficiently' because he was.

I can remember having a conversation with him whilst on holiday when I was a teenager. We discussed what it would be like to be caught up in a terrorist attack and I naively explained that, if I found myself under fire, I would grab a gun from somebody and take the rampaging shooter out. I remember him smiling at my innocence.

'Where would you shoot him?' he asked.

'In the head!' I explained.

'No, you never go for the head,' he said, shaking his. 'Too much of a moving target. If someone is running around killing people, their adrenaline is always pumped right up and when they are in such a high state of alert their heads constantly weave about.'

'In the chest!' I said, thinking I'd cracked it.

'No,' he laughed. 'They usually wear body armour. Shoot at their chests and they'll probably live to have a shot back.' I shook my head. I was beat. 'Their pelvic area,' he explained. 'This area stays still even when the legs and upper body sway around. There are main arteries running through the pelvis supplying blood to the legs. Once you take out the hips their blood pressure drops instantly, making them go blind. You can just stroll up and finish them off!' he smiled.

Yes! I'm pleased I didn't get his life and count my blessings I didn't get one of my grandmothers' lives. Miners' wives. At least they didn't have to go down the pit and at least they got to live on average over eight years longer than their hubbies, but they were still hard, short lives full of heartache and pain. Actually, all of this makes me wonder what the miners' strike was actually about. Fighting a war on our own streets because we were so married to the idea of getting that coal to the surface.

Talk to the men who lie idle in my village today and you'll find frustration and anger. They're angry, due to living on top of huge coal reserves they have seen and touched but were prevented from cutting. As for me, I'm pleased they're shut and the coal now lies dormant. It's a hard thing to say without feeling betrayal to my comrades who used up such energy fighting the government, but good riddance to each and every shaft. No cognitive denial here. I don't want to be like those old Irishmen who blanked me all those years ago in London. Ask the men in these villages if they would like to see *their* children put in a cage and dropped down that shaft to cut that coal, and watch each and every one shake their heads.

Looking back now, perhaps those hundreds of pits did have to close. If for no other reason than the environmental argument, though this is a hugely complicated area that because of the shape of our current political system today, lacks fair debate. And anyway, that was not why they were closed.

Margaret Thatcher wanted the coal industry eradicated at all costs because the miners had become too big for their pit boots and might have interfered with her long-term plans to sell off Britain's family silver in the form of every industry the British working classes had built up. A deliberate programme of deindustrialisation. British Steel, British Leyland, British Rail, British Telecom, British Gas, Water, Electric, the Post Office, ship building and many more. Once the blight that was the miner was successfully eradicated, she could sell off the lot, and not to the highest bidder but at a reduced rate to her friends in the Conservative Party who could buy and sell and make a quick buck – and her son. And this she did!

The reason I talk of the environmental issues being complicated is because they are. There is a significantly larger number of trees on the northern hemisphere of planet earth than there were one hundred years ago. The reason for this is that a much more efficient fuel was found: coal. Yet this area is a political hot potato and, for cowardly, careerist politicians, a subject best left alone. The technologies of dealing with dirty coal have advanced dramatically.

Recently the German parliament ignored scientific data and decided to favour wind. They closed down a number of their coal-fired power stations only to find out the scientists were right: it wasn't windy enough and soon large parts of the country were left without power. They reopened a few mothballed mines and fired up two coal-powered power stations. This was unpopular, however, because of pressure from environmentalists. They suddenly discovered coal can be efficiently extracted from the earth, used to generate power and then the unwanted carbons and sulphurs captured and put back underground. The Germans are now at the forefront of this technology. Just like the 5.3 million British Austin Mini motorcars with their revolutionary new front-wheel drive, transverse engine and classic design that took the world by storm in the sixties, we gave up and didn't have the gumption (or funding) to take it to the next level.

The Germans have just made the three millionth BMW Mini and whilst this has been going on we have sold Land Rover to Tata Motors and in 2013 they also gobbled up Jaguar. Tata is an Indian company and are based there. In this same year Britain gave India over one billion pounds in foreign aid. However, this was slashed to a mere £98 million the year after.

I talked about the Industrial Revolution negatively earlier and about how the earth's crust was turned inside out for the need of coal. However, now it's happened, perhaps it might be a good time to draw on the positives.

The place where I was born and now live was at the height of the Industrial Revolution, the hub for all new technologies, the envy of the world, the Silicon Valley of its day. The invention of the railway. Stephenson's Rocket with its coke-powered steam engine. Iron and steel, and the ships it built, the bridges it was bent, hammered and riveted to form. The Sydney Harbour Bridge, and thousands like it, built here and then shipped around the world on steam-driven iron monsters that were built on my doorstep. Cutting-edge technologies developed by Isambard Kingdom Brunel, even more fantastic than his name. Lead mines, tin mines, millions of tons of aluminium. Calcium, sodium, magnesium extracted from seawater and all to advance our quality of life. People like my grandparents and great-grandparents, who had short, hard lives, sacrificing all to be a small cog in a national engine, lubricated by North Sea oil that has been responsible for such massive advances in technologies. Things *we* today benefit from, whilst we sleep safely in our beds and from the minute we wake up. And the reason we wake up for thirty-two years more than they did. And the reason we, unlike them, get to see our grandchildren become adults.

To me, the technologies most people don't realise we have are nothing short of miracles. We have become blind to what has miraculously been achieved and what is still being unbelievably achieved today. We live in societies that have become so incredibly complex they probably shouldn't work, but do. There are people down our sewers now, people up pylons, manmade satellites up in space, hundreds of thousands of men and women tirelessly working in research labs day and night, humans far away from their families on oil rigs and we give them no thought whatsoever, as we turn on a tap, click on Facebook, start our cars, pop a pill or flick on a light. Modern-day miracles like the national grid, a vast and far-reaching marvel, built over generations that now depicts perfectly just how cleverly enhanced innovations can benefit all of society. Yes, for profit, but what the hell!

Technologies that should against all odds fail but for some reason work perfectly, or if they do falter, they are put right without us needing to know. Simple technologies that improve our sight now we are living almost twice as long as we did only four generations ago. Remove the world's spectacles and contact lenses today, and watch chaos prevail on planet earth tomorrow. Who would have thought we would have an invention that sits on our face, enabling us to see, in most cases for most of our lives, yet as we stare at the world through its engineered glass, we are blind to it?

And where is all that forward thinking now? Lost? Surely we are still good inventors yet it seems our research and development centres do nothing but export their good ideas despite us being in the right place with the perfect platform to take them to the next level. Clean coal, electric cars, whatever is next . . . It seems to me we behave like Newcastle United. As soon as one of their home-grown players comes through the ranks and pops in a few goals he's sold to the highest bidder whilst the team itself, despite having a fantastic history, bobs around below mid-table desperately hoping to avoid relegation. Ah well, too late perhaps. All our forefathers and mothers built up lost. Pity. Perhaps we could have picked up the baton and kept making life better for our children, like they did theirs. Like I said earlier, I'm not married to the idea of coal but what I am married to is good sensible debate and acting on true unbiased scientific actual data.

It seems to me there is less debate than ever. I see huge groups of people who have closed their minds. Some think it's a good idea to super glue their bare arses to a road or a train because they want us to upgrade our cavity wall insulation. Some might chain themselves to a tree that has probably only survived because of coal because they want us to tidy up the planet despite them not being capable of tidying their own bedrooms.

This new generation (my kids included) use up more energy, travel more, have more electronic devices and consume more resources than any generation before them; a generation who have made the word 'ungrateful' woefully inadequate.

Whilst I have been writing this book Covid-19 has swept the planet. The research and development labs of the UK were the first to produce a credible vaccine. The unique structure of our national healthcare system left us in possession of the largest collection of on-hand data essential to beating the pandemic's blight. AstraZeneca was almost taken over in 2014 when Pfizer, an American pharmaceutical giant, offered $218 billion. If that had happened, the USA would now be enjoying, just like in every other sector of British innovation, the benefits of years of

British research and development. Dodged a bullet there. Maybe we are learning.

Perhaps I think like this because I don't take a simple thing like reading for granted or because the learning it brought hit me as a sceptical adult rather than a gullible child; or because I've seen vast areas of our planet that have none of what we have. Could it be the enormous contrast of my wife's upbringing next to mine? Or perhaps it's because I've grown up in the middle of such monumental changes. Could be a little of all of those reasons that never has me thinking, *why is there poverty?* But, *how did we manage to create wealth?* Not, *why do we have hunger?* But, *where does all the food come from?* Not, *why disease?* But, *who the hell found all the cures?* After all, before poverty, there wasn't *even* poverty! My grandparents knew of little else but hunger and disease. Pity they didn't get to see what to me appear as miraculous human initiatives on a mass scale along with their amazing effects on everyday life.

The way the mines were closed and the reasons for doing it should never be forgotten. For a so-called developed nation to treat its subjects with such contempt was disgraceful and deserves no forgiveness. Margaret Thatcher died in the Ritz Hotel, London, of a stroke in 2013. On the day she died and on the day of her funeral, nobody I know worked. We put up flags, drank lots and danced into the night. For this I have, or will never have, regret. You probably have difficulty understanding this depth of hatred and that I can understand. But if you had walked under my skies on the same pothole-laden paths as I had, then believe me, you too would have drunk champagne and danced with me into those nights. And just to be clear, we did not celebrate because we were naive enough to imagine because of her death things might now get better. It was spite!

236

After all, she was only one death while the fatalities created by the tsunami of poverty, deprivation, alcoholism, divorce and addiction to illegal and prescription drugs which Thatcher's policies triggered is still gathering momentum here today.

As British industries were having their throats cut, Thatcher gave huge grants to foreign investors to invest in my area. She unashamedly advertised the North East as a great place to build your factories as there is a huge pool of already trained cheap labour there. Cheap labour! That was me, my brothers, my father and my community. Sunderland airport was closed and sold to Japanese investors and the Nissan car plant sprung up on my doorstep. She gave them millions of pounds in grants to build it whilst the British car industry – along with British Steel which depended on it – lay bleeding on the floor. Robert McAlpine won the multi-million-pound contract to build the plant. Sir Robert McAlpine was the chairman of the Conservative Party at the time. Legalised corruption at the very highest level and nobody interested. One of my brothers and lots of my friends work there today. Pound for pound they get less than they used to get for working at the village pit over quarter of a century ago. They have no choice. They have no voice. The pension fund they paid into for years as miners is sitting in the government's coffers and they have no other way of putting bread on the table.

21

My education

The comprehensive school I went to is now a care home for the elderly. I don't hate that school or the teachers who bellowed loud in its classrooms and corridors. I don't need revenge. Things were different then. Like one of those underdeveloped countries I travelled through and stared at in disbelief in my younger days, where people get their heads chopped off for what they think or what they refuse to think and women are not allowed to show their hair, drive a car or to be educated. Countries we accept mistreat their people, because it's 'different there'. The people in charge, all those years ago, were working with a different standard of morals. Who knows, some of my teachers might have been Japanese prisoners of war or sat on that Dakota with my father. Strange as it may sound, I miss those morals and though the fact my mother had to come to school because a teacher had beaten me with a massive shoe instead of the purposely provided legal stick was probably an indication society's moral compass had us steering a few degrees off course, I still believe, amongst it all, there was some good.

I am convinced that how we treat people in our wider communities should be based on how we treat our own children. I was brought up to take responsibility for my own actions and

I hope I've passed that on. 'Dragged up proppa,' as I like to say. An ethos of, 'if you mess up, you put it right,' sitting on a strong foundation of sometimes having to be 'cruel to be kind'. Pulling at my ears and wiggling my tongue at Old Mrs Bateman cost me that week's orange, yet taught me much. However, I fear today's compass is spinning uncontrollably, offering no direction, leaving us sitting on a more unsteady foundation of being 'kind to be cruel', where nobody learns from their mistakes and nothing is ever anybody's fault. Where the offender has become the 'too easily offended'. Another area I find I differ from most is that I believe it morally reprehensible to respect all and believe respect should only be awarded to those we judge have earned it.

For a morally fit and lean society to function or even blossom, I believe respect might be better hard-earned. I have recently found myself in environments where there is respect saturation, where the currency of respect seems to have suffered soaring inflation. I've witnessed people who have too much respect to spend and I don't like how it manifests itself or what it breeds. To me, these people appear to have not learned the value of learning or listening and don't even know when to shut the fuck up! Where I grew up, respect was something you had to work at or even fight for and I believe everybody striving individually on their own righteous paths to achieve this is what created that warm environment and was the reason all around me was caring, safe and honest. A strong community spirit.

Sorry about that, God! Hope 'righteous' is not one of your words! I'll get my editor to check it out with that woman sitting by her desk in Southampton and if she says you thought of it first, I'll replace it with, 'morally justifiable'. Or are those yours as well?

If somebody trashes their state-owned house, they are given

a fresh one to trash again. If somebody keeps eating until they weigh seventy stone, resulting in the fire brigade having to demolish the front of their house in order to transport them to hospital by crane, we must all take a proportion of the blame; society's fault! How could WE let this happen? If somebody takes heroin, it's an illness and they can't be blamed, therefore the system will supplement their habit with methadone. If somebody becomes an alcoholic, they are given extra money on top of their social security for drink.

I know people in their mid-thirties who have never worked, have kids, drink, take drugs and have trashed over a dozen houses yet they are treated with what to me seems to be unearned respect by the authorities. Don't get me wrong, I don't think these people should be refused help; on the contrary. But I don't believe it is possible to successfully help a person until there is some level of personal responsibility taken. A good friend of mine works in a drug rehabilitation centre and talks of how she has been watching the same faces coming through the door for daily handouts since she started working there. She has worked there for over twenty-five years. The war on drugs can't be won using kindness!

I've watched the system here become a not-fit-for-purpose, cruel enabler that does nothing but strip the poor souls it is supposed to assist of all pride and self-worth, transforming them into a completely dependent group. What strikes me most about this situation is that the middle-class employees of the poverty industries, namely the social worker, health workers and wrongly named 'do-gooders', who have created, implemented and maintained this monster, then have the audacity to turn back and refer to it and them as 'the underclass'. Progressive, apparently, yet all around me everything is getting far, far worse. I have a dear friend who is an undertaker in Hartlepool.

He is now dealing with just as many under thirty-fives as elderly. How and who measures progression, I wonder?

A couple of years ago a young man went on a rampage. He got onto the roof of a house in a nearby town and threw bricks and tiles into the street. He was there for five hours; he was filmed and it went viral. He went to jail where, because he had assaulted a serving police officer, he became a cult figure. A hero! Such a hero that somebody in my village took a premeditated decision and decide to copy his actions last year. He too stayed on the roof for several hours throwing building materials onto the street and onto the cars below, causing thousands and thousands of pounds of damage. Concerned by his anti-social behaviour, a public meeting was held by local councillors. As a local landlord I was invited, which surprised me, as the vandal had no landlord. The house he had entered and then climbed on top of belonged to a young girl he had been trying to strike up a relationship with. He had been to my office and asked for a tenancy but had been flatly refused because he didn't have the right demeanour needed to make him a desirable neighbour, looked like he was on drugs and had no history of being a decent tenant (he didn't know how to listen or when to shut the fuck up!).

To my astonishment an elected member stood up and blamed the police for their delayed response and how they had not tried in any way to bring him to safety. To my further astonishment a policeman followed him up and defended their role. He said that the fire brigade had been even slower to attend and said how perhaps they were probably more equipped to have dealt with him. He then went on to point out that he was supposed to receive regular visits from his social worker but because of a lack of resources he had not been seen for several months. His probation officer was also brought into the argument. He was supposed to see him weekly but hadn't for months. The policeman then spoke of how he had experienced a very unhappy childhood before mentioning that rogue landlords might need to take some of the blame.

I got to stand and ask a question towards the end, but first I pointed out that the system was already in place for him to not be able to get a house and landlord. I then asked, 'We've heard the police blamed today. We've heard the fire brigade blamed today. We've heard the social worker and probation officer blamed today, then his upbringing and now his non-existent landlord. Could I please take this opportunity to ask everybody here today what proportion of the blame for this crime, bearing in mind it was a premeditated copy-cat crime, do you think should be appointed to the man who committed it?'

I made this point because it seems nothing is anybody's fault any more. Imagine asking our parents' generation (our elders) who should be blamed in this situation. Imagine asking them to take even one per cent of the blame for the man on the roof or the seventy-stone man and the growing numbers like him. They would laugh at us and tell us when people knew they would have to take full responsibility for their own actions, stuff like that didn't happen.

Are we ignoring all we were taught?

Don't get me wrong, I realise it's a multi-faceted problem and I know it's more than just the 'Thatcher factor' to blame for the death of communities and social structure here. However, I do believe it was her targeted ideology of deindustrialisation that triggered this decline and the reason for the vast disparities between here and every other region of our country that are being suffered today. No single person, beast or group of people has ever survived having their heart ripped out and my community is no exception.

Fatherless families are another factor and by-product of

these policies. The men around here have had the lead stripped out of their pencils and have been left with no self-worth. Most young men don't work and those who do have demeaning unrewarding jobs with no future. This makes creating a settled home environment difficult. I see this all day, every day on a huge scale. When my youngest was fifteen and in his last year of comprehensive he was in a class of twenty-eight and only six kids in his class had fathers at home.

Smaller families, I believe, are another. I know lots of kids who have grown up as the only child and their demeanour and behaviour is noticeably different to that of my own children. Mainly in their levels of self-confidence. If a boy grows up with only a mother and no siblings around to bounce off or to put him in his place, then his childhood becomes unnaturally extended. If like in lots of cases, the mother is single because of an unpleasant break-up, then this will be picked up on. Endless days of mothers discussing with other single mothers how unreliable and unneeded men are does nothing for the confidence of a boy who is one day supposed to become a compatible mate and competent father. As for young girls in the same position, growing up estranged from male roles and also thinking men are not needed … Well, what can I say? My wife works as a nursery teacher now and tells of how an alarming number of new three- or four-year-old children starting school for the first time are terrified of men.

Illegal and legal drugs are by far the biggest factor here. To progress, people need to focus on what is right there in front of them, but after scoring on the streets or sitting opposite their GP their heads are sent elsewhere? Drug-related deaths in the UK have been rising by a steady 5 per cent annually for the last twenty-five years yet there is no mention of changing failed policies.

How I see these problems being dealt with by the authorities is not so much as overparenting but overmothering. I'm sure when the welfare state and our National Health Service were born together with the social services and benefit system in the late forties it was implemented and then managed by men. As were most families then; patriarchies. Now the demographics of our education, health, law enforcement, courts and social care management systems have undergone a radical levelling up of gender (and rightly so), has there been a softening? I know the difference between my father's parenting and my mother's. She would never have stood up in a court of law and pleaded with a magistrate to please put her son in jail, that's for sure! But my father did, and that worked better for all. Whatever has gone wrong needs sorting and sorting quick, and if it *is* because of a softening due to a kinder, more forgiving and compassionate leadership at the very top of our health, care and legal systems, then somebody needs to wake up, be honest and perform some radical staff retraining soon, because our sisters and brothers are dying prematurely on a vast scale here.

A few years ago, my brother retired from the RAF. He returned home and bought a bungalow a few doors away from my mother; very nice, until a drug addict beat him to his near death in front of his wife. I watched for four days as the drug abuser stood in court and denied all, despite overwhelming forensic, CCTV and witness evidence being presented. The jury returned within one hour with a guilty verdict and the judge (referred to by my brother's barrister as a 'hard-hitting man') sent the culprit to jail for six years and nine months. We never found out why he did it. It was the fourth time he had attacked someone in this manner.

Nine months later he was back on the village streets. He openly boasted that whilst inside he had started to attend the chapel, befriended the vicar before convincing her to write a report for the governor. He met the governor; she organised a meeting with the parole panel and it was agreed he could go home before Christmas. How nice!

He laughed as he explained to somebody I know that he spent so much time with his head bowed in that fuckin' chapel he was almost starting to believe in all that God and Jesus shite!

My brother was fifty-eight when this happened. He was sixty-two last month. He and his wife don't leave their house at night.

I don't know the solution. We can't instruct couples to stay together (like they used to). We can't tell them to have bigger families (like they used to). What the 'experts' always speak of is having better role models. Well, good luck with that one, there's some work to do there! This generation have given up on TV. My kids laugh at me if I watch the BBC; they see it as retro and most of their friends don't see any real people because they never look up from their smartphones, the content of which is unlicensed and impossible to regulate. However, what I do know is that these pockets of deprivation are geographically easily identified and are not everywhere. Surely that's a start!

Today the pupils from my village travel by bus to a nearby town to be educated. The pupils in that school get less than half per head spent on them as a kid who is fortunate enough to have been born in the south of England. And so, the tsunami rolls on, engulfing the next generation and drowning them before they've had chance to take their first breath. The education budget for County Durham has just been cut again for the third consecutive year. Perhaps I should write a letter of thanks to the Department of Education in London. I'm sure it's a very grand building, situated down there somewhere and full of very fine and dandy people.

Dear sirs, dames, lords and noble men,

Thanks for nothing but I've ended up very comfortable in life without you,
     it would read.
Sorry for the delay. I might have written to you sooner, but at the age of fifty-five I've not long been taught to write by somebody from Surrey who, in a class size of only twenty-two, you educated properly. No hard feelings. In fact, I'd like to say a very special thank you for the sustained lack of funding, huge class numbers of thirty-eight and sheer neglect you showed me back then and still show my people today. Thanks, thanks and thanks again for all your hard work in redirecting funds to the more affluent areas of the country because you connect better with those people. Your people! And once again, a huge, huge thank you for not supplying my school with the adequate resources that might have had me reading and writing. Who knows what might have become of me, if I had been literate? (Actually, I think I know the answer to that one. A TV repair man!)
P.S. Please find enclosed a letter from Robert Chance that I have written for him because he cannot. It has Robert's name on it but actually represents thousands of my people. People your deliberate actions ensured have no vision, could never be heard and still have no voice today. The mute people you have made every effort to make sure have remained in the Dark Ages, where nothing shines out because they have never been given the tools or knowledge to create or the knowhow to get it out.

THANK YOU FOR NOTHING!
Robert (NO) Chance

22

The north/south divide

Recently, I entered some of my work into a northern working-class writers' competition. It was a piece about the colliery villages up here being like blackholes for literature. They suck everything in but nowt can ever get back owt! I soon received correspondence, asking me to please confirm that, if successful, I would be willing to travel up north to Liverpool to accept a prize? It would take me four hours to drive to Liverpool and my compass would be reading south! I did not reply. Who are these people? Are they from the same belly of pups as those who think it is acceptable to pay a construction worker in Edinburgh a third less than their southern counterpart? People say to me, when I compare my southern wages to my northern wage, 'Ah, yes, but the wages have always been higher down south because it costs more to live there!' Research shows this is not quite true. The disparity in working-class wages did not appear until the fifties and actually, just before and after the Second World War, if it was a bigger pay packet you were chasing, the west coast of England was the place to be. Around the importing and exporting industrial heartlands of Liverpool and Manchester. Anyway, surely it only costs more to live down south because the people there are given a bigger income to live on? Are we, by accepting this, not enabling the unfairness of this situation to at best be ignored and at worst grow? Have we just accepted it's grim up north!

I've heard the argument that the reason a southern worker is paid more is because research proves that a southern worker produces more per hour. Well, there's a chicken and egg scenario if ever there was! After years of underinvestment, treating people like dogs whilst underpaying them, perhaps workers *do* start dragging their heels!

My brother worked at the Nissan car plant in Sunderland for almost ten years. They were given an annual bonus based on a percentage of the company's profits each year. This would normally manifest itself as an extra three to four hundred pounds every May and though not a life-changing sum, would boost morale on the factory floor. The designers at the plant designed a new car (Nissan QASHQAI). Everybody worked hard, performed lots of overtime, got the new line up and running and production started ahead of schedule. Sales of the car were a huge success and after the first twelve months their percentage-based bonuses were issued to the well-deserving workers at almost four thousand pounds per head, followed closely by a letter explaining that because of money needed for future investment in the company the bonus scheme was to be revoked with immediate effect. My brother made his thoughts known and was sacked at the age of sixty-two. Without reason!

Should it be acceptable for a doctor, fireman or teacher down south to be given more money to live on than somebody doing exactly the same job a few hundred miles north? Or could they never afford to notch down and live like them up there? Perhaps I've got it all wrong and these people are just worth more. Perhaps they *should* be given more money and perhaps *two* votes to our one. Perhaps it shouldn't just be your postcode that determines how much you are given to live on but whether you are male or female, short or tall or the colour of your skin?

Is paying a northerner almost half of what you pay a southerner a prejudice that nobody but I can see? I suppose the most disappointing or even embarrassing thing to admit to myself is there was once a time when I first arrived in the big city as a young bricklayer and thought the locals getting a much bigger wage than I was just life. Like somebody from the Windrush generation walking through a cinema door marked *BLACKS ONLY*, I was downtrodden, numb and brainwashed by the system I had just come through.

If the argument *is* because the cost of living down south is higher, then why not lift the wages up north to suit and let the country even out? It's not only wages, it's the allocation of investment, grants and funding and this is easy to control. Roads, rail, education, health, money spent on flood defences is a fine example. Cumbria is the wettest county in the British Isles yet the amount of rain that falls is irrelevant when it comes to the allocation of money for fighting floods. Apparently, it's fairer when allocating finances to work with postcodes than scientific data. The closer to London you are, the more you get. The Thames gets the Thames Barrier (almost one billion pounds in today's money) while we accept thousands of homes and businesses in and around the city of York being submerged in water every few years. Last year I watched some London-based minister explaining to a TV camera that the government is not King Canute and it is not all about spending money on infrastructure. He went on to say that sometimes nature just can't be beaten. Try telling that to the Dutch. They live free from the risk of flooding despite most of their country being under sea level. This is directly due to 'money spent on infrastructure'. I have worked with Dutch people and have spent time there and they laugh and joke about our flooding.

Why don't we get some of these so-called government experts to work out where exactly the financial borders are (Watford Gap and the Welsh and Scottish borders, I reckon). And when they identify just where they are, then surely they could use another shower of experts, or the same ones, to drag that border just a few miles east, west and right up north to above the Shetland Islands? After all, surely these borders are only manmade and could be driven back easily by injecting real money into real projects in the right areas?

And again, I don't mean handouts. We learned long ago, if you give somebody in a third-world country a bowl of cereal, it helps them for twenty-four hours. If you give them a bag of grain and a hoe, then with some relatively cheap monitoring we can help them for life. Instead of giving someone a fish, give them a fishing rod or a net; a boat even. We've seen some great sustainable projects implemented globally yet it appears from where I'm standing, we are not so clever when implementing such projects in our own backyard.

I'm not out to force men to swap their bowler hats for cloth caps, but surely we today have to make sure that Britain is a developed enough nation to offer our children's generation the opportunity to pick up and put on which hat they feel fits?

If I am ever in need of a sharp reminder of just how powerful the people are that control our money, I simply watch their news. It happened last week and makes me laugh. The BBC announced 'GOOD NEWS! House prices are starting to rise again, which is a sure sign the economy is strong.' How Orwellian! We are a nation of subjects only ever three wage packets away from being thrown on the streets and are kept down to a level where we can only just afford the basics. It's not just the BBC; the rhetoric spewed out by most mainstream media outlets has us (the working classes) convinced that if we were given more and our wages were 'allowed to get out of control', we would be poorer. Really! If we are given more money, we'll be poorer! Mmmmm. Like I said earlier, I was there in the seventies and watched the so-called suffering. Young working people could afford things called houses!

You have a roof over your head, but don't actually own it. You will spend a lifetime giving a bank £400,000 for a property that you are convinced you paid £160,000 for. You can now get a mortgage over thirty-five years! They even have a big knob they can turn up if the economy lifts and we start getting too good of a deal and have big ideas of ridding ourselves of debt before we die. The big knob has 'the interest rate' written on it. If the average house price in this country was 50p (instead of £258,000), we (the working classes) would be much better off. We could have shelter and no debt and the banker would have to fuck off and make a real living elsewhere.

If the BBC announced the price of food was starting to rise, would we celebrate this and perceive it as good news? We all have to buy food and we all have to live under a roof. I have three boys and they will ultimately have to buy one each. People who say their houses are worth a lot of money are deluded. Unless they sell that house and live in a tent bought for £9.99, that money can never be theirs. If you die and leave your house to your children, they can tax that money when you're lying dead underground, in order to keep the wheels of their greasy machine oiled.

If the financial capital that Thatcher promised would replace industry gets it wrong, the government bails them out with our taxes and when they have paid most of it back, they let them off with the rest even though it's our money. Almost 90 per cent of the money in this country belongs to less than 5 per cent of the population and they are predominantly involved in finance. I'm sure the very man who first said, 'An Englishman's home is his castle,' was actually sitting in a castle. Probably in his counting house and mortgage-free.

Somebody must have spotted the north/south divide; the government set up the Northern Powerhouse. It is a government-run committee of highly paid, rejected-by-the-voter ex-politicians and unelected advisers who are supposed to concentrate on sorting out the disparity. The man they first put in charge of the Northern Powerhouse was Michael fuckin' Heseltine! Sorry, Baron Michael Ray Dibdin Fuckin' Heseltine! The very man whose fingerprints are all over the knife that cut the throats of everything my forefathers had built up. The fox in charge of the coop!

John Prescott was part of that committee for a short time but threw in the towel. I watched him make a speech and he said something like this. 'It's a "job for the boys" organisation that can't see over the Pennines, and does nothing but monitor the seismic economic disparity between north and south whilst making sure it remains.'

It was like a political bomb went off, just as I fell out of secondary school, killing some, blasting some of us to the far corners of the world, whilst leaving some poor souls blackened, lame and smouldering in the ashes. What happened to Lynda Phillips, I hear you ask? Did she marry Adam Ant? Did she fuck! She married a man who was an expert at staying on sickness benefits even though he was perfectly fit. He was so good at this people would go to him for advice. They would knock on his door, he would show them how to fill in their benefit forms, how to hide their wellbeing and how to appear ill. A common trick – still used today – is to soak your feet in a bucket of diesel the night before your interview with the

252

dreaded panel of sickness benefit doctors who try their best to meet targets set by the government and certify you fit for work even though there is none. The trick of having your skin breaking down and peeling from your feet could win somebody a month or two of benefits without having to see another doctor and the cream you would be prescribed would have your skin back to normal in three days. Just one of the ways people learned to survive.

The last time I spoke with Lynda she was recovering from a mental breakdown after being divorced, being left on her own in a mid-terrace house with drug addicts living on each side. She couldn't leave the house without it being burgled and had become a prisoner in her own home. The situation only got better when one drug addict murdered another over a £10 bag of something and a group of them were taken into prison where they were allowed to openly discuss their new lives with their many followers on Facebook whilst we pay for their methadone.

I told Lynda about my writing and she laughed.

'You never stayed in a classroom long enough to learn how to read and write, you were an expert in getting kicked out,' she reminded me.

I asked for her email address so I could send what I had written about her, but she said the drug users had nicked her iPad, computer and phone.

What happened to Perfect Pete Clarke the prefect, I also hear you ask? Well, he got a job in the local bank as a clerk but was made redundant in his forties after the death of communities saw the rich banks quickly deserting a sinking ship, pulling the plug and boarding up their high street branches. Peter Clarke, the headmaster's role model, a redundant bank clerk. What a success! Certainly left his mark there, if only with his black ink stamper. Most of those destined for the pit from my English class joined the army when they finally realised British Coal had fallen victim to Thatcher's final solution.

About three years after we had left school one of them, Kev Laws, stole an army wagon, deserted and parked it outside his mother's house. I remember asking him why he'd fallen out with the army and him smiling and explaining, 'They weren't happy with the way I wanted to run it!' About twenty of us got in the back of his troop carrier and went to Newcastle night-clubbing. I think he'd hit the self-destruct button because he drove back drunk, was arrested the next morning by military police and nobody has seen him since.

Alan Ladalor I saw in London about five years after we'd left school. He was getting on the tube with a group of girls. He looked happy and was wearing a very nice red minidress and six-inch heels. He didn't see me, I made sure of that. It wasn't that I didn't want to catch up with him, but it was the happiest I'd ever seen him and he looked like the last thing he needed was a bastard like me reminding him of where he'd come from.

Robert Chance, the guy from the supermarket and my English class, didn't get a very good deal. After a few low-paid jobs, which he struggled to hold down, probably because of his illiteracy, he wound up suffering from mental illness or what the doctors up here get chastised for calling 'Rotten Life Syndrome'. After a lifetime on prescription happy pills, he looks twice as old as he actually is, has lost his chirp and owns dark sunken eyes from which comes a thousand-mile stare you would normally only associate with a dementia sufferer. I find it difficult to talk to him without becoming distressed. Poor Robert, one of those left smouldering in the ashes, I fear.

My village has become a ghetto, with a financial, naked to

the eye, concentration camp style fence surrounding it that is difficult for those trapped inside to penetrate. There *are* holes in the fence but if you're not willing to leave those you love behind, fit enough to scale the mesh, industrious enough to dig under or sharp enough to recognise a 'get out' when you see one, you can quite easily find yourself stuck on its wrong side for ever.

When I was young there was a thriving main street support-ing four butcher shops, half a dozen bakers, two shoe shops, a pet shop, two newsagents, five greengrocers, a couple of book-ies, two barbers, five or six hair salons, three banks, a Co-op supermarket, a small department store, two fish shops, eleven pubs and clubs, two off-licences, a dentist's, a solicitor's office, a launderette, two cafes and for when you became completely exhausted of shopping there was a couple of undertakers there to carry you away. There was even a couple of gift shops. Today, whilst looking around the place, one might think they're viewing a scene from the film *Shaun of the Dead*. It's knackered and other than if you want a kebab, a spin on an electronic roulette wheel, to get a tattoo or take a lesson on how to beat somebody up using martial arts, then it is a ghost town. I moved out twenty years ago. Only four miles away. Deserting a sinking ship, you might say, but if you're bringing up children and you have a chance to get on the other side of the wire, believe me, you jump at it.

My village and the surrounding villages have the highest rate of people on sickness benefit in the UK. The highest rate of people claiming housing benefit. The highest rate of people being on invalidity benefit, the lowest average age for people on incapacity benefit and by far the highest rate of people who have been on invalidity benefit for the longest period of time. The lowest rate of car ownership in Britain. The highest rate of unemployment. The lowest rate of home ownership. And believe it or not, over the last ten years, whilst life expectancy for men has not gone up or down, for women around here it has actually dropped. This is the only place in the UK where the life expectancy for women is dropping! If you can afford to buy one, a two-bedroom terraced house can be bought for less than ten thousand pounds, yet few people can.

Three days ago, I was in my local hardware store; it's one of the only survivors despite it being burgled countless times. The owner, Stewart, often jokes, 'Business is booming! There are so many surrounding properties boarded up, I'm making a fortune selling electric sanders to window cleaners.' He's a fine example of 'if you don't laugh, you'll cry!' An elderly lady entered and asked for some curtain hooks. They were 65p for a pack of twenty and after turning her purse inside out, she apologised for wasting Stewart's time.

'Could you keep them behind the counter and I'll call back in a fortnight?' she asked, before saying her goodbyes and shuffling out. There are over 170 billionaires in the UK and though I'm not one of them I did find myself running down the street and making sure she got her hooks. Perhaps the lesson in life handed down to me from Old Mrs Butterfield with her half-pound bag of mushrooms had a bigger influence on me than she could have ever known. I know that lady and I knew her husband. He worked underground in the village pit with my father. He worked there for over thirty years but died of pit lung. Surely she and all like her deserve better?

It is almost thirty years since the last pit closed and despite different governments coming and going, the situation, just like the life expectancy of our women, is continuing to spiral down. Food banks have sprung up everywhere and just like charity buckets that are rattled for homeless people, or 'Help for

Heroes', we simply accept their existence. One of my brothers manages a food bank only three miles from where I live. It gives away over half a million pounds worth of food per year. The final nail in the coffin of my struggling village high street. A load of wrongly named do-gooders giving thousands of pounds of goods away on its doorstep. The opposite of sustainability. This is not just an old chapel dishing out a few tins; oh no! They have offices, vans, paid managers and trained staff. They have to meet health standards and hold the correct public liability insurances. They are a new branch of the poverty industry and have replaced small businesses!

An ex-staff member informed me that once a month, by appointment, a minibus full of school teachers will pull up outside and use the food bank. It needs money here. Some of that foreign aid (after all, this place doesn't look like modern-day Britain) or that sixty-seven billion the government have raped and reduced to forty billion which was stripped from the miners' pension fund might help. To be fair, it *was* the forefathers of the very people that are suffering the most who paid that money in. Boris made a 'categorical' pledge in his 2019 election campaign whilst in Mansfield that 'no miner would be out of pocket' if he got into power. He should remember the votes he got from here were borrowed.

Let's talk about the complex issue of poverty. I've told you of my childhood. Was that a poor upbringing? Relative to my mother's and my father's childhood it was luxury. Like I said earlier, I had loving parents, have only happy memories and never went to bed hungry. Yet we had very little. What do we understand as poverty today? We see images on our TVs of children on rubbish dumps in far-away countries collecting plastic bottles in an effort to get themselves above the 'dollar a day' poverty bracket. That is undoubtedly poverty but the relationship between this, what I have lived through and what I see in my community today confuses me.

The more I study the subject, the more I realise poverty is not all about money. Unlike when I was a child. The people here are not financially poor, yet all around me might appear to an outsider as poverty personified. There must be millions of pounds being dropped in here to pay for this dysfunctionality yet from what I can see very little hits the ground. Soaked up by the 'poverty industry'. Social services, health centres, care workers, not to mention the policing bill. Yet less and less is being achieved.

The people who say 'it's no good just throwing money at a situation' I now realise might be right. However, I'm sure the very same people who are in charge of the money know nothing of this situation on the ground here. It costs over five thousand pounds to keep a drug user in a house for one month. There are hundreds in my village. It costs even more when he or she has a stint in jail. Over one million pounds when they murder one another. A few brave decisions could save millions of wrongly directed tax payers' pounds.

As for us workers, the less you have, the more painful austerity feels. The suppression of wages has me laying bricks for the very same money I was getting when I first met my wife thirty years ago. When I met her, she was taking home £992 per month for being a nurse. Thirty years later she works more hours teaching disadvantaged toddlers and takes home £1,003 per month. £11 more! The official figures show the average family income around here has risen in the last twelve years by 65p a week. The average overall wealth (including owned assets) of a family in the North of England has risen by 11 per cent in the last ten years yet the same family in the south-east has seen theirs rise by 81 per cent in the same period according to ONS government figures.

The stagnation of wages has been a massive problem but the standard of jobs has also taken a plunge. I don't hear men bragging in the pub about how many millions of tons of coal they have produced any more and I don't see great swathes of proud men walking their families down to the yards to see a ship launched that they have put their heart and soul into for the last few years. The pride has disappeared and been replaced with call centres and distribution centres and the like, where people feel their time spent there is unappreciated and pointless. They have no prospect of bettering themselves, there is a lack of dignity and everybody I know is working harder than ever for less. My wife and I are testament to this. There are four million people on zero-hour contracts in this country. These people ring up every Sunday night to find out if they have a job on Monday morning. I suspect a high percentage of those people are up north.

I've heard politicians on TV arguing that some people like working like this. That doesn't mean it's morally right! Thousands of miners argued in 1859 that their family income would be halved when the government stopped them taking their women and children under eleven down the pit but we know that now to be the right decision. And anyway, when did they start listening to the minority? From four million you will always find the few who don't understand what deal they should be getting. Early in the twentieth century there were groups of women arguing they didn't want the vote, 'politics is men's stuff', and they were happy to let their husbands deal with complicated things like 'elections'. Did we listen to them?

This part of Britain deserves proper well-paid manufacturing jobs for men and women. It needs the people in charge to realise that Thatcher's policy of deindustrialising Britain was a backward step which has left us behind globally. The people here were proud to produce, to manufacture and I can't see a solution to this region's woes, other than putting its heart back in by re-industrialisation.

I spoke to our local MP a few years ago and asked him what he thought his biggest achievement was whilst he had been in office, to which he replied, he was proud he'd helped Morrisons get planning permission for a supermarket in his town (half a mile from its struggling high street) and he had won money to build an arts centre where they have set up a new theatre dance group. That's all fine and dandy but this place needs more Fred Dibnahs and fewer Fred Astaires. We here have the perfect platform to start the next industrial revolution. A more modern, greener revolution inclusive of women. However, this is not on any agenda and is not what our politicians are striving for.

The local politicians who held office when I was a school-boy were real people who had once lived a normal life, paid tax and had actually worked for a living. They were ex-train drivers or miners. People alive to local issues. Working people who had stumbled upon wrongs in their communities or in the workplace and had passionately devoted themselves to the cause of putting things right. People who knew their electorate. Now we have career politicians. They appear to me as sincere as those red fortune-telling cellophane fish we used to get in Christmas crackers when I was a child. You lay them in your palm and the heat from the hand curls the fish, letting you know if one day you'll be wealthy or poor or if you are in love or it's just a fever, just before you slip it in the bin, over-come with disappointment and the feeling of being taken for a fool.

These people have been to university, learned how to never answer a question and how to lie. They can talk for hours without saying a word. Each one a Jack of small talk and a master of the irrelevant. They do nothing. The politicians who are not from here don't care. The politicians who are from here are looking down at us from this newly constructed social balcony and have never been so detached from the real people. And all of the time the community I love and the people who made it what it was are rotting in hell.

Michael fuckin' Heseltine! FFS.

23

So where are my politics today?

I filled in an internet political score card the other day. Try it next time you have half an hour to completely waste. It asks your opinion on a range of subjects somebody somewhere has decided are political and at the end you press a button and it lets you know where you are on a left-to-right basis on the political scale. I filled in all the boxes, pressed the button. The results showed I was somewhere between a Marxist and a commie! Fancy that!

'Do you believe somebody who commits a crime can be rehabilitated?' it asked.

I must confess to looking deeply at myself when filling in those boxes. Would I drive a van full of stolen contraband around the streets of London today? Definitely not! Would I steal a gangster's coal money from under his nose? Definitely not! Would I steal silver from a hotel's kitchen? Definitely not! Couldn't even bring myself to whip a chocolate Curly Wurly or a warm bottle of milk from a Tory's step these days! I wonder why?

I'd like to think I have completely changed, but fear it's not so. I would like to think it's because I wouldn't dare, but deep down I know I would. Sadly, and this probably sounds shallow, but I fear it's only because I no longer need to. Well, I suppose rehabilitation due to economic circumstance still qualifies as rehabilitation. In fact, I'm probably living proof of what could be achieved economically. However, I must confess it is quite comforting to know if things get sticky or go completely tits up, I could always fall back on old skills and simply reoffend.

So on a more serious note, where are my politics today?

Well, unlike some, I don't feel oppressed. And unlike some again, I'm proud of who I am and I'm proud of those poor bastards who gave all to get me here. There is a growing culture of people wanting to be labelled as oppressed; it's trendy! Well, sorry, but I don't see you as oppressed and you're certainly not as oppressed as the people who built those nice warm learning institutes you're probably sat in. I think people labelling themselves as oppressed is dangerous and I'll explain my reasons for that soon.

These people remind me of my grandfather's comment when I flicked on his TV and showed him Sid Vicious singing with the Sex Pistols for the first time in the late seventies. They finished a three-minute track, I switched off his TV and after looking around the room for half a minute or so he took a deep breath and muttered, 'We need another war!'

I'm not saying we need another war; his comment made me laugh but stayed with me. I think he found this new generation who were not, for the first time in a long time, being ordered to put on a tin hat and grab a gun to fight with, screaming into a mic about the lousy hand they'd been dealt a little confusing.

I fear war. Perhaps it's a healthy fear we all should possess. Perhaps growing up with hand grenades instead of candlesticks on each end of the mantelpiece, the father I had, and then being part of the first generation to see all new wars displayed in colour in the corner of our living rooms has instilled this healthy fear. Korea, Suez, Aden, Vietnam, Ireland, Cambodia, the Gulf

War, Syria, the Bosnian War, Kosovo, Afghanistan, the Falklands, Iraq, Libya, Yemen, the global war on terrorism . . .

I think it's safe to say, the older we get, the wiser we get. That's why the native Red Indians of North America and many other cultures rely heavily on their elders as decision-makers.

There's also unarguable data to show the older we become, the more conservative our thinking becomes. Let's just digest this for a minute. Does this mean it's wiser to be conservative sooner? Scary! I don't like to use the word conservative, I lived through the Thatcher years, so let's say this instead: the older we get, the more the naivety of the left irritates us. The Labour Party wanting to drop the voting age to sixteen! Sorry, but I was sixteen once and fighting for a Russian-style Marxist coup on the streets of Britain from the rear of a stolen ice cream van, FFS.

People in their twenties pulling down statues, setting fire to flags and attacking policemen? People shouting untruths such as 'All cops are bastards!' and carrying placards reading *Defund the Police!* which incidentally has now become an actual policy. I'm sorry but because of the mistakes I've made and the changes I've seen I don't believe they have been alive long enough to have a full understanding of the consequences these policies might inflict, and apart from that, I can't help but view them as an embarrassment to those like myself who still consider themselves 'of the left'.

Whilst being involved in these protests and/or attending our universities I believe these people are being submerged in a culture of group identity politics, or tribalism. With help from their mentors, and armed with old Marxist doctrine they mistake as newfound wisdom, they do, by sheer numbers, successfully overwhelm the conservative thinkers in their tribe and because of the localised personal success experienced they become convinced they are overwhelming conservatives nationally. They are not. I see their actions having the opposite effect and have watched them successfully erode the very timbers of what was once a creditable opposition party. My party. The Tories have never had it so good. Jeremy Corbyn becoming leader of the Labour Party and then being replaced with Sir Keir Starmer has been the greatest gift to be dropped into the lap of the Conservative movement of Britain since Michael Foot.

I'm not sure if my perception of socialism has modernised or slipped, but the socialism I see portrayed today, and the way I see it losing its appeal whilst struggling to fit into our modern-day western world, makes it look suitable for nothing but the past.

From what I can tell, everyone is completely addicted to the benefits of choice and capitalist consumerism, where yesterday's luxuries soon become today's necessities. Perhaps if the socialists put more vigour into pointing out that capitalist-style choices are just an illusion, then perhaps they might make some ground. Surely there's nobody in the UK daft enough to actually believe they can send their kids to any school. What if you are working on the minimum wage and have no car? Perhaps we could all send our kids to Eton!

A great choice of hospitals or doctors' surgeries! Really? I think most people would be elated to get through the front door of their nearest one. The choice on today's supermarket shelves is truly something, but they might appear empty if there's nowt in your purse. I wonder if there really is a big enough moron out there who has been successfully convinced that now they have been awarded the choice of who they buy their water, gas and electric from, it's got cheaper? Earlier in my lifetime all of these natural resources belonged to us, the working people. England (not Wales or Scotland) is the only country on the planet that has sold its water to foreign investors.

'Illusion of choice', there's a subject for another day. Or another book!

When my father's generation returned from the Second

World War victorious, they expected more. The mood had changed and the lucky who got to come home were not about to ditch their tin hats, adopt cloth caps and start serving the capitalist gentry, or in their case, coal owners. Within two years the nationalisation of British industries had taken hold. The National Health Service, a social housing programme and the welfare system were born and the ethos of the worker had changed. The fact these policies were so illustriously radical is, to me, blatant proof our careerist politicians today are lesser, shallow, more selfish and the people in charge back then cared less about themselves, resulting in them being thinkers with more foresight, who thought hundreds of years ahead rather than their next five years' salary. So good were these policies that over seventy years on we are almost in a position where there is hardly an organisation, political party (left or right) or even a single politician who would dare to mess with them and expect to survive politically. Everybody who has dared to undermine its foundations (Gordon Brown and his PFI, Thatcher and private health) is damned to the past!

The socialists I witnessed at the beginning of my life were people like my father or, more so, my grandfather. He worked in a state-owned mine, owned by the National Coal Board. He lived in a state-owned house, owned by the National Coal Board. He was a member of the National Union of Mineworkers that would fiercely defend the rights of the British working man, and for the first time he got paid holidays and was given the promise of a pension. He was allocated fourteen bags of coal per month from the colliery. He paid a pittance to the nationalised 'non-profit-making' Electric Board and a much smaller amount to the state-run Water Board every three months. He didn't even own his own front step but it was kept well scrubbed. Actually all he personally owned were the clothes on his back and a scattering of furniture but he was proud. Proud because he was contributing to a fair system. He knew if he or his fellow man needed a roof over their heads, fell on hard times physically or financially, there was now a safety net he was helping knit that would catch all.

They had won a Second World War; fifty-six million people had died but finally blatant improvements for working-class British families were being implemented. At the end of the war two hundred and seventy people from my village were brought from caves and huts on the beach that had been their home and given newly built council houses not far from the clifftops (the council estate I grew up in). I am only fifty-five years young but know people who spent their childhood living on my local beach. Good proud socialists whose lives were improved dramatically by the implementation of brave socialist policies.

Asking myself, *so where's that socialist today?* has me reaching for a telescope! He certainly can't be sighted in my village!

It seems to me that being a socialist today has become, inexplicably, nothing more than a badge of honour or trend. And as for a proud or, God forbid, patriotic socialist, I think they're extinct. Most of the self-proclaimed socialists I know locally live in the bosom of the welfare state. It seems to me a true socialist today is someone who has nowt but is prepared to share that nowt with only members of his tightly knitted tribe.

I've given much thought to the political spectrum and now that I can do my own research by reading, I have been busy obsessively stripping this subject to the bone. Before the research, I fully expected to be repulsed by the actions of the far right but what did surprise me was how I was equally appalled by the abhorrent actions of the extreme left.

The first thing to observe from history is, be it from the left or right, before the persecution can begin, a group of people must first be identified and recognise themselves as oppressed for a period of time. This normally then manifests into street protests (unrest). This is why I believe this initial recognition of oppression is dangerous. It's always the first stage and the trigger needed.

I've looked at the Nazi atrocities. Their victims clear and targeted. One race, or doctrine or whatever you wish to define it as, purposely ridding the world of another group of people because of an ideology. Us against them. Motivated by hatred.

Let's look at the communist and Marxist atrocities. Their victims more unclear. Their ideology and common goal modelled on a system of a shared utopia. A levelling up. People for the people. A goal of complete equality. Motivated by an apparent fairness and virtue.

A big difference, yet the outcome of each as tragic as the next. From what I've read, it appears to me the left is historically more dangerous than the right and I have drawn this conclusion based on two pieces of evidence.

One: it's easier, cheaper, faster and therefore more successful to get somebody to follow an apparently virtuous ideology than one based on hate. We saw this in Nazi Germany; not only did Hitler require a massive amount of financial backing and industrial might but the only way he could successfully manipulate his foot soldiers (every day working-class people) was with an ethos of terror: 'Do as you are told or you and your family could be next!'

Two: there are hundreds of millions more rotting skulls in the killing fields of Cambodia, Russia and China than there ever were in Nazi Germany. Uncomfortable but true.

Only 9 per cent of Nazis were brought to account for the suffering caused by their behaviour. It doesn't sound a lot but it's 9 per cent more than were brought to account under the left. Pol Pot killed two million before living a full life and dying in 1998 of natural causes in his own country. Chairman Mao of China lived in his own country before dying at the ripe old age of eighty-three after killing sixty million people or more. Because Karl Marx didn't own a plot of land (how could he?) he was buried in Highgate, London, in 1883 (somebody must have paid for his plot). In 1954 the Communist Party of Great Britain had his headstone etched. It reads, *Workers of all lands unite*. Sorry, but didn't the Russians try that one, leading to one hundred and twenty million working-class people being murdered? Vladimir Lenin died whilst in office of natural causes. Joseph Stalin killed between twenty-seven and twenty-nine million in his death camps before he died of natural causes whilst in office.

Each Nazi death camp has a memorial to mark where it once stood. Good! We must never forget. I know of no equivalent in Russia or China to visit. But these places must exist. Perhaps it has been best judged they should be forgotten. After all, they were only doing their best for mankind! Forgive me for comparing the huge historical breakdown of some of the world's most powerful nations to where I live today. I realise they are hardly on the same scale but to me there are parallels. There are whole groups of people in my village that will not deal with or communicate with other groups in the same community.

It was never like this at the beginning of my life!

Now I can read and have read, it seems to me our education institutes at all levels might be telling only half the story. My wife, my three sons and I have been through four different education systems in Britain and have all been alerted to the horrors of national socialism but not to the horrors of communism or Marxism. To me, it seems it should be no less acceptable for an educated academic in this country or anywhere in the developed west to announce themselves a Marxist than a neo-Nazi, yet one fifth do.

24

My village and me

About fifteen years ago my phone rang early one morning. It was my mother. Panicked, she explained my father had collapsed at their home. Age was starting to sink its teeth into him and he had lost his broad stance and had recently become shrunken. I was across their front door in minutes to find my father on the floor. His head had caught something on the way down and he was bleeding heavily. His blood-sugar levels were sky high and he appeared delirious. Within minutes, I stood back as two paramedics knelt with him and performed their magic. He looked hopeless. Beaten by life itself. It was the first time I'd seen him like this. He had always taken charge of the room he was in but here he was not even in charge of himself. They brought in a wheelchair and lifted him into it. One of the paramedics knelt in front of him and looked into his spinning eyes.

'How are you feeling, Tommy?' he asked.

'Champion! Thinking about starting another family!' came the answer.

'This is the generation I joined up to serve,' smiled one paramedic to the other as he wrapped a blanket around my old man's shoulders.

My father was right. He was, in fact, 'champion!' He hadn't

seen a good friend shot to pieces for decades, he hadn't watched one of his young brothers or sisters lowered into the ground for well over half a century, he had not had to bury one of his own (his biggest fear), he was in good hands and didn't have to worry about his parachute failing and flickering like a roman candle. Nowt to whinge about!

Apparently the most stressful experience we have to endure in Britain today is a house move. Oh, and Christmas is up there! All that choice and all that spending! Hard times!

I've entered an extra world now, a world of writers, editors, authors, agents; academics. People my dad might have described as 'educated folk'. They make me smile inside. They read my stuff and assume we have something in common. They will let you know in the first minute of meeting you they regard themselves as 'of the left'. It's like a ritual, as if they are kindly welcoming you into their tribe. They might volunteer to work in a charity shop or in a food bank once a week and think this gives them the right to badge themselves up as lefties or even socialists. They remind me of the 'church people' in my village when I was young. Their houses better kept than most, their front step well scrubbed. It didn't matter if they were staunch Catholic or practising Methodists, they were convinced they were a cut above. My father would refer to them as the 'snurges'. I was never sure where the word 'snurges' came from but I knew perfectly what it meant. His own word for a working-class snob, I guess. They would dress conservatively, wouldn't allow their offspring (if any) to mix with the like of me, look down their noses at people who used the village pubs and if your football landed in their garden, they would burst it with a knife and put it in their very clean bin. Morally they could afford to do this because come Sunday, redemption for all sins would be achieved, cleansing the soul, ready to get it filthy again the following week.

Somebody working in a food bank handing a 'bag for life' of donated goods over to the needy then driving home in their BMW doesn't really cut it for me, sorry. Even if the BMW is electric. I see them as part of the problem. Enabling society to behave dysfunctionally whilst helping what should never be accepted, be accepted. As anybody who's brought up a child knows, dependency can grow ugly.

A friend of mine who works in the food bank managed by my brother talks of people ringing the food bank and complaining about the quality of the goods they have had delivered to the door. 'Somebody rang yesterday and complained that they had asked for Lurpak but when they emptied their bags, they found only Stork SB,' she said.

Sponsoring dependency is cruel. Independent responsibility delivers fulfilment and a sense of purpose or, better still, a sense of achievement, thus creating a body of self-worth fundamental to a successful life. Dependency does not!

The people using those food banks might find fulfilment if they were to march to 10 Downing Street with some sort of strategy and proposal to end food banks once and for all. They might sleep better that night, even if hungry. When I ask my brother, who runs the local food bank, how long it's going to be there, he frowns and doesn't get my question. As a cog in the wheel of the poverty industry, he is making a handsome career out of it and has stopped thinking about why it exists.

The very existence or initial need for a food bank should set social alarm bells ringing, provoking an immediate positive reaction, resulting in the ridding of its very existence thereafter. If the underlying reasons were tackled head on and everybody was helped to live full independent lives, what would these volunteering weekend 'socialists' do, I wonder? Church perhaps!

There are more food banks in the UK than McDonald's

outlets. Not sure what that says about the distribution of wealth in the fifth richest nation on the planet.

Am I right- or left-wing because I see a Britain without food banks?

I know a man who now buys an ounce of skunk for £120 every Friday because he gets food parcels every Monday and Thursday. And he's not alone!

Back to what I said earlier about treating our wider communities or the whole of society as you would treat your own children, with a 'cruel to be kind' compassion! Getting them ready for the real world. If society needs money, make it fit a washing machine, push a tea trolley around a hospital, point a chimney stack, plant bulbs in the park, go live in a caravan and pick fruit, cut somebody's grass or sit at a desk selling holidays. Who knows, society might enjoy it and find out what it's good at. Talents could be found! Relationships formed. People might discover a new self-worth, impossible to achieve from stretching out a hand. I had this debate with my agent. He works in a food bank once a week. I put this to him:

'If creating groups of people like drug addicts given methadone, people who have no intention of ever working but are given a regular income and a house, people who, because they are alcoholics, are given more money than those who are not, for drink, was such a good idea, then why not treat your kids the same way?

'You have plenty of money,' I put to him. 'Why don't you set up direct debits for your two young sons and give them each a few grand a month whilst telling them it's pointless going to school, university or reading any more? Tell them you've done all the groundwork and all they need to do is sit back, play games and enjoy?'

He thought for a while . . .

'Because they would never reach their full potential,' came the answer.

I rest my case!

I suppose this comes across as right wing or even Thatcherite to some, but believe me, I want the best for these people, care passionately about them and don't like what they are being morphed into: zombies!

If a young person sits in a house that doesn't belong to them, taking drugs supplied to them by the system, and dies before they reach the age of forty, then the people who have implemented and assisted this situation are not perceived as cruel but caring and compassionate. If there was a body of people who were to suggest stopping what is happening right away, removing that person from that rented house, getting them to work, not paying for the drink and drugs, then they would be labelled as right wing and cruel. I know lots of people in this position, including members of my own family.

Sorry if this piece seems out of context. I argued hard with myself about slipping it in but it did eventually win its place due to its absolute relevance.

Glen, my brother, has one less daughter today. His daughter Abbie died last night. From what we can gather she was murdered, kicked to death because of a drug debt. She was highly intelligent, very funny and thirty-three years old.

If I was to stand on a stage with my arm around a girl's shoulders in front of ten thousand people and say, 'This person here has done over fifty burglaries, the last one being this morning. She is addicted to heroin and is on her way to jail. Put your hand up if you think we should stop her going to jail, crowd-fund our monies by setting up a direct debit of fifty pence each (£5,000 per month), rent this person a house, buy her new furniture plus new kitchen appliances, then set up a system where we pay for a methadone programme, pay her rent and council tax plus benefits with a social care package involving a team of trained social workers to deliver her methadone and food parcels, leaving her free in the community to burgle some more,' despite the meagre individual financial commitment required I believe not a hand would be raised! Yet it is exactly what is going on. I know a methadone programme costs almost two thousand pounds per month; my friend told me. He is a pharmacist and told me whilst I was building an orangery the same size as my house on his two-hundred-year-old mansion last summer.

Perhaps we should ask the same ten thousand or perhaps a fresh ten thousand to raise a hand if they think there being more drugs available in Britain's jails than there are on its streets is a situation we should accept. It's not accepted by most developed nations. Not a hand would be raised, yet still it goes on. Ninety-three per cent of all crime in the UK is drug or alcohol related, costing us over nineteen billion pounds a year, yet the system does the very opposite to drying criminals out.

Ask the ten thousand if they think the users of food banks should be swabbed for drugs (this can be done for less than one pound) and then if they are clean and have genuinely fallen on hard times, they get food. Tell them to raise a hand if they think somebody who tests positive and can't afford food because they are buying drugs should still be given food just like the genuine case? Yet that's what's going on.

I'm privileged today. I have a twenty-three-year-old son and I often find myself socialising with his large circle of friends, most of whom have now finished university. One young lady is now working as a social worker in Newcastle and is fully aware that lots of the duties she is asked to perform only enable the situation of her clients to worsen.

'What would happen if you approached your boss and suggested a more abrupt but successful approach?' I asked.

'I'd be reminded I must always follow protocol,' came the answer.

One of the young men is a policeman and is appalled by a system that forces them to treat known criminals with the same level of respect as their victims. He laughs when explaining that almost everybody he puts in front of the courts appears straight back on the streets because the whole judicial system is so completely naive due to them being from this newly formed social bracket (snurges) who are completely out of touch with how real people live.

'What would happen if you refused to show criminals respect?' I asked.

'I'm still in my probation period and would probably be reminded it would be in my interest to do so,' came the answer.

One particularly bright young lady is a school teacher and speaks of how all methods normally used to bring discipline to a classroom have recently been stripped away by the new generation of bureaucrats from above and so learning in her classroom is down to virtually zero.

'The people who impose these methods on us can have never stepped into a class!' she laughs with despair.

The last tool left in the box was exclusion from the classroom, but even that is not permitted as it has now been newly labelled by the 'progressive thinkers' upstairs as a form of victimisation. She told me of teachers bribing children in a one-hour lesson by telling them, 'If you promise to do fifteen minutes' work, then you can play on your iPads for the other forty-five!' She explained to me how she doesn't feel safe in her class. She talks of this year's leavers being completely unfit for the workplace. She's right! I've tried unsuccessfully to employ some of them.

'What would happen if you shouted at them or excluded the ring leader?' I asked.

I think you know the answer!

Once a community slips and spirals, it's difficult to catch. Decent people no longer want to be there, those who can, move away and the remaining housing becomes cheap. A housing association can buy a terraced house here for £1, the only stipulation being they must buy ten. Some do and because the locals won't live in them, they enter into contracts with local social services and the national probation service. They then fill them up with what the few remaining locals describe as undesirables. I know this because I have a letting office in the village and I am constantly approached by these services. I will not deal with them!

To rehouse an unnaturally high concentration of troubled souls who have just been released from various institutions for various reasons tips the balance and makes it difficult for an existing community to soak up and deal with, at grass roots level, its once manageable native social problems that historically it has always successfully achieved. How this manifests itself into ordinary everyday life is that I do not know anybody in my village (and I know hundreds) who, in the last few years, has not suffered a burglary. I don't know a tradesperson who has not had their van broken into and their tools or equipment stolen at least once, probably twice. And I know hundreds of them too.

I don't believe there is a shop or any other business that has not been broken into and robbed at least three times. Even the local dentist has pulled his shutters down and gone! It is constant. Every night. My brother's pub has been hit over twenty times in four years. The hairdresser's. My letting office, only two weeks ago. My building office two months ago. My factory unit, where I keep my building equipment, was cleaned out last summer. The only surviving butcher wiped clean of meat in the dead of the night only weeks ago. The long-suffering hardware shop owner who takes most of his stock home every night in a van, robbed. Even the funeral parlour had its doors kicked off in the early hours of the morning only a few months ago for the sake of a Help for Heroes charity box. He'd just buried a veteran. The thieves took the box and the key for his hearse, then used it to ram raid the village cafe before driving it into the sea.

My brother had brilliant CCTV footage of two unmasked men taking his tills from the bar in his pub. He rang the police and was told he would have to make an appointment online if he wanted somebody to come out and at the moment appointments are running at about five weeks. He has a list of thirty-four crimes committed against him and his staff ranging from vehicle theft to serious assault, none of which have resulted in a single conviction or even an attempted prosecution. Less than 5 per cent of burglaries are solved nationally and I suspect the disparities that exist in public spending reflect in those figures locally. It has to be zero per cent here.

Last week, my next-door neighbour had the back doors pulled off his van and two lawnmowers taken. A forensic team turned up in a van with *Crime Investigation Unit* written on it. As an experiment I approached them and struck up a conversation. 'I know exactly who took the lawnmowers,' I informed them. 'I have CCTV footage of the crime and I recognise them and know where they live.' To which one of the young ladies in police uniform replied, 'Sorry, but we're just here to see if there is any forensic evidence!'

As a builder, I am at the moment rebuilding a house for a man who stood up to local yobs in the village and reported their antisocial behaviour. For this his house, car and caravan have been burned to the ground. He was lucky to escape with his wife and two young children. No convictions! I know a man who was shot because he owed somebody £115. My neighbour, a headmaster, had his house burgled just weeks before Christmas last year. They ransacked every room, before taking his children's presents away in his wife's car. Two months later whilst doing the local school run his wife spotted her car and followed it back to the address of a known criminal. She reported it and was told that because the case was now closed there could be no further investigation. Her husband put in an official complaint resulting in the police eventually attending the address only to report back they had checked out the car and it was legally owned by the new owners despite my neighbours having the original documents for the car in their house. No further investigation! No prosecution! I could tell you over one hundred similar tales, over a dozen involving myself. There are regular murders. People run up drug debts with dealers then suddenly go missing and are never seen again. It's like the Wild West! The place is on its fuckin' knees!

Perhaps people *are* treating wider society like their own children. I know parenting has changed radically in a relatively short space of time. Not many kids 'dragged up proppa' today. I see evidence of this all around me, not just extended childhoods but adults treated like children. However, allowing this overparenting to seep into our health, education, legal and social service systems is, from what I can see, shattering people's lives and has already ruined my community.

Let me tell you a true story about a good friend of mine that personifies why I think like this.

Dean King taught himself to be a painter and decorator and has worked for me on a casual on-off basis over the last fifteen years. A very sensitive man, Dean hit rock bottom after splitting from his partner. After experiencing difficulty getting regular access to his young daughter his mental state worsened. Because of this he stopped working and started drinking. One morning about four months ago he went to sign on at the dole office at nine a.m. and the kind lady behind the desk asked if he had been drinking. She could smell beer on his breath.

'Oh yes, the first thing I do when I wake in the morning is have four tins,' Dean explained.

'Are you registered with us as an alcoholic?' she quizzed, looking at her computer screen.

'Don't think so,' replied Dean. The lady asked him how long he'd been drinking and he explained he had probably been drinking too much for the last three years. She tapped away at her keypad, rang the GP surgery over the road, got him an emergency appointment and asked him to call back and see her after he had seen the doctor. He visited the doctor and she helped him fill in some papers. He then returned over the road with the relevant forms that proved he had, in fact, been an alcoholic for the last three years. The lady thanked him for the paperwork and he left. One week later he received a Giro cheque for nearly two thousand pounds. This money was his back payment for all the extra money he should have been receiving for being an alcoholic. I know this because I had been knocking on his door, he had been granted access to his daughter and I had just about talked him into coming back to work.

The money he received rid him of all enthusiasm for work and he started to drink heavier than ever. I spoke to him about one month ago and my parting words were, 'I'll see ya later, Dean, and don't forget to give me a ring when the money runs out!' Dean was buried in the local cemetery last Thursday. He was thirty-eight years old and his daughter is ten. If that is not murder, then it must at least be corporate manslaughter.

This is common. I know a plasterer who received £2,200 for

the same reason three years ago and despite being only fifty years old, has not worked since. The drink has rendered him incapacitated. He will never work again. I know a heroin user who put a compensation claim into the NHS and has received £2,400 because it has now been proved the heroin substitute (methadone) she has been taking for years is responsible for rotting her teeth. I also know a man who has just received £1,800 for the same reason.

Is that lady at the dole office and the doctor, who probably live next door to one another in a gated community somewhere on Planet Perfect, so detached from reality that they actually believe these people will use this money wisely to build new lives? Do they know they are killing people with what they perceive as a kindness? My people!

Alison, a girl I grew up only a couple of streets away from and who is now one of my wife's closest friends, has been the manager of the village community centre for almost two decades. The building provides a whole host of activities for all ages and has become a much-needed hub. A place to go. Alison is in a unique position. She knows exactly what's happening on the ground but also gets to meet the decision-makers from up above. Only annually, of course, when she has to stare across a boardroom into a noble panel of dignitaries and beg for her job and the funding that might keep her afloat for twelve more months. She then has to perform a presentation explaining what she achieved with last year's money before going on to hopefully justify her and the building's existence.

Following this, she has an agonising few weeks while she waits for her appraisal and to find out if she will keep her job and get funding. She dares not ask for more money. She long ago learned to keep her head down, to not rock the boat. I know her very well. She is full of goodness and harbours a genuine fear of being got rid of or, worse still, replaced by someone who doesn't care. Someone who can't connect to the people and their complex problems, recognise their needs, identify and help with their struggles.

So, there we have the disconnect encapsulated. The expert on the ground is too scared to speak up. Not wanting to appear 'troublesome' or, worse still, not daring to appear 'too angry'. Somebody with years of experience and full of not just good ideas for change but simple common-sense solutions, not only ignored and having to live a life of cliff-edge uncertainty (unlike the panel of dignitaries) but completely and purposely frozen out.

'How can SHE possibly have a valuable opinion if she connects with that lot down there?'

25

The collapse of the red wall

The Tories cleaned up in this neck of the woods in the last election. There were seats in County Durham that turned from red to blue for the first time in over one hundred years. The industrial and traditional labour heartlands of the North. The disconnect between the Labour Party and working people, for me and most people, stretches back as far as Gordon Brown and his election campaign of 2010. His disastrous encounter with the formidable Mrs Duffy who raised what she believed to be legitimate concerns about her grandchildren finding it hard to find work because of the Labour Party's open-door policy on immigration, only to be talked over, ignored and then called a bigot from the back of his Jaguar as he forgot he'd left his mic on, was a wake-up call for the working classes. 'The leader of our party, a snurge!'

I didn't want to mention Brexit in this book but it's almost as difficult as trying to explain Noel Edmonds to somebody who hasn't seen him before, without using the word 'bastard!'

The Labour Party leader sitting on the fence on such an important issue as leaving Europe typifies exactly what's the matter with Westminster politics today. Politicians once got paid for their opinion. They would let you know their thoughts and if you agreed, you might vote for them. The fact Corbyn imagined if he kept his thoughts to himself, he might retain his credibility was blatant proof he had become so disconnected from reality and how democracy is supposed to function, he was (as they say up here) 'not fit to shovel shit!' You could have given Boris's job to Basil Brush and he would have cleaned up and walked into number ten after the election shouting, 'Boom! Boom!'

The big shame was that Jeremy Corbyn insulting the British public like he did not only finished him, but finished the Labour Party too, leaving us up here high and dry. We'll have to get over it. Just like we accept that though Christianity has all but disappeared, it left us with a strong foundation that shaped our morals, laws even, we must now accept that though the Labour movement left the welfare state and the National Health Service, it also has now disappeared.

The people here drew the conclusion that if the party itself let things go 'that far', it also can't be 'fit to shovel shit'. This was and is a political disaster for the UK as a credible opposition party nipping at the heels of an elected government is a healthy situation for all. That's over with now, leaving the Conservatives to enjoy a wide-open road with the knowledge they can drive as dangerously and as recklessly as they like.

I believe the left-wing bias of academic leaders at our schools, colleges and universities is one of the reasons our democratic system is spinning around with one oar in the water today. There are academics who say their teachings are harmless and when their students leave and enter the workplace, they quickly forget all and slip away quietly into the capitalist world. They might have a point, this might happen eventually, but what is not harmless is the atmosphere created by these huge institutions built by the tax payer. I believe this atmosphere also poisoned the air of the Labour Party's meeting rooms and conference halls and after breathing that air, its members became so disillusioned with identity politics they actually decided it might be acceptable to wind back the clock, ignore history and try another Michael Foot. This was not harmless! It is widely understood in America today that if Hillary Clinton had not played the identity politics game towards the end of her last election campaign, which she lost by the smallest of margins, she would have almost certainly been the first female president ever in charge of the most powerful nation on the planet, instead of Trump. Every time a leading politician, here or over the pond, reaches out to the minorities, average Joe sitting in the middle ground thinks, *but what about us?* Especially during austerity. It divides the nation rather than bringing it together.

What was also very damaging was the general tone of rhetoric from Labour politicians that seemed to promote a patronising message that if you voted for Brexit, you must be less intelligent. Unbeknown to the working classes of Britain, the Labour Party membership had been highjacked by a majority of 82 per cent middle class, but because of an overall rhetoric of 'we know best' this was starting to seep out, creating a new awakening.

Emily Thornberry's mocking and disrespectful tweet about a white van man with England flags hanging from the windows of his two-up, two-down was a fine example. Surely the left in the UK can see this? If this Conservative government serves a full term, the Labour Party will have only been in office for thirteen years in the last half a century. Like I said, this is not harmless; we are unrepresented and the present system here is causing anguish to my people!

The unions are another issue. Running parallel with the political party they fund, unions are also losing members at a vast rate. Just like the Labour Party, the employees of the biggest unions no longer move there from the factory floor because of merit or their credibility but spill out of our universities with degrees. They get very well paid for managing everybody's monthly subs but they have, long ago, lost sight of who they are supposed to be representing. We have seen the former leader of Unite (Len McCluskey) giving a Labour MP £250,000 after a single phone call (the most a leader is allowed to dish out without consulting anybody) to set up a remain campaign and then more monies soon after a referendum result involving almost thirty-four million (mostly working-class) people delivered the opposite result.

Since the Labour Party endorsed the EU's open-door policy HGV drivers' wages have stagnated for over twenty years (where have the unions been?). I know two wagon drivers from my village who have packed in work and gone on the dole because they are financially better off doing so. They were getting fewer pounds in their hands per week than they were a quarter of a century ago. Now that we have left the EU and discovered we have a shortage of British wagon drivers the very union representing the transport workers (URTU) has snapped into action. Recently, they landed in parliament and tried unsuccessfully to lobby a Tory government to open the floodgates to one hundred thousand drivers from overseas. They argued that if this was not permitted, HGV drivers (the people they are supposed to represent and the very people who pay their wages) might demand a pay increase for the first time in decades, putting the large corporate institutions that employ them in a rather weak position. Unbelievable! A union alongside its party campaigning to protect some of the largest and most profitable organisations by stifling its own members' wages. Don't think many wagon drivers will be paying their £14.14 per month for much longer!

A few months ago BBC News reported that Tesco needed

five thousand drivers and had asked for government intervention and help. They were having a bad year, and had last year made only £1.7 billion in profits (£2.4 billion this year!). Their chief executive earned £1.6 million in the same year. It would take one of his lorry drivers over fifty-seven years to earn that. Perhaps we should put a fresh ten thousand people in that room and ask them to raise a hand if they think us tax payers should pay to train Tesco's lorry drivers to drive Tesco's lorries full of Tesco's goods?

Sir Keir Starmer is currently asking the government to help these corporations and lengthen the visas of the few remaining European drivers. Putting him at the helm of our old party has done nothing but widen this disconnect. For the second time in history the British working man and woman actually feel they have more in common with an 'Eton boy' called Boris than the leader of the Labour Party. People don't change their voting habits after a century lightly; they have to be wronged. And this wronging has to be prolonged, sustained and affect their day-to-day lives.

Corbyn was a throwback, a disaster, but only one part of a three-tier problem. I'm not a clinical psychologist. In fact, you know what I am: I'm a bricklayer who probably should never have been shown how to read and write. However, what I did know about people, and the Labour Party didn't know, was that whether it is wrong or right or left or right, what people want most in life is the best for their children. That's what motivated my father to sit on that Dakota in 1945 and at the bottom of that shaft with *NEVVER AGAIN* tattooed on his arm for fourteen years thereafter. It's also what motivates most working-class people and when that energy is correctly enhanced, continues to help western societies to improve at the vast rate they have done previously. For this to work and for communities to blossom, the system must first reward hard work whilst also appearing to be fair. And here sits problem number two.

My community and the people who make it up are split in two. The working men and women feel robbed. If you refuse to work and can't afford a house, you are given one. If your gas boiler dies and you are working, it costs £1,100 for a replacement. If you are not working, you are given one for nothing. If you work and pay 12 per cent national insurance plus 20 per cent income tax, a prescription will cost you £9.15. If you don't work and don't contribute, it will cost you nothing. If you work, you pay for all opticians and dental works. If you don't, it's free. If you work, you pay monthly council tax. If you don't, you pay none. Children's school meals ... the list goes on.

The subject of social mobility confuses me. From what I can tell it rarely goes other than one way. Up! You rarely get the offspring of the academic middle-class couple wanting to be a hospital porter and, if they did, they would be 'such a disappointment, where did we go wrong?' However, what I do know is, the working man and woman in this part of the country was, at the time of the election, very angry. Angry, because of constant reminders that if you work, you are no better off. My daughter-in-law is a fully qualified state-registered theatre nurse, lives in rented accommodation with my five-year-old grandson and works five shifts per week in a busy hospital in Perth. She has done the figures and informs me, if she was to stop going to work tomorrow, she would only be £80 per month poorer. She is getting up and going to work for an extra twenty quid a week. How can that be right?

The most painful kick in the privates for the average care worker, factory worker, retail worker, construction worker or service industry worker, and the subject that upsets them most, was and still is family cars. I hear this all day, every day from everybody I know. Britain has seen 4.3 million mobility cars put on its roads. This equates to 10 per cent of annual UK car sales today. These cars are provided by the social services for people who for one reason or another cannot afford to buy one. I know people who travel to work every day in old cars they struggle to keep road-worthy and on pedal bikes, whilst their neighbours, who don't work, travel around in brand-new cars. The argument being that the taxpayer is not paying for these cars and the people who have them are paying for them because they are allowed to spend their benefits how they wish is not washing with the workers. The workers feel they pay their benefits! I don't know why it's the car that upsets people more than anything else. Probably because the car is a very in-your-face visual possession and probably because, not long ago, they were recognised as a display of wealth; status symbols even.

The benefit system is national yet the resentment I see displayed is more regional. I go to London and people don't see it as a problem. They accept the working have an obligation to help those who can't. So why the disparity in attitudes? To answer this question, we must look at the disparity of incomes. If you are on fifty-plus grand a year, the difference between you and the unemployed person next door is significant. If you live in the struggling ex-coalfields of Durham and your family's weekly income has risen by only sixty-five pence over the last twelve years whilst benefits have gone up by almost half again, in the same period, the difference is insignificant. Don't get me wrong, I don't believe the benefit system should be scrapped (tweaked perhaps). I believe it's the suppression of wages that is responsible for the division and the brewing resentment here and this is what needs to be addressed.

When people are vexed, they look for someone or something to blame. At the time of the last election 1.5 million people were registered unemployed in the UK. At the same time there were 3.7 million Europeans working in the UK. The people here blame this for the suppression of their wages and believed that Brexit was the light at the end of the tunnel. The democratic vote for Brexit being ignored for three years, plus the intelligence of the more working-class areas like Sunderland and Hartlepool being openly joked about on TV and referred to as an embarrassment to the party was the final nail in the Labour Party's coffin. Forty-one per cent of families where I live are recognised as low-income families.

Boris Johnson was promising to honour the referendum result and he was there to vote for. He put his cards on the table and everybody knew where he stood. As for Jeremy Corbyn . . . well, what can I say? If someone sits in a police interview room and answers, 'No comment, no comment, no comment,' to every question asked, I assume them guilty. I suppose my thinking is, *If I were in that position and innocent, I would be explaining my life away.*

'I was in the chip shop at seven thirty and walked down the street and through my mother's front door. *Coronation Street* was on the telly!' would be my spiel.

The Labour Party stood for nowt! The loyal socialists of yesteryear, the new generation of young lefties, the working classes of the north, my community and me, looked at our old party for strength and direction and got, 'No Comment!'

What could people do? Have a stab at what Corbyn might be thinking and vote for him on the off chance he might be like-minded? Vote for posh boy Boris? Vote for the Liberals who were promising a 'people's vote' because the previous referendum had been a vote by a different species? Or vote for the Brexit Party, who were exclaiming they wanted Brexit done but were not interested in running the country?

Or not vote at all?

If the ground was shaking in Durham on election day in 2019, it wasn't the usual settling of old mineworks but the rumble of our grandparents turning in their graves.

Hundreds of years of fighting and striking, suffragettes throwing themselves in front of horses and here we were with the best option being Tory or to not fuckin' bother. The people must have thought the clowns had taken over the circus. And I'm sure those not-too-long-ago images on our TVs of identical triplets Cameron, Clegg and Miliband politely squabbling had already helped flick off the last glimmers of interest from most. An army of advisers and spin doctors behind each one. Three awful humans, all career politicians and each as clever as the next at not letting the question asked influence the answer delivered. What is particularly sad is this new generation of voters now believe the inert wax models depicted as politicians on our screens today are historically typical. Worse still, they think if someone passionately speaks their mind, or lets their own opinion slip, they are stupid and a loose cannon.

The chasm between the Labour Party and working people has widened. Whilst I have been writing this book the constituency of Hartlepool has fallen to the Tories for the first time in its long industrial history. Diane Abbott commented, 'It is not possible to blame Jeremy Corbyn for this result as he had left his post over six months previously!' These Labour MPs who profess to know how we all think but are then surprised by our actions need to realise that it's not that we are backing the wrong horse rather that it is them that are weighing our horse down.

There have been studies done and their findings are worrying. They show our shambolic system has not just turned young people apathetic but worse. They are actually turning against the idea of democracy. I believe we should take this very seriously indeed. A survey conducted by a Cambridge think tank concluded more young people than old believe that having a strong leader who doesn't have to answer to a parliament would be a better way of running our country. Fifteen per cent of people born in the eighties think having a democratic system is a bad thing.

I've never felt I was force-fed politics as a child, more moulded by the issues that surrounded me.

'Why did you have to go to war, Dad?'

'Why are you on strike, Dad?'

'Why did everybody clap when the man you were nasty to walked out of the pub, Dad?'

'Why are you crying, Mam?'

We don't teach our children politics or about our democracy in today's schools. I don't get it! I suppose it would be a difficult one to pull off, without individual teachers being biased. The Tories are not about to let the teachers and lecturers have an influence over tomorrow's voters when such a high percentage of them have a Marxist or at least some left-wing tilt, yet something needs to happen. Students are taught history from a government-set syllabus that reads like a novel with the last few chapters ripped out, leaving them with a disconnect between how yesterday mouldered today, and how changes made today could alter their landscape tomorrow.

In my building business I employ lots of young people as apprentices. I've lost count of how many times a young kid has approached me to complain their wages are short. When I explain it's because of their coming of age and because they are now eighteen they have just started to pay tax, I always get the same reaction.

'So where does the money go?' Or, 'But I don't want to pay it!'

To which I always answer, with a smile, 'Welcome to the real world, Sonny Boy!'

It appears to me, teaching our kids maths and English but not how to survive in the system they have no option but to be in is not only a madness but extremely dangerous.

I know a thirty-five-year-old roofer who, only a few days ago, celebrated when receiving news, by phone, that his wife and the mother of his four children had just been diagnosed with a condition that will eventually leave her blind. This is real, and is what is going on out there on the factory floor! I heard him gleefully boasting to a bricklayer that not only will he now qualify and get paid to be her carer and not have to work again but he can now apply for a brand-new motability car.

'There's another thing I'll have to pay for!' said the bricklayer.

'Don't be stupid!' laughed the roofer. 'You don't pay for the car, you idiot, the government does!'

Some four hundred years ago, a great thinker from a high-class social bracket did something quite radical. He dared to teach some of his uneducated servants to read and found they picked it up. To his amazement, some went on to use their imaginations and successfully write down their thoughts. This disturbed him, and provoked some further, more far-reaching thoughts, which eventually resulted in a theory. *Perhaps everybody has the potential to be clever if they are given the opportunity to be educated.* He then projected his thinking a step further. *Perhaps,* he wondered, *if more people were educated, might society benefit or could this even result in wider social improvements?*

He organised a further experiment, hoping it might prove the validity of the first. He invited all the best brains to meet in an amphitheatre. The greatest mathematicians, philosophers and theologians turned up only to be confronted with a clear glass milk-churn-size vase full of birds' eggs stood tall on a table. It was full to the top of hens' eggs, duck eggs, goose eggs and quail eggs and the assembly of intellectuals were given time to walk around and study the vase before being asked to write down how many eggs they thought it might contain. They were then asked to sit back as three thousand so-called uneducated plebs were quickly made to file past the vase before they, too, were asked to have a guess. They recorded what the plebs said, did the numbers, taking the average from the educated dignitaries then the average from the uneducated peasants. The elite intellectuals' guess was nowhere near, yet the subservient plebs were just about spot on!

This caused much upset, provoking huge debate among the elite. The mathematicians arguing it must be because of the number of plebs being greater than that of the intellectuals. The philosophers arguing if the plebs were so witless, then the greater the number used, the more multiplied their stupidity should become and therefore the greater their inaccuracy should be. And the church leaders, fearing for their safe and comfortable privilege, arguing the whole thing must be a fix, the plebs must have been acting on a tip-off or they had been secretly infiltrated with a majority of educated persons or helped by God. Or the devil!

The stonemasons, weavers, market stallholders, agricultural workers and domestic servants being better decision-makers than the political elite was not a theory that could be accepted by the privileged few; they saw this as a direct threat to their credibility as leaders and resulted in that great thinker being chased away to live a life in exile for having what we now might recognise as socialist beliefs. (Sent to his bedroom without pudding!)

From what I can see from here on the ground, the massive

disconnect and lack of awareness of how the system is supposed to work, together with the absence of any sense of belonging, is growing. The founders of our welfare state would be spinning in their graves. It's not being looked after. In reality, the Labour Party should probably be the group caring for and protecting our system from abuse. After all, despite stealing the initial idea from the Liberal Party it was probably their greatest achievement! Yet because the wheels have fallen off, they can't even get to the position required to achieve this.

Like I said earlier, I believe Britain needs a new generation of subservient MPs and I think this will happen naturally. Soon, I hope! Not a party of the left or right but a party where the MPs are servants to their polled members and take their direction from them. I believe the days of a clumsy system where voters latch on to one person who they can only hope might represent their will are, because of information technology, numbered. It's already happening and can't be stopped. Nicola Sturgeon and even Boris Johnson have performed numerous U-turns recently on key issues because of very quickly whipped-up internet campaigns. Boris Johnson made an announcement yesterday and after fifty-seven minutes he withdrew what he said and was apologising for his remarks. Over one hundred thousand kids walked out of Australia's schools last week and conducted street marches because of global warming. When thousands of people unite on a single issue the careerist politicians latch on to them. The tail is wagging the dog now and this is happening because of the iPhone.

The members of this new party could be from all corners of the political and social spectrum. That social worker, that policeman, that school teacher I spoke of earlier could be instrumental in change! Those groups of tens of thousands who have not yet raised a hand could at last have a voice. It could be a 'people's party' and take its direction from a constant polling of real people from all walks of life. This would at least instil an unbiased awareness. It's not as if us uneducated plebeians would have to travel miles to an amphitheatre to stare through a vase full of different-sized eggs; it could now be done very quickly, using the devices in our pockets and handbags. If we can tell Tesco or Asda what we want, what's stopping us telling our local MP what we want? I suppose how the system of 'eggs in a vase' would manifest itself in today's high-tech world would be to look more like 'ask the audience' instead of 'phone a friend'. After all, I don't believe anybody has ever won the top prize on *Who Wants to Be a Millionaire?* without relying on the audience. Sometimes less than half of the audience know the answer yet once they are polled and the other half have an educated stab, probably based on their individual life experiences or gut feeling, leaving the minority to have a pop for an option you are certain it is not, you almost always get the most reliable answer simmering to the top.

And I don't see the structure of our political system altering (ever!) but just like the Monster Raving Loony Party or the Liberal Democrats, this new party will simply latch on to the side of the existing system we are familiar with.

How I hope this develops is, somebody puts up to be an MP for a certain area, polls their constituents once a month on subjects that are chosen by and are important to those particular people and to that particular area and then that MP, regardless of his or her beliefs, goes to parliament armed with the will of their people to argue their case. And I'm not talking, 'how often would you like your bins to be emptied?' Unless, of course, that's the top issue in that area, in which case, please can I live there! These new MPs would behave like barristers being instructed to do their best whether prosecuting or defending. They would be motivated by the sheer desire to deliver *their* people *their* will. After all, a barrister doesn't defend a rapist because they have an affection for rapists but because they have an understanding of how they must do their best for the overall system to function fairly.

Information technology has been used to improve and make more efficient nearly every part of our lives and I hope it's not finished, yet it seems to me that our electoral system still seems locked in the past. One person walking down to their local school, church or community centre every five years with a white card in their hand whilst 34 per cent (over one third!) of eligible voters remain oblivious or have something more important to do that day.

I hope this happens soon, cutting out irrelevant, to most, centralised metropolitan-driven manifestos and eradicating safe seats for lazy careerists. Just like when I was a child, a prospective MP would have no option but to get to know their people and about local issues in order to be successful. We could browse on our phones what questions they were about to ask before an election and if they were out of touch and not relevant to what might affect us in our everyday lives, we could simply go for one of the more traditional left or right parties with their carved-in-stone manifestos and this would show democratically at the ballot box.

How could somebody armed with nothing but their own opinion credibly argue across the floor of the House of Commons with someone who has communicated with thousands (or millions) of people and is asking for exactly what they want? The will of the people! If one of these new generation of MPs was asked their opinion on a newly developing situation, they wouldn't have to, like our present-day politicians, avoid the question, but simply say, 'I'm sorry, I dare not to presume what my people might think, but I shall ask them and find out before acting according to their will!'

Best I keep quiet! I might be sent up to my bedroom without

pudding for having socialist or even populist views or, better still, chased somewhere nice and hot to spend a life in exile by those who have enjoyed power for far too long. Well, fuck 'em! And let's remember, who knew best how many eggs were in that vase? Us!

To be fair to the feckless elite, they have never been any good at the practical stuff like getting themselves dressed or counting eggs; after all, they have always had someone to do that sort of thing for them. Someone like you!

If this pandemic has taught us anything, we must have at least learned that the working classes of Britain are just as essential, or more essential to this country than the top brass. The hospital cleaner with a disinfectant bucket has been rightly highlighted as more important, or at least *as* important as their local MP. Whilst generally the middle and upper classes had jobs that could be done from home, us hands-on working classes such as front-line health workers have been out there.

If you feel I've painted a picture depicting well-off people sitting in the safety of their own homes whilst we have produced, manufactured and delivered everything they needed, it's probably because I have, as that is exactly what happened. This has resulted in twice as many from the working classes (per head) dying of Covid-19 than those of that higher social bracket. The statistics resemble the 1912 fatality list from the sinking of the *Titanic* where if you were working class, you had zero or very little chance of survival, if you were middle class, you had half a chance of a seat on a lifeboat and if you were upper class, the chances were you sailed off into the sun.

Perhaps now that a bright light has been shone on the worth of working people, we might see change?

When I worked in Australia, everybody I met knew how

their country worked. It is compulsory under federal law for an eligible voter to vote there. They see it as a hard fought-for gift. They would interrogate me and make sure I was paying into their system. They loathed what they called freeloaders. They had some sort of merit or point system in place. If someone finished school and had a year out, usually to surf, they would lose a certain number of points per year. The more points lost, the less dole they could claim. An incentive-based system! The complete opposite to the way our system works. I would get people coming onto my building sites asking for work because they needed to 'get their points back up'. They would explain that because they had not worked and contributed for a few years it wasn't worth them signing on. I admired this system, not only because it got people to work but because of the political awareness it created. The people who were pushed back into paying tax wanted to know who they were giving that money to and how it was to be spent. They had a pride in their system and their country. They scrubbed their front steps.

In 1961 a patriotic John F. Kennedy said: 'Ask not what your country can do for you – ask what you can do for your country.' I like that! Does that make me a lefty or a righty. To me, this statement from the lips of the leader of the free world sounds almost socialist. After all, is that not a direct call for people to stop thinking about themselves and concentrate on the greater good? Embracing our wider communities. Can't imagine a British leader being so brave today. Shame!

I am aware that most great thinkers parallel being patriotic to being narrow-minded. I get that. Every one believing the country they just happen to be born in, the best. I've lived in better and worse countries than England, but I do believe it is healthy for all nations to like themselves first if only as an extension of their wider communities. I believe it instils a sense of pride and belonging essential for a nation's wellbeing. After all, if a person doesn't believe the ground below them is partly theirs, what's to stop them dropping litter on it.

This incentive-led system might first appear cruel, but as I said earlier, I know lots of people in their sixties who have not worked since their thirties and are financially much better off than those who have worked all their lives. Surely a system where the people who are contributing and paying for others are not rewarded for their generosity is a crueller system?

My eldest brother has just qualified for his state pension. He has contributed to the system for forty-seven years and gets three pounds fifty-five more per week than somebody who has not contributed one penny. That to me seems cruel. Surely a more constant contributor should be rewarded for their years of generosity by way of a more generous state pension?

Put that to the ten thousand!

The sooner this generation use the technologies to hand to put these issues to the nation, the better for all!

But who am I to say? Probably starting to sound like the twat standing at the bar on his fifth pint, shouting to everybody who passes, 'And I tell you who else I don't like!'

Ah well . . .

26

Why write this book?

I suppose the reason I've written this is because I feel I've been wronged. Not just me but my generation, my part of the world, my almost extinct community, my people. I suppose another reason might be that I know lots of my generation could never write this and that puts a weight on me. If like me, you feel you have something to shout about, silence can feel like a lie.

To see my whole community not progressing is frustrating but watching its destruction tears at my heart. Everything and everybody dying, if not already dead.

When I visited Auschwitz last year, I read an account of a man who miraculously survived. Twelve of them would make a soup from one small onion thrown over the fence by a passing kid. The soup was thin and weak yet it was all they had. All who shared that soup perished and only he survived. He still makes that soup today. He puts one small, rotted onion in a pan with three pints of rainwater, boils it for one hour and eats it over a number of days. Surely he doesn't want to relive those days? Perhaps he's scared to forget. So strong is his emotion, it makes the piss-weak soup taste good. He might harbour a fear of his memory fading. A duty to keep the light burning. If *he* loses those images, that's it, gone for ever! Or perhaps to him, it tastes of hope, the future and everything that must be kept alive.

When I was ten, I would stare at those cast-iron pit pullies from the classroom window. They would strike a fear and a dread in me I could physically feel in my chest and the very pit of my stomach. The pullies are long gone now, yet the empty skyline that was once a mere backdrop but now hangs in their place still gives me that same ache in my guts today. I hated those pullies yet I long to see them again. Why is this? Is it because we don't like change? Try to put a new railway through somebody's back garden and see how hard they fight; try to remove an old railway from the bottom of somebody's back garden and watch them fight some more. Are these emotions stirred because we only remember the good times and strive hopelessly to wind back the clock as we yearn for their warmth? Does the inner core of my psyche actually believe if we re-erected that massive steel structure and planted those pullies back on top tomorrow, my dad would come back to life, buy me a nice new shiny bike or walk my mother home from the village dance and we could live it all over again?

I don't know what it is. Perhaps I was happier then; more carefree, no responsibilities. No mortgage, no bills, no kids to worry about. These things might get us down more than we realise, leaving us with a subconscious lust for those lost days that contained only innocence. Who knows? It could be a more caveman emotion than we know, a primeval instinct even? I was fitter and more aware back then, my senses keener, my eyes sharper. Could be it's nothing more than my less conscious inner self that wants me to be back there. An instinctive survival mechanism built into our very inner being that has evolved for no other reason than self-preservation. So that we might compete to be a more successful hunter and more attractive mate. Is the old Jewish survivor eating his pissy soup for no other reason than his soul is telling him that it might help him survive the next holocaust? Who knows? I'll let the boffins sort that one out whilst I stare at that naked skyline hanging where the pithead once stood with a bowl of scouse stew and enjoy the warm ache it gives, that feels so closely related to love.

Why write at all?

Being able to write, I fear, had taken the edge off straight thinking. Pushed it into second place perhaps. I can't be wholly sure what I think about a subject now until I've written about it. 'Put it to the pen!' I'm not complaining. Ridding myself of illiteracy felt like being unshackled from the village idiot; and anyway, even if I did want my ignorance back, too late. That's it, gone!

Unusual, I suppose, my wife being my teacher. I like to think we have learned from one another, though that's probably a bit one-sided, if not ungrateful. It wasn't all plain sailing or alto-gether as romantic as it probably sounds. There have been times when I have heard Wendy say that perhaps if she had known how intense the fire would burn, she might not have struck that match. I think this refers to the times I get an idea that needs exploring and needs to be written before it fades, slips away and can't be found. The times I ignore her one o'clock call, get stuck at my desk and forget to go to bed for a night. I think she just worries about me. I suppose it is romantic in that sense. Her fault anyway – she already knew when she struck that match I don't do things by halves. Her words, but it does make me wonder why we write at all.

Perhaps we write because we are engineered to reproduce. Leave our mark. Or want to live for ever. Do we really think that our thoughts might be so important they should remain when we are no more? Will someone reading my work long after my passing make me feel alive again? I think not, but probably hope so. Being human makes us fear our passing being irrelevant. Is that it? Is my obsession to write fuelled only by a desire to leave a stack of books behind, taller and broader than I ever was? Is it an urge to speak from beyond the grave generated by a mere selfish ego?

I feel I have always written. There was just a time I couldn't get it down on paper. A life split in two, I suppose. Before having this ability, they were only thoughts, their only audience myself. Before silence equalled betrayal. But being able to write down a thought shines a light on it. Puts it under the microscope. This has responsibility. If I wrote down all that swims around inside my head, I might now be behind bars. As a thought leaves the psyche and travels the arm towards the pen, that arm must filter. Once free of the broad shoulder, it is slowed by the thinning of the limb. Keeping its precision whilst fighting for its voice, its flow becomes restricted at the bottle-neck wrist. At this point, though remaining true, it can be softened. A rant tamed. Or sent back for a braver day when I might dare. Across the palm and down into the finger the thought will flow, slowing all the way. The final editor the fingertip that touches the cheap plastic of the pen. A last chance to send it back before it leaps from flesh and becomes inert, black and white and shared. All need not be true. After all, that's what they call fiction. Poetic licence! But to me it needs to be believable. Like some Motown star from the seventies who promised he had us a 'one-way ticket to the moo-oo-oon.' He didn't, but boy, we danced.

Why write at all?

Might it be nothing but a work ethic? A deep ingrained work ethic you inherit and pass on to your own, perhaps in a selfish effort to rid yourself of its tight grip? It doesn't work. The enthusiasm for expression as equal in the building of the brick-by-brick house as the word-by-word novel. I take part blame to have got myself into my thirties without the ability to read or write and I suppose this makes me a little bit of a fool. Yet to now have that gift and let it idle, I am certain, would make me the biggest fool the world might ever see.

Sorry, it's one o'clock. Must go! I'll let her know the book is finished. She will be pleased!

Pip x

Acknowledgements (Thanks)

First of all, I must say a special thanks to both our National and my local Education Authorities for NOWT!

Thank you to New Writing North and the Arts Council, who truly reach out to the underdog.

I would also like to say a big thank you to my wife, Wendy, for introducing me to the miracle of reading and magic of books. Thank you Najma Rashid for giving me the confidence to go from reading to writing.

Thank you Pauline Long of Easington Writers for showing me what can be done and what should not be done with the English language. A special thanks to Darren Clish and Doug Johnstone for their wise words along the way. Thank you Calum Watson for direction. Thank you Michael Chaplin for being that direction. Thank you Stan for your ideas, this book in particular. Thank you Bernard Hall for getting me started again when I'd all but given up. Thanks to Kris Doyle and Matt Cole for the soapbox under my feet. Thanks to Ellie Mann for getting me from biro to laptop. Thank you Tony, my brother, and all others who believed. And thank you again Wendy for your patience, the ten thousand cups of tea slipped quietly by my side and our children. The reason for it all.

Pip x

Where did it all go?

A naked skyline, pit heads past,
    the rigging chopped up, the pullies scrapped.
Nee men and boys dropped by cage,
    nee hard men, packed in, with boys nee age.
Gone the steel track with its click and clack,
    that hacked at my sleep while the sky was black.
Nowt to see of the silver steel lines,
    toiling spoil from now-gone mines.
Once mine to train, then train to blast,
    history the heat, the orange blast cast.
Nee fiery glow viewed from pit heaps a-distant,
    nee bangs, nee steam puff from cast-iron piston.
Nee still-hot girders, no cast set hard.
    Nee trains, nee tracks to riverside yards.
Nee stork-tall canes that would dip and peck
    at brand-new steel, the hull, the deck.
Redundant land where girder met sheet,
    where white-hot rivets sparked to cleat.
Where are the men that swarmed the streets
    like busy black ants building the fleet,
each one a cog with an aim and a task,
    walking with purpose, a bait bag, a flask?

Dragged Up Proppa

Where are the men that marched proud to the pit,
    in the cover of night, before skies were lit?
I miss the men that bragged across ale,
    one million ton shifted, a ship set sail,
a train wheel cast, a bridge shipped away,
    a boiler made, I long for that day.
All hidden now, like cobbles 'neath tar,
    I long for me Muther and miss me Dar.

Pip Fallow, January 2023